Culture and Identity in African and Caribbean Theatre

By

Osita Okagbue

Published by

Adonis & Abbey Publishers Ltd
P.O. Box 43418
London
SE11 4XZ
http://www.adonis-abbey.com
Email: editor@adonis-abbey.com

First edition, September 2009

Copyright 2009 © Osita Okagbue

British Library Cataloguing-in-Publication Data

A catalogue record for this book is available from the British Library

ISBN: 9781905068609 (I IB)

The moral right of the author has been asserted

Culture and Identity in African and Caribbean Theatre

By

Osita Okagbue

Adonis & Abbey
Publishers Ltd

Dedication

I dedicate this book to my sister, Ngozika Uchenna Okagbue, who against all odds chiefly made this book possible by translating all the Francophone play texts for me.

CONTENTS

ACKNOWLEDGEMENTS

This book has taken a very long time to write and in the process so much debt has been accumulated which must now be repaid by way of acknowledgement. I owe a great deal to Professor Martin Banham, Emeritus Professor of African Theatre at Leeds University where the initial research for the study was carried out under his supervision, a great many thanks, Martin. Professor Emmanuel Obiechina made my trip to Leeds possible and has remained my academic mentor and support throughout the years; I remain grateful Prof. I am greatly indebted to my late sister, Ngozi Uchenna Okagbue, for her wonderful and painstaking translation of the French plays; I am sorry I did not complete the work before you left, but here is to you; you will always be with us. I am grateful to the British Academy and the Arts and Humanities Research Board (AHRC) who awarded me research leave and travel grants in 2000 that enabled me to begin work on the research and proposal that finally became the book. I need also to acknowledge my good friend and colleague from way back, Dr Victor Ukaegbu of Northampton University, who made very useful comments on the work; John Ginman, the Head, Department of Drama at Goldsmiths, who encouraged and generously supported the publication of this book; and Mike Idemili, who assisted me tremendously when I first visited Dakar to begin my research into Francophone African theatre and performance. I am grateful to my brother, Ifeanyi, and my sister-in-law, Obiageli, who have always supported my work. I must thank also Dr Jideofor Adibe, of Adonis and Abbey Publishers, London, for suggesting the writing of this book and for supporting and waiting patiently for me to finish it.

However, the greater gratitude is to my wife, Amaka, without whose support and 'gentle' reminders this book and all my work would not have been possible. Finally, my children, Solumkene, Chiemelum and Nedonna, who yet again endured my spells of inattention and the many times away from home; I say, you will always be first and special.

Chapter 1

INTRODUCTION: SLAVERY, COLONIALISM AND AFRICAN AND CARIBBEAN EXPERIENCE

Moments in African History

Africa came into contact with Europe in two ways; first, through slavery, and second through colonialism. And as a result of trans-Atlantic slavery, Africa is bound to the Americas and the Caribbean by an umbilical cord whose point of origin can be traced to the slave coasts of West Africa and the historic dispatch of the first batch of slaves from the port of Lagos in 1444 by the Portuguese under the authority of the Papal Bull of Pope Nicholas V. Thereafter, between 1444 and 1807, an estimated fourteen million Africans were transported under the inhuman conditions of the 'middle passage' from West Africa to the various islands of the Caribbean, and to North and South America. An identifiable product of this forced migration is the shared cultural bond which exists between black peoples in Africa and those in the African Diasporas. Africa was the shared point of dispersal and has in many ways remained the original source of forms of cultural expression for black peoples around the world. An examination of the shared cultural denominators and what they mean for African peoples and peoples of African descent is the object of this study. A look at plays from Africa and the Caribbean will reveal that in spite of time and distance, and in spite of all manner of cultural emasculation of the slaves by the slave masters in the New World, Africa refused to die in the souls of her dispersed children irrespective of where history and circumstances had flung them on the globe. However, it would be wrong to deny that slavery and colonialism had left distinct marks on the individual as well as collective psyches of both the slaves and the colonised. The book will examine the effects of Africa's double experience and encounter with Europe because the tragic position of African peoples today is due, first to their being enslaved and later their becoming colonised.

Culturally, slavery and colonialism were two very momentous incidents in African and African-Caribbean histories, and the low esteem in which Africans and peoples of African descent in the Caribbean are held in world opinion and affairs today can be attributed to the occurrence of these two episodes in history and the ideological and myth-making superstructure used to justify them. Slavery involves a negation of the freedom of the enslaved, just as colonialism involves a similar negation of the freedom of the colonised. And in spite of the seeming superficial differences in the strategies and circumstances, colonialism was just another form of slavery; it is the enslavement of a whole nation or people in their own lands and in their own homes. However, because they knew that their actions were wrong, the perpetrators of trans-Atlantic slavery and European colonialism sought ways to justify their acts, not only to others but also to themselves. Thus there was the necessity for a knowledge generating and dissemination machinery designed to defend and justify the enslavement and colonisation of African peoples - what Edward Said refers to as the orientalist apparatus (see Said, 1978).

A plethora of reasons was put forward by those who defended trans-Atlantic slavery and African colonisation and every branch of knowledge and intellectual arsenal available was deployed to find cultural, psychological, religious or biological legitimacy for the slave and colonial enterprises. Among these were ideologues and myth-makers, and the works of these slave and colonial apologists and the effects that they produced will be the subject of this first chapter. The damage they did and repairing this damage is the concern of African and African Caribbean playwrights whose plays are looked at in this study. The plays through counter-discursive strategies present alternative narratives and images that call to question, or are outright refutations of the images which had been put out by colonial and slave apologists through tropes and mythologies of black and African savagery and inferiority.

However, the dramatists were not alone in this refutation of slave and colonial master narratives and it may be useful to introduce the views of the counter ideologues of slavery and colonialism who in their works expose the underlying motives and nature of trans-Atlantic slave trade and European colonialism. These writers are unanimous in their view that both Atlantic Negro slavery and African colonisation were, in fact, carefully thought-out and ruthlessly executed adventures motivated purely by economics. A foremost advocate of this view and group is Eric Williams, the well-known historian of European capitalism and the Atlantic slave trade. Williams saw the origin of Negro slavery as economic and not racial and for him:

> . . . it had to do not with the color of the laborer, but the cheapness of the labor. As compared with Indian and white labor, Negro slavery was eminently superior. The features of the man, his hair, color, dentifrice,

his 'sub-human' characteristics, so widely pleaded, were only later rationalizations to justify a simple economic fact . . . the colonies needed labor and resorted to Negro labor because it was cheapest and best (Williams, 1945: 19-20).

There is no doubt that the slaves were cheaply bought as the scene from *The Trial of Dedan Kimathi* (1976) shows. The play highlights the unequal nature of the trade exchange between the African chiefs and their European trading partners. In the mimed scene which enacts the Black Man's History, 'several strong black men and a few women . . . are given away for a long posh piece of cloth and a few trinkets' (p, 5). Another historical source points out that 'slaves were bartered for a few yards of calico, a couple of barrels of rum, or a keg of gun powder' (Nichols, 1963: 8). The African chiefs and kings no doubt felt they had a good bargain since whatever they got in exchange for the slaves, must have seemed adequate recompense for getting rid of enemies of war and local undesirables. But the European slavers definitely made huge profits on their investments in the goods used in exchange for their human cargoes across the ocean as is evident in the discussion between two characters in Dennis Scott's *An Echo in the Bone*. Records exist of the enormous profits made by all those who took part in the trade, with profits being sometimes as high as three hundred percent or more.

So, in spite of efforts to prove the contrary to be true, it is clear that the desire for profit was the motivating factor behind trans-Atlantic slave trade. As Daniel Mannix's study concludes:

From the beginning to the end the trade was a denial of any standards except those of profit and loss. A black man was worth exactly what his flesh would bring in the market. If his flesh would bring nothing, he was tossed overboard as if he were a horse with a broken leg (Mannix, 1963: xi).

One of the slavers' comments in Scott's play mentioned above provides an insight into the underlying economic calculations that went into European participation in the slave trade. For this character, the new group of female slaves who embark on the ship are just 'commodities' that he could invest his little earnings in with hope of huge returns in the future:

A New Batch of females. Naked as the day. That's what I should do. Three voyages now, all that money saved, careful I am not like Daniel down there, spending it all on grog. If I add my share for this venture, I

could buy me a young black and settle in the islands. Hire her out
maybe. Then retire for a quiet old age, and nothing to do . . . (*Plays for
Today*, 1985: 88).

European capitalism, with its desire for expansion and profit, had set
in motion the series of activities which led to the colonisation of the
Caribbean islands and subsequently to trans-Atlantic slavery (see
Rodney, 1973: 92). Africa became the target because it could provide the
cheapest and most competent labour to man the sugar, cotton and
tobacco plantations in the Americas and the Caribbean. Africans therefore
became slaves, not because they were seen as inferior to European or
ordained by God to be enslaved. These were rationalisations which came
later as a way of explaining slavery to the slaves or of assuaging the
guilty conscience of Europe.

European capitalism, its national and international expansion in the
later part of the 18th and the early 19th centuries, led to the scramble for
Africa and the subsequent Berlin Conference of 1884. The outcome of the
conference was the arbitrary cutting up and desecration of the African
continent, its peoples and cultures by European colonisers with the tacit
support of their respective governments. Again, and not surprisingly,
those who defended colonialism found justifications for the colonial
enterprise. Notable among them was Octavio Mannoni who, from
studying the Malagasy, concluded that the colonial relationship was the
product as well as the satisfaction of mutual psychological needs of the
coloniser and the colonised (Mannoni, 1965). For Mannoni, the colonised
Malagasy suffers from a 'dependency complex' which needed or craved
the paternal attributes of the European coloniser in order to be satisfied.
His argument is that the colonial relationship had been beneficial to both
the coloniser and the colonised; he of course saw no economic motive in
colonialism. Colonialism, according to Mannoni's theory, was a
psychological phenomenon because not all peoples can be colonised, and
neither can all peoples be colonisers; it follows therefore that Africans
became colonised because psychologically, they were disposed to it and,
by Mannoni's accounts, there were legends which foretold this encounter
and that the natives, in fact, had desired and waited for it.

But for every Mannoni who defended colonialism, there is an Albert
Memmi who disagreed and argued, for instance, that:

the idea of privilege is at the heart of the colonial relationship - and that
privilege is undoubtedly economic . . . the moral or cultural mission of
colonialism is not true, the profit motive is basic. The deprivations of the

colonized are the almost direct result of the advantages secured to the colonizer (1968: 46-7).

This explains the privileges which the coloniser enjoyed and which the native is denied within a colonial context. It is from this that the myth of the laziness and indolence of the African native emerged. Colonialism may have had a different set of assumptions, but its sustaining ideology was the same as that of slavery. Africa and her peoples were inferior, uncivilised and pagan, while Europe was the source of light and civilisation and her peoples were inherently superior to the Africans. All the myths are inspired and sustained by this basic trope.

Thus, in spite of the mask of civilisers and Christianisers which the colonisers donned to hide the true mission of economic plunder and cultural emasculation of Africa and Africans, the truth of the economic motive behind all colonial activity was still evident and obvious to enslaved and colonised Africans. Four plays in this study, *The Trial of Dedan Kimathi,* Ola Rotimi's *Ovonramwen Nogbaisi*, Bernard Dadie's *Béatrice du Congo* and Cheikh Ndao's *L'Exil d'Albouri* deal directly with colonialism, with each exposing the underlying economic motive. Shaw Henderson in *Dedan Kimathi* confides to Kimathi during their confrontation in the latter's prison cell: 'Nations live by strength and self-interest. You challenged our interests: we had to defend them' (*The Trial of Dedan Kimathi*, 34). Vice-consul Phillips in Rotimi's play, however, offers the best exposé of the underlying economic motivation for colonisation when he asks his colleagues:

> What then are we in Africa for? What objective brings us here? Commerce, gentlemen! Commerce brought us to Africa; commerce determines our actions in Africa (*Ovonramwen Nogbaisi*, p. 32).

Myths of Colonialism

Assumptions which underpin an ideology are hardly codified into legal forms or legislation - except in South Africa under apartheid - and neither are they thrown about in unclothed form. They are usually circulated through prevalent popular myths. Myths sometimes function to naturalise the basic assumptions of an ideology. Myth gives a natural justification to a historical intention. It provides a moral basis for a social system, by implying, if not stating specifically, that the given system is right and just (Maughan-Brown, 1985: 10). Myth does not deny things; on the contrary, its function is to talk about them in such a way that it purifies them, makes them innocent and ultimately gives them a natural and eternal justification. It also gives them a clarity which, although not an explanation, amounts to a statement of fact (10). In this respect, therefore, myth and ideology are interdependent, for myth embodies and gives flesh to ideology while the latter supplies the former with its substance and reason for coming into being.

Literature is one major means through which these ideology-loaded myths are propagated as a lot of slave and colonial literatures demonstrate. Shakespeare's *The Tempest* is a case in point and one is not surprised that the two major characters in this classic colonialist play, Caliban and Prospero, provide the title for Mannoni's thesis on the 'psychology of colonisation'. The fractious and unequal power relationship between Prospero and Caliban based on usurpation, deprivation and exploitation is the proto-typical colonial relationship. The manner Shakespeare writes this relationship – making the audience/reader see the relationship from Prospero's point of view instead of Caliban's as Aimé Césaire does in his postcolonial revision of the play, *Une tempête* (1969) – makes Shakespeare's version an endorsement of the colonial trope of the lazy, savage and ungrateful colonised versus the benevolent, industrious and civilising coloniser.

The ideologies which provided the enabling social framework within which Negro slavery and African colonisation took place needed racist mythologies which, unfortunately, have since come to colour the relationship between Africa and Europe, between black people and white people through the centuries. Africa's relationship with and perception by other peoples have also been coloured by the racism of Europe, as knowledge of and contacts with Africa have, in the main, been mediated by Europe. The myths and their effects on both black and white characters in African and African-Caribbean plays will be the focus of this chapter.

Justifying Injustice

Trans-Atlantic slavery was a horrible historical occurrence for many African peoples. The colonisation of Africa which came later was no better. Those responsible for these two major crimes against humanity knew what they were doing was wrong, and, besides, they knew too that their victims also knew that they were being wronged. So, reasons had to be put forward to justify the blatant injustice of both to the victims. Legitimisation of slavery came from virtually all sections of European society, including the Christian church, but mainly from the European academy. As Julio Finn points out:

If the Portuguese had experienced any feelings of conscience about enslaving the Negroes, these were quickly assuaged by the Bull of Pope Nicholas V which authorized them to 'attack, subject and reduce to perpetual slavery the Saracens, pagans and other enemies of Christ southwards from Cape Bogador and including the Coast of Guinea (1988: 25).

The European slavers were therefore helped by the Roman Catholic Church to see themselves as being engaged in a crusade for Christ, since the Negroes, by the pope's definition, were also enemies of Christ who should be made to suffer a lifetime of enslavement for their lack of faith.

The church, as a matter of fact, functioned in two ways during New World slavery. First, it had provided the moral authority and justification for the initial enslavement of Negro peoples. And second, when the 'evangelising' task had been accomplished, it was again the church which through its teachings, ensured that the enslaved accepted their bondage willingly by placing their faith and hope in God and the last judgement. The church also coerced the slaves into denying and abandoning their original religious and traditional values by ensuring that the indigenous African religions neither saw the light of day nor used as rallying points for rebellion. The church performed a similar function during colonialism since the coloniser and the evangelist usually worked together or followed in each other's footsteps. The relationship between colonialism and Christianity is aptly captured in this simple statement: 'When the white men first came here, we had the land and he had the Bible. Then he asked us to close our eyes to pray and when we opened our eyes, we had the Bible and he had the land' ((Ngũgĩ wa Thiong'o, 1972: 33).

The colonised who became christianised suffered a double bondage and loss because, apart from the enforced cultural emasculation which the colonisers practiced, the churches were in fact more successful in making the natives become ashamed of and thereafter to reject their autochthonous cultural values. African beliefs and thought were termed pagan, evil and unbecoming of Christians; this is the attitude of the Europeans in *Béatrice du Congo* and ironically, the newly converted Mani Congo holds the same view. It was extremely difficult for the natives to resist the overwhelming de-culturation process which the church carried out believing that was the only way the gospel could take root and grow. To a large extent, it succeeded since it was through Christianity and its educational system that European conquest was finally entrenched. If not, how does one explain the absolutely unnecessary and farcical wedding of Kĩgũũnda and Wangeci in *I'll Marry When I Want*? The new

7

Christians led by Kīoi and his wife, Jezebel, believe and teach that the traditional wedding which had made the couple man and wife many years previously was no longer binding, and that only a new Christian wedding could give legitimacy in the sight of God to their union and to their two grown up children. One can also mention Simon Pilkings in Wole Soyinka's *Death and the King's Horseman* who sees Elesin's suicide as a barbaric act which he had to stop. Elesin had to be protected from himself; this is another example of the paternalistic protective attitude often adopted by the colonisers to enable them interfere and deal with Africans as children who had to be taught by grown up Europe how to live safely and wisely. The metaphysical dimension and implications for the Yoruba world of Elesin's willing suicide never comes into reckoning as Simon and his armed police officers step into the ritual chamber to arrest the king's horseman. Ironically, however, in stopping the rite Pilkings destroys utterly the life of the man he was attempting to save, as well as threatening the very foundation of the Yoruba world.

But more damaging than the papal tag of Africans as pagans was the plethora of stereotypes invented by European academies which led the way in the attempt to give credence to the strongly but widely circulating belief that 'blacks were nearer to animals and biological half-wits' (Finn, 1988: 22) who could only be good and useful in God's scheme of things as slaves. This is the core myth which slave and colonial discourses shaped and reshaped to explain and justify the enslavement and colonisation of African peoples. The notion of white superiority and black inferiority which underpinned slave and colonial social structures and relationships was predicated on this assumption. So, the more debased and culturally emasculated the slaves or African natives became the more elevated and secure the European slave masters and colonisers felt. The transition from inferiorising only the slaves to extending it to include the whole of Africa and black peoples was systematic and happened over time.

When the European slave traders first arrived on the African coasts, because they needed Africans to trade with or supply them the slaves, they had to accord some respect and humanity to the chiefs and others who controlled all coastal trade. They treated the chiefs as partners and paid all the taxes and duties imposed on trade by the chiefs. Thus, only those who were unfortunate to be caught suffered the systematic dehumanisation which New World slavery demanded. The African chiefs, for their part, sold prisoners of war, criminals or those found to have committed abominable acts against the land and also who normally would have been required to pay with their lives. This practice changed though when the trade went into full swing and demand became high – raids, kidnapping and abductions were also used as ways of acquiring slaves. The trade scene in *The Trial of Dedan Kimathi*, as well as illustrating the imbalance in the trade exchange between the African chiefs and the Europeans, also significantly shows that the trade was between equals who were merely exchanging goods which each needed from the other. The sale into slavery of the Warrior and his entire command in Soyinka's *A Dance of the Forests* shows that in Africa it was mainly offenders who were sold into slavery prior to the Atlantic slave trade. The Warrior and his men refuse to obey Mata Kharibu's order for them to go to war over Madam Tortoise's marital gymnastics. The point, however, is that there was no question of inferiority or superiority between the African and European slave traders. The New World slaves became inferior and sub-human because that was the only way to make them work without appropriate pay and without the hope of freedom. It was also the only way to make it natural for the Europeans to exploit the African slaves and their labour for nothing since they could not be expected to pay human wages to non-humans.

The slaves in Scott's *An Echo in the Bone* are not in the least perceived nor are they treated as humans by the white slavers on the ship. It may be useful here to compare slaves in Africa and those in the New World. Trans-Atlantic slave trade did not introduce slavery into Africa since prior to that it was customary for the nobles and well-to-do to acquire slaves who helped out on the farms, in household work, or in trade as Kofi Ako does in Ama Ata Aidoo's *Anowa*. But in selling the slaves to Europeans, the African slave trader could not have imagined that the treatment which the white slave-owner would give the slaves would be any different from that which slaves in Africa received - at the least the slave in an African household was recognised and treated as a human being and therefore enjoyed certain rights. Also, the slave in an African setting stood the chance of working his or her way to freedom and becoming a full and free member of their new society if they so desired. And in most cases, the slaves became integral members of the families which had owned them previously and they were usually taken into account in matters affecting the family. In certain parts of Kalabari (Nigeria), for instance, some former slaves rose to become heads of the very families which previously owned them. This illustrates the degree of freedom and social mobility which the slaves in Africa enjoyed, something that slaves in the New World were never allowed.

Thus, slavery as an institution was not new to Africans; what was new and different was the treatment given to the slaves, as well as the racist ideology behind this new form of slavery. The slave in Africa was never seen as an inferior person in any way; unlucky maybe, but never the non-human that he/she became in the New World. In the Caribbean and the Americas, he/she lacked the humanity which would have linked him/her to the master thereby making the inhuman treatment received from the latter unacceptable – such as having their tongues slashed for spitting in disgust at what their captors were doing to them on the slave ships in *An Echo in the Bone*. The slaves were chained, brutalised and denied a voice because that was the only way to get them to perform the role which had been chosen for them by their tormentors. They were made into animals so that they would not be paid for their labour, and so their humanity does not stand to accuse the inhumanity of their tormentors.

With colonialism it was not possible to continue to make the claim that Africans were not full human beings, even though some of the racist notions from slavery had taken root and were found to be quite handy in the colonial context. Africans became barbarians, savages and cannibals who warred constantly, killed and ate each other. Because of this, it was possible for Europe to take up a self-assigned mantle of benevolence to save Africans from each other and from themselves. This 'saving mission' is set in motion in *Death and the King's Horseman* when Simon Pilkings prevents Elesin from committing ritual suicide as demanded by his honoured office of horseman to the dead king. This role of benevolent protector was used time and again to justify the presence of Europe, especially in situations when the colonised Africans rose to demand the dismantling of the colonial structure, such as during the Mau Mau uprising in Kenya in the 1950s, the subject of *The Trial of Dedan Kimathi*. If Europe was to withdraw its protective and civilising presence, Africa would revert to darkness and savagery. The white race was a superior race; it was the adult who had to protect and lead the child by the hand. Europe was to guide infant Africa to light and maturity. Little wonder the numerous myths, which emphasise the infantile nature of Africans, such as J. Hunt who is convinced that 'the intellect of a black adult could not exceed that of a fourteen year old European' (Finn, 1988: 23). Such views of Africa were born and supported by pseudo-scientific theories, such as the fallacy that 'the African makes very little use of his frontal lobes' and from which follows the conclusion that the 'normal African is a lobotomized European' (Fanon, 1967: 244). Interestingly, it is this same idea which forms the centre-piece of Mannoni's theory of 'dependency complex' and 'abandonment neurosis' which he argues underpinned the encounter between the Malagasy and European colonisers. The Malagasy were happy in their colonisation because of the comforting fatherly presence of Europe:

> Europeans have helped to allay the Malagasy's anxiety by making him feel that objective danger has been removed. His view of the world has changed and the presence of Europeans has made his world seem a safer place. The child is comforted when the father takes it by the hand (Mannoni, 1965: 149).

Europe is the father of the child, Africa, and by colonising the latter, the former was only fulfilling a natural role; after all, according to Mannoni, long before the Europeans came, local legends foretold their coming. The Malagasy even prepared and hoped for it because of their dependency need which the meeting would satisfy. Thus a mainly historical event is cleverly presented as a natural and cultural phenomenon through a myth of dependence and abandonment.

The many master narratives, myths and tropes which helped to explain and support both trans-Atlantic slavery and African colonisation were deployed over an extended period of time. Edward Tyson is credited with the theory that the Pygmies of Central Africa were the missing link between man and ape (Finn, 1988: 23). Of course, in time, what was used initially to refer to a single aboriginal African group came to be used for the entire Negro race. Negroes dully became a stage in the evolution of humans from apes. But this in reality was an attempt to fixate the Negro at a stage in human evolution - that is, the Negro stopped at a point in human development and has stood still ever since. This idea Walcott ironically makes his race-hating and Negro-bashing Lestrade express in *Dream on Monkey Mountain* as he pompously lectures his black prison wards on creation:

> In the beginning was the ape, and the ape had no name and so God call him man. Now there were various tribes of the ape . . . and God looked at his handiwork, and saw it was good. For some of the apes had straighten their backbone, and start walking upright, but there was one tribe unfortunately that lingered behind, and that was the nigger (*Dream on Monkey Mountain and Other Plays*, p. 216-7).

For Lestrade and the view he represents, the Negro stopped at the hunched animal stage which Europe had passed, and thus, properly speaking, the Negro was not yet a human being.

Slavery and colonialism, as contexts of unequal relationships, needed social structures based on domination, oppression and exploitation and these structures could only be developed and maintained through acts of violence, physical as well as mental. During trans-Atlantic slavery, to justify the traffic in human beings, it was necessary to create an appropriate image of the black human cargo of the slave ships, images that made them less than human, nearer to beasts than to humans. The need to make the slaves less than human, one can argue, must have arisen from a Christian anxiety since accepting the slaves as human beings with souls, created by the same God the white slavers worshipped would have run counter to the Christian doctrine of the equality of all human beings before God. Therefore, only if the slaves were not real people could the good Christian profess that God had ordained slavery as part of his scheme for the world (Broderick, 1973: 11). Alternatively, in accord with the papal bull, if the slaves were from a heathen race, then enslaving them became a way of bringing them into the Christian fold and to God. It is not surprising that the slavers in *An Echo in the Bone* never for once refer to the slaves as human beings, rather they are only described in zoological terms, such as 'dreadful animals', 'filthy beasts', 'heathen brutes', and 'these creatures'. And when they are not beasts, they are 'property' or 'goods' owned by other people. Lestrade routinely refers to the black prisoners who are his companions on the journey to Africa as simply 'you apes'.

Robert Knox (1791-1862, a Scottish surgeon whose anthropological views were profoundly racist) concludes that blacks 'lacked the grand qualities which distinguish man from animals and as such they were beyond the pale of civilization' (in Broderick, 1973: 11, see also Knox, 1850). And many more tried to prove that black people were not humans and it is hardly surprising that Thomas Carlyle should, with conviction, call a black man 'the indolent two-legged cattle' who 'should be forced to work' because of his ' indisputable and perpetual right to be compelled . . . to do competent work for his living'. The black man, according to Carlyle, alone of all wild men could live among civilised men, but that he could be useful in God's creation as a perpetual servant. Underpinning all these theories and assumptions was a wholesome contempt for black people and a conviction that they belonged to a sub-specie of humans, much lower than the specie to which white peoples belonged (11).

These ideas about the inferiority of black and African peoples freely circulated among the slaves and those who enslaved them. The purpose was to make the slaves to begin to doubt their very humanity because the social structure needed it and already ensured the systematic erosion of that humanity. The structure also tried to make the slaves believe that they deserved the humiliation which they got. And, on the other hand, to make the harsh and inhuman treatment meted out to the slaves, both during the Middle Passage and in the plantations of the New World, less offensive to the refined moral sensibilities of an acquiescing Europe, the slaves were painted as despondent, lazy, beastly, wicked, indolent and savage, and so they needed to be flogged mercilessly in order to get them to do any useful work or to stay docile and tame. The key thesis of this theory of black slaves being animals is that humans are the central point of creation and it is God's design that humans should control and deploy every other element in nature to a useful purpose. And so, by enslaving and putting to work the savage beasts of the African continent, Europeans saw themselves as fulfilling God's grand design in creating the world. When it became impossible not to accept the humanity of the black slaves, the act of enslaving and removing them from Africa was cleverly presented as an act of saving them from their savage homes and thereby placing them within the realms of civilisation and Christian salvation. Implied in this, of course, is the idea that the best thing that could have happened to black Africans was their coming into contact with Europe and Christianity. This was the moral mission which Europe had assumed in its relationship with Africa during the slave period and which was also adopted during the era of colonisation; that both enslavement and colonisation happened for the benefit of African peoples.

Just like slavery, colonialism was an economic act, but other reasons were put forward to explain and justify it, to both the colonised and the coloniser. Europe's obdurate image of Africa had been formed during the era of the slave trade mainly from accounts of travellers and the slave traders themselves, and this image was reinforced effectively and became entrenched during the colonial era. The image was not particularly favourable, not with its insistence on the notion of Africa as the 'Dark Continent', the dark mysterious womb of the world where rules of civilised behaviour did not exist. This is the image that informs one of the classics of Western European literature, Joseph Conrad's *Heart of Darkness*, with its portrayal of native elemental savagery and unbridled nature. Underlying and informing this view of Africa and her peoples is a

Eurocentric contempt which, in spite of all the evidence to the contrary provided by abolitionist literature of the 18th and 19th centuries, has persisted. The view that stressed African barbarity and depravity remained and was constantly reinforced by the pseudo-scientific racism of the 19th Century (Reynolds, 1985: 106). This view, that influenced greatly the organization of colonial regimes after the scramble for Africa, persists today and is still present in a lot of Western European literature about Africa and Africans. In deed, some of the peoples of African descent in the Caribbean know Africa through such literature, which may perhaps explain why Pa Ben in Trevor Rhone's *Old Story Time* could say of Len's stay in Africa:

> letter come from all over the place, as far as Africa. A nuh little fret we fret for him, for we know say if lion or tiger never eat him raw, the savages in the bush would catch him, cook him up as stew and devour him (p, 22).

Of course, one acknowledges Rhone's implied irony in this scene, but it is still a view of Africa held by many in the Caribbean which the play is trying to debunk, especially Miss Aggy who herself sees nothing good in being a black person.

One of the justifying myths of colonialism was that of proselytising and civilising Europeans who had taken it upon themselves to take the benighted children of Africa out of their darkness and savagery. However, the so called moral and cultural mission of colonisation was just a ruse with which to cover up the fundamental economic motive. And when this civilising myth lost its potency, it was supplanted by the myth of the lazy and indolent native. The aim of the latter myth was to prove that the colonised was poor, marginalised and without privileges simply because of these natural attributes, while the coloniser enjoyed his great privileges because of his proven attributes of industry and spirit of adventure. It is in light of this pervasive myth that one can begin to understand the basis of the claim of the enraged settler in *The Trial of Dedan Kimathi* who blames Kimathi and his freedom fighters for threatening to upset the colonial *status quo*. And for a man who apparently was a nobody back in his native Scotland, the life he had in colonial Kenya was too good a thing to let go easily - in Kenya, the fact of being a white man, had guaranteed him a superior social position and immense property by virtue of the colonial utopian myth which represented colonised lands as virgin lands that belonged to nobody.

Underpinning much colonialist discourse and thinking is the recurrent trope which had been used to justify the removal of land from its native owners so the agents of the colonising power could expand and enjoy immense wealth and privileges in the colony. The whole of America, for instance, was virgin land when it was 'discovered' by Christopher Columbus when he accidentally landed in the Bahamas in 1492 instead of India. Perhaps, the autochthonous groups later germinated like unwanted mushrooms that had to be systematically exterminated to keep intact the myth of virgin and unoccupied lands. In the same way, the Scottish explorer, Mungo Park, discovered the River Niger in West Africa, and perhaps all the peoples living along its long bank which traverses many countries and who depended on it for their livelihood and wealth had not even been aware of its existence. However, in colonial literature the colonisers always managed to chance on territories that belonged to no one, territories which they made bold to claim and tame for their respective nations and monarchs, using, of course, the labours, willing or coerced, of the native populations. The colonial conquest of the earth, as Conrad's Marlow concludes, mostly meant taking 'it [the earth] away from those who have a different complexion or slightly flatter noses than ourselves' and 'it was not a pretty thing when you look at it too much' (Conrad, 1962: 7).

The colonial myth of utopian outposts of civilisation with untamed landscapes was meant to achieve one major objective - to confer the status of hero on the coloniser. It did so by depicting the original encounter between the coloniser and the colonised as the archetypal encounter between civilisation and savagery, between order and chaos. If the land was not owned by anybody, then colonisation had not deprived anybody of land or rights. Thus, the settler in *The Trial of Dedan Kimathi* refuses to see Kimathi and the Kenyan natives as having any land rights to fight for. And because the Kenyans were deemed to have no rights to the land, all colonial attempts to explain the Mau Mau war sought the reasons everywhere else but the key area of contention - the fact that lands had been expropriated from the Kenyan peoples by the colonising British and the Kenyans now wanted their lands back.

Colonial historiography, in the main, explained Mau Mau as the product of an 'anxious conflictual situation in a people who had lost the constraining and supportive influence of their own culture' but 'had not lost their magic modes of thinking'. These natives, one of the colonial historians, Carothers, concludes, had fallen prey 'to some sophisticated egotists' who exploited the cultural lacuna to lead them into rebellion and inevitably back into savagery and barbarity (quoted in Maughan-Brown, 1985: 50). Other colonial scholars put forward pretty much the same explanation, which was that Mau Mau was a return to savagery, the collapse of the African mind in the face of pressures to which the modern world and its technology was subjecting it; it was a neurotic reaction of the natives to a feeling of being abandoned by the colonising father, it was simply a reversion to barbarism. But all these were, not surprisingly, dependent to an astonishing degree on a reproduction and rearrangement of the basic elements of the core trope of colonialism – of African primitivism, atavism, regression, savagery, and of course, intellectual and physical inferiority. There was no place for or mention of the socio-economic and political origins of the uprising because that would have undermined the basic ideology with which the colonisers and settlers justified their presence in and stranglehold on the whole of Kenya. Curiously enough, they, it would seem, sometimes believed in these lies themselves, considering the obvious conviction with which they sometimes preached the legitimacy and merit of the colonial presence as the enraged settler does in *The Trial Dedan Kimathi*:

> Settler: [*pointing his gun at Kimathi as he is whisked out of the court and screaming at the top of his voice*]: Bloody bastard Mau Mau . . . . Fucking black monkey. Listen, you'll die now, wog. . . Look at me. I am no idler.
> I may not be a Delamere or a Grogan
> But I am a worker
> I came to this country as a soldier
> A simple soldier
> Fighting against banks, mortgages
> the colonial office, the whole lot
> on my back
> You think it was easy?
> And when I thought I would
> sit down and enjoy the fruits of my labour
> You struck
> I had perfect relationship with my boys
> They were happy on my farm. . . gave them everything
> they needed
> They loved me. . .
> Then that devil, Field Marshal, came . . .
> Poisoned simple minds
> led astray their God-fearing souls
> With his black mumbo jumbo . . . (28-9).

Thus, in this virgin land that was Kenya there is no place or mention of the Gikuyu, the Embu, the Meru, the Luo, the Masai, and all the other ethnic groups - the aboriginal peoples who owned and utilised the land long before the colonial invasion. In colonial thinking and reckoning, these groups were written out of the scheme of things and from the pages of history so that the colonisers could get blown into romantic heroes in mortal combat with mythical villains for the control of the Dark Continent.

In most colonial historiography of the Benin Kingdom, Oba Ovonramwen Nogbaisi is represented as a blood-thirsty tyrant who feasted on the flesh of his enemies and sometimes on that of his loyal subjects. So, when the British invaded his kingdom and defeated him, it was meant to appear as if they had saved the people of Benin from the scourge of this villainous ruler. The same classic colonial encounter between the forces of light and those of darkness, civilisation and primitivism, order and chaos is played out in the historical representations of the Punitive Expedition against the Kingdom of Benin by the British in 1897. This is the trope of most colonial/imperial literature and historiography which was fed to Europeans, as well as to the colonial and postcolonial child who went through the brainwashing of the colonial educational system, especially under the ideologically uncompromising missionaries. Little wonder that racism has continued into the postcolonial and neo-colonial era, in spite of the fact that slavery and colonialism are now history. The attitudes engendered by such literature are ingrained and self-regenerating. For the colonial child, the effects of this assault through racist colonial literature and practices as they grew into adulthood will be the concern of the next chapter.

This chapter does not claim to have exhausted the myths created and used during the eras of trans-Atlantic slavery and European colonialism to debase and dehumanise African peoples and cultures. But the few that have been highlighted here represent a fair sample of the corpus of mythological lore of the slave and colonial times. The core myths have been shaped and reshaped throughout history and in different contexts to serve the needs of Europe, while ensuring the continued suffering of an Africa deprived of a voice. And in whichever way it is looked at, in the contact with Europe, whether during slavery or during colonialism, Africa was the loser. Newton, one of the well-known slavers, puts this very well when he wrote that:

It may be safely affirmed that from our first settlement on the coast until abolition of the slave trade in 1807, we did not confer one lasting benefit upon the people (Mannix, 1963: 33).

And for colonialism, Kimathi's words to Shaw Henderson, the judge at his trial, sums it up: 'With the British we have been the losers all the way' (*The Trial of Dedan Kimathi*, p 34). On both counts, Africa was the loser, while the myths have sought to make claims to the contrary.

The central trope of the justifying myths used during trans-Atlantic slavery and colonisation in the late 19th and early 20th centuries was that Africans were barbaric, atavistic, primitive, bestial, and Africa was the 'dark continent' and going to it was like going back into primordial time and space to encounter humanity in its pristine state, before culture and before civilisation. This image of Africa as the dark womb of the world is the origin of the many stereotypes which have dogged peoples of African descent through slavery and into the colonial era and after. Patrick Brantlinger's summary resonates with the central argument put forward by the dramatists studied in this book:

The myth of the Dark Continent was thus a Victorian invention. As part of a larger discourse about empire, it was shaped by political and economic pressures and also by the psychology of blaming the victim through which Europeans projected many of their own darkest impulses onto Africans. The product of the transition - or trans-valuation - from abolitionism to imperialism, the myth of the Dark Continent defined slavery as the offspring of tribal savagery and portrayed white explorers and missionaries as the leaders of a Christian crusade that would vanquish the forces of darkness.... When the taint of slavery fused with sensational reports about cannibalism, witchcraft, and apparently shameless sexual customs, Victorian Africa emerged draped in that pall of darkness that the Victorians themselves accepted as reality
(in Gates, 1986: 185).

Ironically, the myths did have effects on the Africans and it is the echo which the images arising from them elicited in the enslaved and the colonised that will be looked at in the next two chapters.

Chapter 2

MENDING A DAMAGED PSYCHE

For African peoples, the two encounters with Europe, first in the form of slavery and second during colonisation, had a traumatic impact on individual and collective psyches. No understanding of the many problems which Africans and peoples of African descent face in the world today, irrespective of where they are located, can be complete without a full understanding of trans-Atlantic slavery and European colonisation of Africa. It is probably right to say that every person of African descent in the world today must have, directly or vicariously, participated in or experienced the psychic dislocation which both trans-Atlantic slavery and African colonisation had brought about.

Trans-Atlantic slavery created the first major African Diaspora communities and in doing so introduced the complex dimensions of black and African experience in world history. About eighty percent of the population of the Caribbean and ten percent of North and South America are products of a slave history who are still seeking to understand who they are in their places of 'exile'. In Africa, on the other hand, a significant percentage of the productive population passed through a colonial experience. Both slavery and colonialism had left in their wakes men and women no longer sure of themselves, especially when confronted with the humiliating presence of the other. And although, strictly speaking, the problems of black people in Africa are not the same as those of blacks in the Caribbean and the Americas, in contact with white peoples, there is not much difference because the effects of their dehumanising experiences have not gone away. Besides, for most white people, a black person is just a black person, irrespective of their histories, geographical locations and circumstances. The tendency to stereotype and generalise about races and cultures, a carry over from slave and colonial mythologies, is still evident today in black-white relations. The Caribbean person of African descent is worse off than the African person having undergone a double process of enslavement and colonisation. This perhaps accounts for what appears to be an identity void in which they find themselves. They appear to lack the cultural bed which had cushioned the fall of their African brothers and sisters as a result of colonial racism, denigration and dehumanisation. Africans in the continent, in the main, were able to retain firm links with the cultures of their ancestors, as Soyinka's Yoruba characters in *Death and the King's Horseman*, and the majority of the indigenous population in *L'Exil d'Albouri* and *Béatrice du Congo* demonstrate. Whatever encounters these characters had with the colonial invaders was from the security of their indigenous cultures. African-Caribbean peoples, on the other hand, because of long years of physical separation, only have distant memories of their African cultures or relive them in their dreams where they lie buried in their unconscious. This, not surprisingly, is a preoccupation of a significant number of characters of African descent in African-Caribbean literature and theatre - good examples of such characters are found in *Dream on Monkey Mountain* and *An Echo in the Bone*.

The process of emasculation and inferiorisation of black peoples of African descent began with the trans-Atlantic slave trade, and continued during colonialism. As pointed out in the previous chapter, this process was achieved through the fabrication and mass circulation of racist myths of white superiority in opposition to black inferiority; white humanness contrasted to black animalism. As much as possible, the white slave owners and colonisers when in contact with black people adopted an 'inauthentic attitude' that produced only an 'I-it' relationship (Tirykian in Gordon and Gergen, 1968: 77). This form of relationship often is characterised by a tendency on the part of the inauthentic party to fixate the other at the ontogenetic level by insisting on perceiving and treating the other as if they were objects. It was a gradual but conscious process of objectification which sought to arrest for black people the process of becoming, to somehow force that process to collapse and become permanently fixed at the ontogenetic level - thus to proceed to perceive and treat black people as if they were still at a stage of human evolution which white people had gone beyond a long time ago. The result was that the individual so treated was forced to become a-temporal with daily routines becoming the only way of life which the individual understood or which had meaning. In reality, once an individual reached this state he or she became a defeated person, neither questioning nor seeking to attack the social structure responsible for their oppression. This was the kind of person that slavery and colonialism wanted. The two practices sought to induce a state of stagnation or rut on enslaved and colonised African peoples; to make of them, men and women of the present, with neither a past nor a future (Tirykian, p.88). And to some degree, this succeeded as is evident by the extremely comic, a-temporal and cultureless characters that one finds in a number of African and Caribbean plays.

Trans-Atlantic slavery marked the beginning of the uprooting, humiliation, dehumanisation and subsequent alienation of Caribbean peoples of African descent. Removed forcibly from their ancestral homes in Africa, and thrown into a bewildering and physically hostile New World dominated by Europeans who, it appeared were bent on bending or breaking them to achieve their economic goal, the African slaves for the first time became aware of their blackness. But they also realised that their terrible experiences in the New World arose from it. It is thus hardly surprising that a loss of faith in the self began. If to be black meant to suffer, as the situation in the plantations must have been, then it was a great curse to have been born black. And as if that was not enough, by a systematic process of de-culturation and dehumanisation, the slaves were made to lose their names, their languages and worlds embodied in their cultures which they had carried with them from Africa. That they were able to cling on to some elements of their African cultures was, according to Emmanuel Obiechina (1986: 101-60), a testament to their indomitable wills which refused to die in the face of a merciless and relentless assault. These elements of Africa which refused to die in the souls of her dispersed children in the Diaspora constitute the 'African survivals' in the Caribbean and the Americas, survivals which are reflected strongly in the theatre and literature of African peoples in the Diaspora. These survivals, the book argues, are responsible for the similarities between African and African-Caribbean cultures, forms of artistic expression and hence the similarities in the plays.

What the slave owners attacked was the slaves' personalities, their total concept and images of themselves as men and women. And they all but succeeded because what the slaves retained of their originary beings were not allowed any freedom of expression and with time an atrophying process inevitably set in as can be seen in the impurity of the survivals in Caribbean society today and in the theatre. But even with the lack of complete success on the part of the slave owners, enough damage was still done, especially on the easily impressionable minds of the children who saw their parents being ground in the emasculating mills and fields of plantation slavery. The self-doubt of the parent, as we shall see later, became etched in the mind of the child, and the slave master completed the psychic humiliation for the slave child through the cultural imperialism of the classrooms of slave and colonial education.

That the slave or colonial child was so affected is hardly surprising since the process of developing a concept of the self starts from childhood when the child begins to construct ideas of who they are in relation to others and to their environment. This notion of the self 'is created by the child from past experiences but it in turn affects future experience' (Mischel, 1976: 249). The process involves impressions of other people and of the world, an integration and organisation of a vast load of information from the past, as well as expectations for the future. As Mischel again points out:

> The roots of our self-concepts are the impressions and evaluations that other people have of us in our interactions with them throughout the course of life (249).

However, the impressions and evaluations which matter most to the child are those of their 'significant others', and for the slave or colonial child, of course, it was his parents and their masters of course. What kind of self-concept would one expect a slave child to develop, given the peculiar environment and social structure into which he or she was born and their parents' (the starting point of their self-concept construction) position within the social structure? Would it be a personality with a well-polished and positive self-image or one ashamed by the very fact and circumstance of their birth? Answers to these questions are provided by African-Caribbean plays which offer an array of characters who seem to curse the fact of their being black and who would do anything to escape from this damaging limitation imposed by their race and skin colour. Makak in *Dream on Monkey Mountain*, Miss Aggy in *Old Story Time*, Jean in Matura's *Meetings*, some of the characters in Daniel Boukman's *Orphée nègre* (in *Chants* 1993, see also Upton, 1998) and a host of others are examples of characters engaged in a desperate struggle to escape from the prison of their race and skin colour.

As it had been for the slave child, so it was for the colonial child as every individual is invariably a child of their culture and of their society, and of course of their special experiences within both (see Parsons, 1968: 21). Both the slave child and the colonial child grew up in cultures of repression and silence. Their respective societies were ones of dominance and oppression, societies in which their fathers and mothers were dominated and oppressed, in which they were treated as less than human and they had no power to set the course of their lives or those of their children.

Even then, it was not only the slave or colonised children who were affected by the all-round assault on the black psyche. The fathers and mothers were affected too, being the direct objects of the cultural and psychological attack. As Ngugi wa Thiong'o points out:

To control a people's culture is to control their tools of self-definition in relationship to others. . . . For colonialism this involved two aspects of the same process: the destruction or the deliberate undervaluing of a people's culture, their art, dances, religions, history, geography, education, orature and literature, and the conscious elevation of the language of the colonizer (1986: 16).

If, as was the case in all the colonies, the native languages of the colonised were degraded, if their cultures were denigrated, if everything about them was made to appear ugly, primitive, debased, then conversely, everything of the coloniser became beautiful, civilised and elevated. And so, when the coloniser systematically turned the colonised into a spineless, cultureless object it is not surprising that when this object-person attempted to define himself or herself as Souris or Makak do in *Dream on Monkey Mountain*, only negative images could be summoned because all their lives had turned out negative because of slavery and colonialism and the dehumanising structures which sustained them. Creating a self-image requires going into oneself, and the self consists of:

the 'I' or subject - the one who acts, the doer in the world and who tries to control it; then the 'Me' - the object, the observed, the acted upon (Mischel, 1976: 249).

When one focuses attention on the self what one usually encounters is the 'me'. So, when the slave or colonised native looked at himself, what he saw was only the object 'me' which corresponded to a negative and powerless individual. And this was the image that confronted the child as he or she began to construct his or her identity as part of the rituals of infancy. Every child wants a hero for a father, but the slave and colonial environments left no such heroes to satisfy the longing in the children of slaves and colonised peoples. The latter therefore sought their heroes elsewhere, and of course there were imperial colonial and slave literatures to provide them with numerous white heroes whose heroisms were achieved at the expense of black villains, devils and monsters. And because the child did not like the non-heroic portraits of the fathers and mothers, he began to identify with the 'other' who was heroic, just as their parents after a while had begun to imitate the oppressor in order to escape oppression and humiliation. This need by the oppressed (slaves and colonised peoples) to escape through imitation or 'mimicry' is responsible for the curious identification of the oppressed with the oppressor which Memmi describes in his portrait of the colonised and the coloniser. He writes that what surprises about the negative portrait of the colonised is,

> the echo that it excites in the colonized himself. Constantly confronted with this image of himself, set forth and imposed on all institutions and in every human act, how could the colonized help reacting to his portrait? It cannot leave him indifferent and remain a veneer which, like an insult, blows away with the wind. He ends up recognizing it as one would a detested nickname which has become a familiar description. The accusation disturbs and worries him even more because he admires and fears his accuser . . . . Wilfully created and spread by the colonizer, this mythical and degrading portrait ends up being accepted and lived with to an extent by the colonized. It thus acquires a certain amount of reality and contributes to the true portrait of the colonized (1974: 87).

Fanon sees this as but a dangerous movement towards a disintegrated psychic structure. The yearning to escape from the humiliating prison of their skin and race is believed by some to be achievable only through whiteness. This precisely is the choice Miss Aggy makes in *Old Story Time*. In her case, because it appears to be no longer possible for her because of old age, she projects this desire onto her son, Len, who she must transform at all costs - first through education and hopefully through marriage to a long-haired white girl. The same desire is also at the root of Lestrade's psychosis in *Dream on Monkey Mountain*. Lestrade yearns to be accepted into white society by becoming an agent of the law and helping to put the 'natives' (niggers) down. Makak, on the other hand, longs for escape from his skin through a union with the White Goddess of his dreams. These characters are summed up by Fanon when he writes:

> Out of the blackest part of my soul, across the zebra striping of my mind, surges this desire to be suddenly white. I wish to be acknowledged not as black but as white ... who but a white woman can do this for me? By loving me she proves that I am worthy of white love. I am loved like a white man, I am a white man (1967: 63).

And by possessing the white woman or object, the black psychotic hopes to possess or become a part of white culture. This explains both Miss Aggy's obsession and Makak's hallucinatory desires.

This is the problem of the colonised in the grip of psychic alienation. It must be noted though that very often the degree of alienation is in proportion to the level and depth of education and contact with European culture. This is more obvious in Africa where a majority of the natives, in spite of the colonial presence, had retained links with their indigenous cultures. Caribbean peoples of African descent, on the other hand, having gone through the double process of cultural emasculation, suffer a higher degree of alienation and the desire to escape from the social limitations imposed on them by their skin colour is more as Fanon shows in *Black Skins White Masks*. The problem for African and Caribbean societies today, it seems, is that there are still a lot of these 'apes of white culture' whose condition is better known as 'colonial mentality'. For those who have gone far along the road away from their African and African-Caribbean cultures, the process of return to roots is slow and needs proper guidance. As Memmi warns:

> The colonizer lives on for a long time in the decolonized man and we will have to wait longer still before we see that really new man (1968: 88).

Here then is the relevance of the playwrights being studied here. Their works are characterised by a sense of purpose and an inward looking approach. Their plays are specifically addressed to black and African peoples and their analyses are of the characters as well as of the audience. Another characteristic of this drama is that unlike the Negritude writers (such as Leopold Sedar Senghor in his poetry), the dramatists do not protest their blackness or the existence of black African or African-Caribbean cultures, nor do they create referential counter-myths that present European cultures as negative and African ones as positive. They also differ from the Negritude writers in the counter-discourse and counter-narrative strategies they use to challenge white distortions and denigration of black peoples' histories and cultures. Chinua Achebe speaks for these dramatists when he writes that his task as a postcolonial writer is,

> to help my society regain belief in itself and put away the complexes of years of degradation and self-abasement. For no thinking African can escape the pain of the wound in our souls.... The writer cannot expect to be excused from the task of re-educating and regeneration that must be done (1973: 3).

The oppression and emasculation which Africa and African-Caribbean peoples experienced under slavery or colonialism had without a doubt left a mark on their psyches. The writers are concerned with helping the formerly enslaved or colonised black peoples to re-emerge from racial despair to reclaim and re-assert their cultures, histories and identities. They hope to help black people fashion new images of themselves, by helping them retrieve their sense of self previously lost. This task involves helping Africans and Caribbean peoples of African descent to re-examine themselves and to find out about their histories, to re-evaluate their collective and individual experiences. All the myths about African and Negro inferiority, laziness and indolence, lack of history and culture, excessive sexuality, low intelligence, savagery and bestiality, had to be exposed as lies that underpinned the tropes of slave and colonial discourse. As Fanon says:

> Negroes are savages, brutes, illiterates. But in my own case I knew these statements were false. There was a myth of the Negro that had to be destroyed at all costs (1967: 117).

In exploding these myths, what the writers want to achieve is, consciously or unconsciously, to help their African and African-Caribbean peoples to free themselves of the complexes that have been developed as a result of slave and the colonial environments.

Although African and Caribbean peoples passed through relatively similar experiences, the quest for self-retrieval it seems is pursued in widely differing ways by the dramatists and characters in the plays. These differences are easily noticeable, not only between African and Caribbean writers, but also between writers from the same continent. Broadly speaking, this book identifies two distinct forms which the African and Caribbean journey to cultural retrieval and self-knowledge takes.

In Caribbean theatre, there is a preponderance of the theme of individual search for an understanding of the self and their position in society. This is the theme Walcott, Matura and Rhone explore in *Dream on Monkey Mountain, Meetings* and *Old Story Time* respectively. For these Caribbean playwrights of African descent, the search is a personal one. The African writers, on the other hand, see the search as a collective endeavour and in their plays one hardly encounters characters racked by personal doubts and needing personalised confrontations with history as we do in the Caribbean plays. Rather one finds in the African plays the theme of society in search of its soul, its destiny, culture and history. Scott's *An Echo in the Bone* shares this collective approach with the African plays. Sometimes, as in Soyinka's *Death and the King's Horseman*, the playwright is not concerned with merely stating a historical or cultural fact, but instead strongly makes a case for an African world seriously threatened from within and from without. But, whatever form this quest or search takes, the result is often the same: for the African characters and those in Scott's play, a clearer view of the self through a thorough and more sympathetic understanding of society; and for the Caribbean characters, an acceptance of the nature of society through coming to terms with the self. In sum, the outcome is an African or African-Caribbean personality reconciled and comfortable in mind and body to the fact of their cultural and racial origins.

In general, the writers, in seeking to mend the damage done by the myths that had been used to justify slavery and colonial atrocities, try, not to create counter-myths that denigrate Europe and Europeans, but instead to re-create and re-present African and African-Caribbean histories shorn of all the distortions, or simply by counter-discursively creating positive characters who do not resemble the stereotypes of slave and colonial discourses. Oba Nogbaisi, Dedan Kimathi, Dona Béatrice, Chaka, Cetsewayo, King Albouri are examples of African historical personages whose images are both regenerated and recuperated. Occasionally when they present such characters, they are intentionally made the butt of derisive laughter. So, exploiting the power of literature which had been the weapon of slave and colonial institutions, African and Caribbean writers lead readers and audiences to re-examine themselves, to begin to see themselves anew, and in the process to begin to ignore all the false images which hitherto had been created of them.

In trying to be a means for African and African-Caribbean peoples to search for and recuperate their denigrated images of themselves, cultures and histories, dramatists adopt three distinct modes of representation. Thus plays have been grouped according to which approach to the search for self-understanding adopted by the dramatist. There are three headings; plays in which characters undertake soul journeys; plays which debunk the myths by challenging the racial archetypes; and finally, plays which reinterpret or reread history. All three approaches involve strategies of counter-discourse and counter-narrativity. The first two types will be discussed in this chapter while the history plays will be looked at in the next chapter.

Journey into the Self

A majority of African-Caribbean dramatists take a different approach in the quest to mend psyches damaged by long years of emasculation under slavery and colonialism. While the African plays present specific events and personages from history from which they recover the heroism of these characters and their times, the Caribbean writers are neither in search of heroes, nor are they interested in presenting history as immutably flowing into and informing the present. Their focus is more on the African-Caribbean person now; they are interested in his or her life, values, and world, but above all, they are interested in his or her alienation in the present. Although fully aware of the historical dimension of the Caribbean psychic dilemma, the majority of the playwrights avoid specific historicity, and for Walcott, arguably the region's greatest poet and dramatist and who has written a trilogy on the Haitian revolution, 'it is not the pressure of the past which torments great poets but the weight of the present' (1978: 40). This appears to be the guiding philosophy of much Caribbean writing. This is not to suggest that the writers run away from the past as that would be untrue. The fact is that where the African writers studied so far work from the past to the present, their Caribbean counterparts look at the present to see what light it can throw on the past. The result however is the same: both sets of dramatists and plays present reconciled and enduring African and African-Caribbean characters that do not fit the European stereotypes of black and African peoples.

Naturally, the quest for the Caribbean writers takes the form of a journey into the self, an examination of an individual consciousness to discover the root cause of the alienation which can be found in the past but which still significantly affects the present. Whenever there is a need to visit the past, as in *Dream on Monkey Mountain* and *An Echo in the Bone*, the past is usually generalised and subjected to the consciousness of an individual self in search of its soul and the causes of events in the present. However, in the second respect, the Caribbean plays resemble the African plays in their shared view that black people have to understand their past, come to terms with it if they ever hope to understand and transcend their present predicament, and through this knowledge to bring about a better future. It is this shared belief in the important link between the past, present and future which serves as a unifying bond between African and African-Caribbean perceptions of the world; a perception which this study argues arises from a unique African metaphysics which recognises and accepts the inter-relationship between all realms of existence, as well as all schemes of time. This worldview is an underlying and ever present influence and motif in the theatres and literatures of Africa and the African diaspora in the Caribbean.

For Caribbean peoples of African descent the issue of identity is a central question, one which most intellectual efforts in the islands address:

In what ways will the black man of the Caribbean come to terms with himself, convert himself to what he is, find his true self in society, and in history? How will he make the synthesis of the diverse historical components of his culture? Under what conditions will he eventually decolonize the socioeconomic structures and the psychological structures which have made life in the Caribbean one of the greatest scandals of the 20th century? (Depestre, 1973: 51)

There are as yet no answers to these philosophical questions which relate to the search for a Caribbean identity. As Depestre again points out, it is a fact that in the Caribbean 'men and women have not yet been able to recover their social character, their profound personality, their humanity and beauty which colonization has alienated' (51).

This is the issue which a play like *Dream on Monkey Mountain* explores through a psycho-analytic process which enables Makak to go into himself to discover his innate contradictions and complexes, his origins, and in the end to come to terms with the fact of his blackness and Afro-Caribbeanness. What happens to Makak as a result of this self-search, and by extension Corporal Lestrade (the mulatto), and the audience of black people, is like the archetypal journey into the centre of being. It is a necessary journey but one in which,

The road is arduous, fraught with perils, because it is, in fact, a rite of passage from the profane to the sacred, from the ephemeral and illusory to reality and eternity, from death to life, from man to divinity. Attaining the centre is equivalent to an ... initiation; yesterday's profane and illusory existence gives place to a new life that is real, enduring and effective (Eliade, 1965: 18).

In this play, Walcott succeeds in fabricating a collective rite of passage for both the characters and for the audience. When Makak and Lestrade emerge from their journey at the end of the play they are newly reborn individuals who appear to be surer of themselves and their place and role within their society. Makak's exuberant shout at the end of his search is 'Now, O God, I am free' (*Dream on Monkey Mountain*, 320) and Lestrade declares 'I was what I am, but now I am myself. . . . My feet grip like roots' (299); both statements confirm the self-discovery and knowledge resulting from the journey they had undertaken.

A similar discovery concludes *An Echo in the Bone* when, once out of the state of possession, the whole Crew family and their assembled friends at the wake come to a fuller understanding of and love for one another. The happy wife, mother and mother-in-law, Rachel, sums up their collective experience:

> We is here, don't it so? No matter what is past you can't stop the blood from drumming, and you can't stop the heart from hoping. We have to hold on to one another. That is all we can do. That is what leave behind (*An Echo in the Bone*, p, 136).

To forewarn the reader of the complex and illogical structure of his dream play, Walcott prefaces *Dream on Monkey Mountain* with Jean-Paul Sartre's essay on psychosis, the latter a preface to Fanon's *The Wretched of the Earth*:

> Thus in certain psychoses the hallucinated person tired of always being insulted by his demon, one fine day starts hearing the voice of an angel who pays him compliments; but the jeers don't stop for all that; only from then on, they alternate with congratulations. This is a defence, but it is also the end of the story. The self is dissociated, and the patient heads for madness (in *Dream on Monkey Mountain*, p, 211).

The audience thus knows what kind of story and characters to expect - individuals buried deep in their personal hallucinations, black schizoids whose only hope of release from their misery is through becoming white like their tormentors. A majority of them are lost in that craze 'for whiteness that does drive niggers mad'. For Makak, this craze is symbolised by his longing for the white apparition, which in Afro-Caribbean folklore is a white diablese, a demon woman of great seductiveness who lures men to their deaths. Makak, the black ugly charcoal vendor, and Lestrade, the mulatto police corporal, are the central characters in the play, and each is locked in his own personal psychosis. But at same time, Makak and Lestrade are different projections of the same person, for it is clear that Lestrade is Makak and Makak is Lestrade; what ties the two together are the white demon woman and the black self-hating Moustique. Walcott's symbolism in this play is complex but effective and its entire structure and texture is multi-layered. Moustique represents Lestrade's and Makak's hatred of their black cultural identities, while the demon woman is all they love and desire about white culture. And it is the tension and pull between these two that creates the alienation or crisis of identity that each feels.

The play is a dream, 'one that exists as much in the given minds of its principal characters as in that of the writer' (*Dream on Monkey Mountain*, p, 208). Walcott here is possibly exploring his own consciousness in search of a reconciliation of personal conflicts of identity; conflicts from childhood which he admits in his essay, 'What the Twilight Says' (in *Dream on Monkey Mountain*, p, 3-40). The image of himself and his twin brother, Roderick, forlorn as they stood and watched a procession of black Salvation Army worshippers who they could not join because they were not of the right colour, but whose music aroused deeply buried ancestral chords in the minds of the two innocent watchers:

> then a kind of march would begin, but one that kept the native beat. Yet, like the long applauded note, joy soared further from the two pale children staring from their upstairs window, wanting to march with that ragged, bare-footed crowd, but who could not because they were not black and poor, until for one of them, watching the shouting limber congregation, that difference became a sadness, that sadness a rage, and that longing to share their lives' ambition so that at least one convert was made (22).

Searching for the self requires courage; it is an act of will which needs patience for 'it is a journey from man back to ape, through a darkness whose terminus is amnesia, and one which every one should make in order to articulate their origins' (5). And in presenting Makak and Lestrade, Walcott, perhaps unconsciously presents himself and the resolution of his crisis of identity. It is a moving theatrical experience because it is born of a sincere act of soul-searching and unburdening, and his poetry reaches sublime heights in this powerful drama. The sounds, which emanate from the events and the characters resonate like echoes from the depth of the soul, haunting and true.

In a dream the unconscious mind is able to let out its fantasies and desires which in waking life are kept suppressed in the sub-conscious; a person is able to give their desires and fantasies wings and there are no limits to where and what heights these can reach as do Makak's in *Dream on Monkey Mountain*. Carl Jung (see Fonagy & Higgit, 1984; Mischel, 1976; and Hall & Lindzey, 1978) argues that the human psyche includes not only a conscious aspect, but also a covert or shadow side which is unconscious. The latter is made up of archetypes consisting of basic elements or primordial images that are usually manifested in dreams or myths. The growth of an individual psyche takes place only when the shadow unfolds and is gradually integrated with the conscious into a coherent pattern. Walcott's characters are able to achieve this at the end of the play. The shadow is the contradictory aspect of the conscious and this is why it is repressed in the first place; but a balanced personality is one

31

in which usually opposing components are successfully reconciled. Lestrade's problem in the play and the reason why he treats Makak so brutally is because he adopts a defence mechanism and Makak is his shadow, which he has to repress or deny - Makak is his black side, which he does not want to acknowledge. When an individual's two sides remain strongly opposed to each other, this can lead to the two contesting for supremacy by being manifested simultaneously. A schizophrenic gap results in which the personality is split into two selves at odds with each other, a condition manifested in different ways in some characters in Caribbean plays. There are some, like Makak and Lestrade, who have reached the extreme stages described by Sartre, and there also those, like Jean in Mustapha Matura's *Meetings*, who continue to suppress, though not always successfully, their shadows. The latter often require progressive systems of defence to be able to cope with their psychic alienation.

The journey to the centre is often littered with pitfalls; but there are also immense psychological benefits for those who undertake it. For those who endure and accept everything they encounter, the reward is peace with and understanding of the self. This is the journey which Makak, and through him Lestrade and the audience make in *Dream on Monkey Mountain*. It is also a journey undertaken vicariously by the characters in *An Echo in the Bone* through Sonson's possession at the wake for his father, Crew. Hugh in *Meetings* makes a similar journey; although his is more at the physical level but his internal conflicts and process of reconciliation with his past are dramatised in much the same way as those of the characters from the other two plays are. His actions throughout are determined by similar psycho-analytical processes, however, his identity problem seem to have stopped short of the psychotic stage which Makak's or Lestrade's had reached.

In general, in the Caribbean plays many of the characters make this journey into the self in order to discover the images and ideas buried in the unconscious, images which constantly demand to be acknowledged. For Walcott (quoted in Lyn, 1980: 50), Caribbean peoples of African descent, especially those of mixed race, must 'perceive in proper perspective that black Atlantis buried in a sea of sand' - that is, they must connect with their unconscious in order to discover their true identity which can only come from a reclaiming and recuperation of their racial and cultural memory. It is significant that only at the moment when he finally arrives at the heart of the jungle (inner self) that Lestrade is able to resolve his crisis of identity. All previous contradictions - his hate-love reactions to blackness - fade away and a new person is born. Likewise, deep in the heart of the forest Makak recovers his humanity and sense of self and could now return to his Caribbean island, fully reconciled to his home and to the fact of being of African-Caribbean ancestry.

Dream on Monkey Mountain dramatises Makak's dream and his periodic hallucinations. He is a man suffering a self-imposed social isolation because of his shame about his skin colour. Makak believes that he is extremely ugly and thus unfit to live among other human beings and so retreats to Monkey Mountain to hide from the world. But escape is not possible for him as he can get neither joy nor release in his insularity for there is also his partner, Moustique, who constantly reminds him that he must descend from his lonely mountain home to rejoin the world. Thus, Makak is inextricably trapped in the nightmare of his skin colour and his desire to break out of this prison through association with white culture is the root cause of his hallucinations. At the mock trial, Makak, in his defence, informs the audience of his aversion to seeing his face's reflection and that it is in order to avoid this ugly sight that he escaped into the mists of Monkey Mountain:

> Sirs, I am sixty years old. I have live all my life like a wild beast in hiding
> . . .
> Is thirty years now I have look in no mirror
> Not a pool of cold water, when I must drink
> I stir my hands first, to break up my image
> (*Dream on Monkey Mountain*, p, 226).

This unacceptable image of himself has to be destroyed permanently, but only by him passing through a 'white mist' so his ugly blackness would be washed away. To achieve this, he creates the white apparition, 'an image and symbol of his longing' which begins to dominate his dreams. Makak's dreams are, however, not altogether negative because they also help him to retrace his roots. Through his dreams he is able to go back to the time of slavery, and then further back to a time before slavery, to his very beginnings in Africa. Using his mind, Makak compels his companions (and the audience/readers vicariously) to sail along with him on his dream boat:

> What power can crawl on the bottom of the sea, or swim in the ocean of the air above us? The mind, the mind, Now, come with me, the mind can bring the dead to life, it can go back, back, back deep into time. It can make a man king, it can make him a beast. Can you hear the sea now, can you hear the sound of suffering, we are moving back now . . . (291).

The Makak who is speaking here is one who has found himself and a voice. This is a lyrical passage, almost like a hypnotic ritual incantation and in it Walcott makes a point crucial to the play: that self discovery for each person is a task which that person has to perform for themselves as the potential to do so lies within each individual. And for the Caribbean persons of African descent this means going into themselves and purging themselves of racial complexes, of wild unrealisable dreams about Africa, and reconciling themselves to their Caribbean island nations and home. For the mulatto, such as Lestrade, and the whole Caribbean culture which, according to Walcott, is also a mulatto (hybrid) culture, maturity and a real sense of self can only come through 'the assimilation of the features of every ancestor' (1978: 38). As Walcott adds, the problem of the Caribbean person is the fact that:

> The law is all he can remember about the past. Slaves, the children of slaves, colonials, then pathetic, unpunctual nationalists . . . . First, we have not wholly sunk into our landscapes . . . our bodies make only light, unlasting impressions on our earth. It is not an earth that has been fed long with the mulch of cultures . . . Everything is immediate, and this immediacy means over-breeding, illegitimacy, migration without remorse. The sprout casually stuck in the soil. The depth of being rooted is related to the shallowness of racial despair. The migratory West Indian feels rootless on his own earth, chafing at its beaches
> (*Dream on Monkey Mountain*, p, 20-1).

Caribbean peoples must reconcile the past, present and the future before they can begin to accept their Caribbeanness. Once they do, their sense of rootlessness would disappear and the acceptance must also include an acceptance of their diverse origins and cultures which have been melding over the centuries. Walcott's abiding message to all Caribbean peoples is for them to recognise the fact that Africa, the Caribbean and Europe meet and merge in the West Indian.

Of dramatic importance is the fact that Makak, using his mind is able to get the other characters to act out his dream with him. Makak is able to bring his 'actors' to act with him because they too have the same fantasies and nightmares that he has. Yet, at another level, the characters are all aspects of the same person, projections of Makak's multi-faceted and tormented personality. The physical process of going deeper and deeper into the forest and to 'Africa' corresponds to the psychological one of getting nearer and nearer to the core of Makak's personality, and what is discovered at the end is Africa which, according to Obiechina (1986), resides in the soul of all Africa's dispersed children living in the diaspora.

Makak's journey is important because it draws Lestrade in pursuit of his own shadow and centre of being, which symbolically is Makak. At the point in the centre of the forest when the two come to a realisation of themselves, the physical meets and corresponds to the psychological in the play. The audience is presented with an action which they can perceive at three levels, proceeding to an inevitable dramatic merging in the scene where all the characters meet in Makak's 'kingdom' in Africa, or more accurately, where they all encounter and accept their common bond which is their blackness and African ancestry.

Makak's periodic dream or full moon madness is a form of psychic revolution, 'an internal convulsion which becomes a periodically necessary purgation of the oppressor or colonizer from the souls of those he has insidiously occupied' (Dawes, 1984). In Makak's case, he has to purge his mind of the oppressive image of his white woman by beheading her in the final scene. The act has to be personal since she is his creation, and only through killing her can he become free of her. Thus, Lestrade is right when he cautions:

> What you behold, my prince, was but an image of your longing. As inaccessible as snow, as fatal as leprosy . . . . You must violate, humiliate, destroy her, otherwise humility will infect you. You will come out in blotches (*Dream on Monkey Mountain*, p, 318).

The White Goddess possesses the imagination and dreams of the other characters as well and it is the image of her which feeds their alienation because of her inaccessibility. They, like Lestrade, want and yet hate her because she is the 'mother of civilization and the confounder of blackness' (*Dream on Monkey Mountain*, p,). This idea of love and hate conforms to the Jungian archetype of primordial desires, which in the case of African-Caribbean peoples is a perceived mix of hatred and desire for white culture. Fanon (1967) has already pointed out that most Antilleans strive to consummate this desire. But for a black person seeking to discover the self, this idea and the desire which it represents has to be expurgated as Lestrade implores Makak to do:

> If you want to discover the beautiful depth of your blackness, nigger, chop off her head . . . . She is the white light that paralysed your mind, that led you into this confusion. It is you who created her, so kill her! Kill her ! (*Dream on Monkey Mountain*, p, 319).

In the end Makak becomes free, after ritually executing both Moustique (the symbol of his black self-hate) and the Apparition (which symbolises his desire for white culture), and what is left is a harmony of black and white symbolised by Lestrade, now reconciled to his mixed-race identity. Walcott's ideal Caribbean is a mulatto (a hybrid) who accepts but transcends both sides of their ancestry - a Lestrade purged of both his obsessive love and admiration for white culture and his extreme anti-black neurosis. Makak is the dark side of Lestrade which he finally accepts, while the latter is the manifestation of Makak's desire to mix with whiteness. Thus, it is not by accident that Lestrade refers to Makak as 'old father' and later as 'grandfather' in the final scene when he comes to accept his cultural and racial identity. Makak's response to Lestrade's plea for acceptance is a statement of oneness: 'Now, he is one of us . . . . They reject half of you. We accept all' (pp. 299-300). Lestrade is finally home to where he belongs, in the bosom of his race. His journey into the self has led to the beginnings of life for him. As it is for Lestrade, so it is for the other characters, and for the audiences of Caribbean peoples. Even Souris, the habitual rogue, admits that Makak's crazed dream was useful after all for it made him realise: 'I believe I am better than I am. He teach me that.... His madness worth more to me than your friendship' (*Dream on Monkey Mountain*, pp. 302-3).

An Echo in the Bone deals with a similar psychic journey which takes the characters back to the beginnings of African-Caribbean history and like many other Caribbean plays by writers of African descent, it leads the audience/reader inevitably back to trans-Atlantic slavery. Unlike *Dream on Monkey Mountain* which represents a personal journey of sorts, *An Echo in the Bone,* as well as being a whodunit murder mystery, is in fact a voyage of discovery into the communal psyche of African-Caribbean peoples because, as Walcott points out in 'The Muse of History':

> For us in the archipelago the tribal memory is salted with the bitter memory of migration . . . the degraded arrival [which] must be seen as the beginning, not the end of our history (1978: 40).

The African-Caribbean person is a product of the slave encounter, and little wonder then, as the plays being studied show, that etched in the unconscious of every Caribbean person of African descent is the painful memory of the 'middle passage', and any excursion into the self inevitably brings the individual face to face with this racial scar. Makak in the speech quoted previously talks about 'the belly of the boat' and 'the sound of suffering'; Marie in Matura's play takes Hugh back to the slave era; and in *An Echo* slavery and its consequences for the descendants in the Caribbean is the main thread of the dramatic action.

The setting for the play is a funeral wake in memory of Crew. As in Walcott's play which uses dream, the possession during the wake is a dramatic device that allows the action to explode the boundaries of time and space in a series of dream-like episodes. Scott's detailed instruction for the setting is significant:

> The action of the play originates in an old sugar barn behind Crew's cottage, nine nights after the killing of estate owner, Mr Charles, and the disappearance of Crew. The action moves through the present, a ship moored off Africa in 1972, Madam's shop two days ago, an auctioneer's shop in 1820, woods near the estate in 1833, Crew's house four years ago, a Great House in 1834, a field in 1937, and outside the Great House last week (*Plays for Today*, p, 75).

Through this explosion of and escape from the confines of sequential time, the characters move through a plethora of seemingly unrelated events which alternate between the present and the past. The illogicality of the action disappears in the end when the long oppressed Crew kills Mr Charles. By going through these actions, the characters are forced to examine their lives, defeated and self-denigrating as they appear, then into the mind of the absent Crew where they find a meaning and some pride for and from his act. This emerges only through the unconscious journey with him through his son, Sonson, across the terrains of racial history in the Caribbean. The play presents a past that is valid and necessary because it helps the present to understand itself. One witnesses in the play a series of events through which, according to Hill, 'characters effortlessly adopt other personas as racial memory is evoked to flash sequences of black slavery, peonage and attendant evils before our eyes' (in *Plays for Today*, p, 1).

Central to *An Echo in the Bone* is a sense of cultural and racial origins. An awareness of cultural and racial roots provides the underlying theme and tension for the main action of the play; it underpins the conflict between Crew and Mr Charles, his oppressor and descendant of the slave master. Their confrontation is also the archetypal confrontation between black and white, and between slave and master. Rachel, the dead man's wife, is proud even in mourning and she has tried to bring up her two sons, Sonson and Jacko, with the same pride in the self and race that their father had. The play suggests that pride in racial origins must be recovered and repossessed by African-Caribbean peoples before they can reclaim and repair their humanity that was bruised and battered under slavery.

Brigit, one of the few characters in the play to have a positive self-image, makes the point that it is not an easy thing for a person to live without respect, especially in their Caribbean home where, as she says, white people still treat black people like dirt. To drive her point home, she is highly critical of Lally for the latter's lack of and nonchalant attitude to self and racial pride:

> I born poor, you hear me, and black and the only thing I have is my pride . . . . And if the owner of this estate should call me and say lie down girl, you don't have nothing to lose, is the same thing I will tell him like I tell all the others - I don't have anything but I have a right to answer no. Black people used to work this land for nothing and they used to treat them like beast, they could mount them anytime . . . . I is not an animal. I is a human being (115).

Brigit, unlike Makak in the previous play, neither desires to have mulattos as a means of socially elevating herself and her children, nor is she prepared to serve as a vehicle for anybody's sexual pleasure, whether black or white. She is the more positive female equivalent of Crew than Rachel is because it is her idea of self and her attitude which are dramatised by Sonson when he becomes his father during the possession scene. This sense of pride, a sense of being a man, independent and with a sense of responsibility for his wife and children which Brigit advocates finds full dramatic expression in the scene in which Crew tells Rachel about his history, about what his past and pride mean to him. When Rachel tells her husband that Master Charles has offered her a job as a housekeeper at the Great House, Crew (the possessed Sonson) explodes:

Sonson: You what?
Rachel: They want a housekeeper up there, Crew
Sonson: You? Housekeeper . . . . Then tell me something. What is to happen to the rest of us when you up there in white Massa house?
Rachel: Brigit in the house, Crew, she will do whatever you say . . . And one night a week, or two . . .
Sonson: You sounding as if everything settle already!
Rachel: I don't know, Crew! I going up there to find out!
Sonson: When you asked me about this?
Rachel: I never ask you . . .
Sonson: Well, you can haul yourself back to the house and put it out of your mind.

Rachel: You making joke!
Sonson: [*threatening*] Try me out
Rachel: You never raise your hand to me once yet. This is not the time
          to start.
Sonson: You think a man have no pride? I must let my woman support
          me, eh?
(126-7).

And later in the same scene, in a desperate effort to make her
understand how he feels, Crew goes back to his origins, to the history of
his family, right up to and through the slave era and after, his religious
attachment to the little piece of land which she was asking him to give up
and move into the city to look for work. Mr Charles, in fact, had been
trying to frustrate him and force him off the land by diverting water
away from it, but Crew is not prepared to give up what he regards as his
own piece of the earth, his only patrimony:

Sonson: I am like a dumb man trying to tell you what happened to him,
          I can only trace this line here in the hard dirt, see? And the line
          going from here to there, and this end is where they bring my
          great grandfather, here, and this is me. If you take away the line
          from the ground I am nothing. I am nobody!
Rachel: The land don't have to take the bread out of your mouth. The
          land is not everything!
Sonson: It is everything! Everything . . . . My father and his father sweat
          for it. It is my birthright that say I am not a slave anymore. I
          don't have to work for no man. I don't have to beg no man for
          bread to pass to my children. And my woman don't have to
          slave in any white man house. I don't care how much they pay
          you! Rachel, love, don't take that away from me.
(128).

This is an earnest cry from a man whose dignity is being seriously
threatened and it is a good thing that Rachel listens and gives up the idea
of becoming a housekeeper to the very person responsible for
undermining her husband's manhood. Crew is proud of his very little
portion of earth because it is a symbol of his freedom and manhood
which he is not prepared to mortgage. He is also proud of his occupation
as a farmer because it enables him to be a master of his own labour and
the product from it.

The intended effect of this scene on the observers - both those within
the play and those outside of it - is to give them an insight into the life
and mind of Crew, a man who killed, not because he was refused the

water he asked for, but because his dignity, integrity and very existence as a man were questioned, even denied, and also because he had suffered so long and Mr Charles seemed determined to prolong his suffering. For Crew, at that moment when Master Charles pushes him down the steps of the Great House and is poised to kick his face, the latter symbolises the long years of oppression and dehumanisation which he, Crew, and his race have suffered from the moment his ancestors stepped ashore from the slave ships. Crew's act is therefore a sudden explosion of a long suppressed rage triggered off by Mr Charles' act of further provocation. To account for this ungovernable and seemingly senseless rage of Crew's, Scott takes his audience carefully through the pages of African-Caribbean history, from which he,

> selects incidents from the near and distant past to show that violence has been inherent in the relations between the two races - with blacks invariably the victims - from the day the first slaving vessel arrived off the coast of Africa (*Plays for Today*, p, 12).

Conventionally, one should be appalled that Crew kills Mr Charles on such a trivial matter as being pushed down the steps. But when one considers the evidence from history, which the dramatist has assembled to explain Crew's seeming 'madness', one begins to understand him and to sympathise with this outrageous behaviour. Crew, like Makak in *Dream on Monkey Mountain*, liberates himself only through this seeming act of violence, for sometimes it needs only violence to confront or escape violence as history has shown only too often

The central message of the play is that persons of African descent in the Caribbean, though poor, should not let their humanity and pride be taken away from them as well. All they have to do is perform one decisive act of liberation to cut the chains that bind them to their socially and psychologically disabling slave history. Even among the slaves on the ship from Africa, Scott presents African slaves who heroically clung to their sense of self and dignity in the face of extreme dehumanising and humiliating actions of the slavers. They managed to retain their humanity, pride and Africanness in their souls and they remained unbroken in spirit as they fought their captors across the middle passage. It is to these that present generations of African peoples in the Caribbean should be thankful for a sense of history, cultural and racial memory. Most of the alienated psyches of black and oppressed people in the Caribbean, and as the plays show, grow from a sense of unrootedness which the harsh treatment suffered under slavery and colonialism had engendered. The key purpose of resurrecting the slave scenes is to use them to enable the present to fully understand where and when the suffering of peoples of African descent in the Caribbean began. Slavery was the beginning of African-Caribbean history, as well as the root cause of African-Caribbean misery; and it is hoped that this knowledge would put paid to the wild longing of some to return to an Africa which had become a distant memory, an Africa which had also contributed to the present predicament of her children in the diaspora. Crew's act, therefore, must be seen as a means of freeing himself from the chains of that horrible past and for the audience, it offers an opportunity for vicarious participation in a bold act of self liberation. The past was a terrible and revolting nightmare, but still it is a past which has to be relived in order to achieve catharsis and an escape from the humiliation and deprivation which it brought about. As in *Dream on Monkey Mountain*, the journey in *An Echo in the Bone* is like visiting the dark corners of a private island, in order to encounter and lay to rest the ghosts of the past. Also like *The Trial of Dedan Kimathi*, Scott's play seeks to restore a measure of confidence to a traumatised communal psyche by confronting it with an uncomfortable collective history.

If *Dream on Monkey Mountain* and *An Echo in the Bone* present audiences with characters undergoing intense psychic revolutions, Matura's *Meetings* is concerned with exploring the aftermath of such a psychic revision and the necessary realignment which follows in its wake. In this simple play - there are just three characters – Hugh (the male protagonist) puts into practice what he had learnt from his psychic journey. Matura, like Scott and Walcott, also believes that this type of psychic re-evaluation which Hugh has undergone should take place in every black person in the Caribbean. By the time the play opens, Hugh was already aware of his alienation, of his incompleteness; he also knew what was missing in his life. In this regard, he was ahead of Makak and Lestrade in Walcott's play, some of the characters in Scott's, as well as Miss Aggy in Rhone's *Old Story Time*. These other characters seem not to fully understand themselves when the reader first meets them, some do not understand themselves at all and so are therefore totally unaware of their alienation. They only become themselves in the end after their respective psychic explorations. Hugh is like Pa Ben and Len in *Old Story Time* and Brigit in *An Echo in the Bone*. These three are never for one moment alienated from their African-Caribbean cultural roots, and neither do they display any sense of inferiority to white characters.

Recognising his alienation, and also recognising what he had to do, all Hugh needed was a guide to lead him back to the soul of his African-Caribbean culture. This is provided by the though absent but still all pervasive Marie, through her granddaughter, Elsa. Between them, these two take Hugh through a slow process of memory recall, spanning his past, beyond his childhood, back to the time of slavery and the slave revolts in Trinidad (the slave rebellions occurred fairly frequently in Trinidad and Tobago between 1770 and 1829). Once again, as was the case in the other Caribbean plays of self and cultural retrieval, the journey stretches back and stops at that archetypal point when the history of African dispersal began, the 'degraded arrival' which, as Walcott pointed out earlier, was the beginning of their history in the Caribbean (1978: 40). The slave experience is central to Afro-Caribbean migration and each play studied so far strongly reinforces this point. The experience provides the dominant image in the communal unconscious of peoples of African descent in the diaspora. To understand themselves, they have to begin there because it is the point at which their cultural and psychological trauma began. They therefore must come to terms with that recurring image of the slave ancestor being ground through the inhumane mills of plantation slavery.

Hugh, unlike Makak and Crew, is not poor; he, in fact, belongs to the elite, the privileged few who have benefited from education and decolonisation. But in spite of his wealth and social status, he is still bugged by a feeling of incompleteness. His wife, Jean, on the other hand, thinks that all that is needed to wipe away feelings of inferiority is by behaving like a white person - eating white food, living a completely white life style, thinking and talking white. She vehemently denies her African-Caribbean identity and, for her, anything to do with traditional black culture is 'bush'. She, in fact, sees the black countryside and the people with the eyes of a white tourist as her comments indicate - black people who live in the country are ignorant noble savages of the Romantics to her. Jean suffers an acute form of 'colonial mentality' in which everything is measured against the slave master's or coloniser's values and frames of reference. For her, otherness is the white world into which she seeks to be admitted at all cost and against which everything has to be judged. Her whole life seems to be a determined fight to impress upon this significant other that she is good, and that whatever is found in the 'developed' world can also be found in her native Trinidad. Unfortunately, her portrayal in the play presents this as a negative kind of assertion because it is not born of a sense of pride in her local roots and customs, beginning, as it does, from a subliminal acceptance of inferiority. For all of Jean's education and 'feminism', she is Memmi's classic case of the colonised still living inside the decolonised.

Her dismissal of Marie as an ignorant old woman who should not meddle in matters well above her competence, especially when such matters concern 'renowned engineers trained abroad', shows Jean's total subscription to the colonial/white view of the black natives as being significantly low in intellection. But Hugh is quick to defend and point out to her the shallow criteria and values on which typical educated Trinidadians based their judgment. And to show her that the natives, though uneducated, are sometimes more knowledgeable than those who are, and, this he feels, is because they are close to their history and culture. Of Marie, he tells Jean:

> Dat woman know so much ting, and she en' read it in no book, is ting she learn for herself and tings that was handed down to her
> (*Play Mas, Independence and Meetings*, p, 82).

Hugh's encounter with Marie launches him on the road to re-education about the history and culture of his people, a culture and history that he had previously denied, and which Jean is still denying and resisting. Marie guides him through the significant moments of the past and as he says in amazement, 'she was telling me tings bout who had houses dere in de old days, wat life was like in de plantations, amazing tings bout de trees . . . de exact spot where the first rebellion of the slaves took place in Trinidad' (82). Through her he learns of the heroism of the maroons who revolted and their relevance to the history of Trinidad. In her simplicity and un-learnedness, she carries within her the history and culture of her island. And in order for Hugh to rid himself of his feelings of incompleteness, he must learn all these from her and his salvation lies in the fact that he is a willing pupil who is full of wonder at every revelation. His desire to 'eat all the old food' leads him to employ Elsa who becomes his second guide in his search for his cultural roots. Through discussing food, Elsa helps Hugh to re-visit the important landmarks of his childhood which he had successfully forgotten – these included memories of kite-flying in the fields as a boy, the mad bulls, sweeping the yards with brooms, and other mundane things, such as whistling. The urge to erase these signposts of the past is unhealthy and in the play Jean represents this tendency which arises from a feeling of inferiority. The play seems to be crying out for Jean to undergo her own psychic shake-up so that her repressed self can emerge like Hugh's to free her from her feelings of shame about her African-Caribbean identity. But she is far too gone to take her chance when it was offered to her. Hugh invites her to join him in his quest to understand the past and history of their people, but she dismisses his effort as a 'regression to barbarity', a movement backwards.

To make a point about the validity of the indigenous way of doing things, Matura shows, through Elsa, that before the sophisticated Europeans implements arrived, black people had ways and implements for handling and tackling their basic human needs, and these had never failed them and therefore are as relevant today as they were hundred years ago. Elsa's rejection of the electrical gadgets is not a condemnation rather her preference for her indigenous tools signifies her belief in the adequacy of the native tools to satisfy her needs. It is significant that she accepts the refrigerator since she does not possess an effective equivalent in her native stock of implements. This goes to show the eclectic nature of her indigenous culture which is willing to accept new ideas when they are better, without necessarily throwing away time-tested ones of her own. Elsa stubbornly refuses to duplicate the tools she needs for her job in Hugh's and Jean's house. It is significant that Hugh does not make or try to talk her into using the new and sophisticated ones at the expense of her own. This signifies his recognition of the usefulness and effectiveness of the indigenous culture. It is a stance which his wife is unable to adopt as she would find such an acceptance a regression to primitive times which would only cast a smudge on her 'been-to' image. Jean is too far gone in her denial of self that she seems incapable of seeing anything positive in black indigenous folks and their way of life. She has reached the point of no return and the audience/reader watches her drift along, knowing that she is doomed to be consumed by the modern values which she has become addicted to. The play ends with her sick and alone in the house, Hugh having made the choice to go up the mountains with Elsa to live among the country folks. Jean, by denying and running away from her past becomes fatally trapped in the present, and hers is a psyche that has gone beyond repair because she consistently refused to know and come to terms with herself.

As far as she is concerned, Hugh's identification with the knowledge and wisdom of the common people was like 'going backwards all the time'. This, however, does not bother Hugh since he seems sure of himself. To Jean's sarcastic comments, his response is:

> I want to know about dem people because dey have a lot ter teach we, about life an we history, we life is based on how dey live, how dey

adapted ter life wen dey come here after slavery (*Play Mas, Independence and Meetings*, p, 102).

These common people, Hugh feels, are the vital link in the chain that binds and leads the present to its past and soul, and cutting that link would be like setting oneself adrift. Hugh having realised this is determined to restore the link; but to his wife, his efforts are simply superstitious behaviour bothering on ignorance, 'Nancy' stories and witchcraft, which no modern educated person should attach much importance to. Hugh tries to point out to her that what mattered was not the superstition or the stories of witchcraft, but rather the underlying reasons behind them, why the people bring such stories into being. He believes that they do so for 'survival and sanity'.

Matura in the play echoes Scott, Walcott and many other Caribbean playwrights in arguing that the Caribbean people will understand the present through an understanding of the past. They should understand their history, the arrival of their ancestors to the islands on the slave ships, and how the African slaves managed to survive the trauma of plantation slavery. A proper understanding of the past, the plays suggest, can only come through the guidance of people like Marie and Elsa who have remained simple, who have not allowed modernity and its pressures and values to dislodge them from their historical links. The two represent the common folk who do not have the material possessions that Hugh and Jean have, but who have things inside them which the others lack. They have their humanity and culture intact. For Hugh:

> Dey stay that way ter give us, people like me, a chance ter see, ter see, how ter live, a nodder way a living, I want ter live like them, ter be like them, simple, uncomplicated (103).

In the end he chooses to join them and he is initiated into the rites of Shango. His acceptance does not mean a rejection of his education or his status in the society – Hugh reminds one of Olunde in Soyinka's *Death and the King's Horseman* who is glad to perform his role as demanded by custom in spite of his training as a doctor in England. What Hugh has done is to search for and discover the part of himself which had been missing, the part that was responsible for his estrangement from his culture. He completes himself at the end of the play by accommodating the diverse and seemingly contradictory elements of his personality and history. The roots go deep as Pa Ben informs his audience in *Old Story Time* and it is nothing one should be ashamed of. Those who search for their roots, like Makak, Lestrade, Hugh and the characters in *An Echo in the Bone*, discover their cultural and historical origins and are thereby restored. But those, like Jean, who scuff at and deny aspects of themselves because they are ashamed of their African-Caribbeanness, remain irredeemably lost, forever trapped in their alienation.

Slaves of the Archetypes

Frantz Fanon insisted that the central theme of his life and work was to teach his black brothers and sisters of the Antilles, and by extension all black and colonised peoples in the world, not to be slaves of the archetypes created for them by the collective unconscious of Europe (1967a: 35). Fanon sought to achieve this, not by creating alternative myths about European inferiority, savagery, bestiality, etc., but rather by proving that the existing myths of negation about black people were all false. That is why, as Sartre points out in his preface to *The Wretched of the Earth* (1967b: 9), Fanon's works are not addressed to white peoples, but to blacks whose lives he discusses. In this respect, he pre-dates the dramatists of cultural and racial affirmation whose works are being discussed in this book, since they too are involved in the same endeavour of exposing as false, the various myths and theories that were used, and are still being used, to suggest that the 'Negro is a stage in the slow evolution of monkey into man' (1967a: 17); that black people are intellectually and physiologically inferior. These negative archetypes of black people are taken on in different ways by the playwrights; some do this obliquely as in the plays that engage with historical and cultural revision such as *The Trial of Dedan Kimathi, Ovonramwen Nogbaisi, George William Gordon, L'Exil d'Albouri, Lat-Dior...* etc. Others, on the other hand, confront the stereotypes directly as in *Dream on Monkey Mountain, Old Story Time, Pantomime, Death and the King's Horseman*, Aimé Césaire's *Une tempête* (*A Tempest*, which is a revision of Shakespeare's *The Tempest*). Most adopt a defensive rejection of the archetypes by creating counter-discursive tales which challenge the images; however, a set of plays, mainly those from the Caribbean which explore the Haitian revolution, adopt a rather ironic tone in the way they present the archetypes/stereotypes. Walcott in particular, in his Haitian trilogy, uses irony to challenge or shame the present into an awareness of the mistakes of the past that need to be addressed if African-Caribbean achievements, socially and politically, are to become a reality. In fact, all the plays of Haitian history – James, Walcott, Césaire and Glissant - see a need to use the mistakes of the great heroes (villains as some of them turned out to be) of that defining moment of African-Caribbean history as a warning and indication of the malaise of contemporary Caribbean societies and their leadership.

Thus, the view that black people are a stage in human evolution from primates is unfortunately held by the Lestrade of the early part of *Dream on Monkey Mountain* when he says while addressing the black prisoners under his charge:

In the beginning was the ape, and the ape had no name, so God called him man. Now there were various tribes of the ape . . . and God looked at his handiwork, and saw that it was good. For some of the apes had straightened their backbone, and start walking upright, but there was one tribe unfortunately that lingered behind, and that was the nigger. Now if you apes will behave like gentlemen . . . (*Dream on Monkey Mountain*, p, 216-7).

Lestrade is not alone in this belief about the evolutionary backwardness of black peoples; Miss Aggy in *Old Story Time* has reached a pathological stage in her acceptance of Negro inferiority. All her life she labours and denies herself comfort, mortgages her dignity and pride to ensure her only son, Len, is lifted above the sub-human prison of their skin colour. The irony in the play is that what should have merited praise and admiration because it is a selfless sacrifice for her son does not because it is achieved at the price of self and race immolation. The only thing that redeems Miss Aggy in the eyes of the audience is her selflessness because, disgraceful and comic as her obsession with white culture is, she is not despicable. The compassion Miss Aggy evokes in the reader or audience is what makes her redemption and the reconciliation between her and her son and his wife, Lois, a welcome conclusion to an interesting and intense drama.

Because she is determined that Len should rise above the limitations of his skin colour, she scolds and beats him mercilessly when she catches him playing with a 'little dutty black gal'. Miss Aggy is an already damaged psyche in dire need of redemption. In her mind is a firmly ingrained negative perception of self, a deep-seated hatred for blackness and a consuming desire to see her son climb up the social ladder; first, through education, second, by not associating with black people, and third, through marriage to 'a nice brown girl with hair down her back'. Her problem arises from an acceptance of inferiority which has inevitably led to her low self-esteem. Two attitudes can result once the process of race immolation begins. The first is that the individual can develop a strong hatred of any person from the other race; or it can go further leading to an equally intense hatred for one's kind. Miss Aggy belongs to the second. Her line of development can be traced thus:

Low self-esteem → self-contempt → idealization of white → frantic efforts to be white → unattainable ideal → hostility to white or introjected white ideal → self-hatred → projected onto other blacks → hatred of other blacks (Kardiner and Oversay, 1968: 259).

Like Makak in *Dream on Monkey Mountain*, Miss Aggy does not end up with a feeling of hostility towards whites. They both rather introject the white ideal - Makak, through his desire for the White Goddess and Miss Aggy, through her son's marriage to Margaret. The difference between the two, however, is that Makak stops short of self-hatred because of the unattainability of his ideal. But Miss Aggy hates herself as a black person, and because of that she hates other black people, especially black women who represent a threat to her hopes of improving her family tree through miscegenation. The hatred and sense of threat are so intense that she invokes the powers of *obeah* to get rid of Lois for coming between her and the realisation of her desire. Her rage at the news of Lois's marriage to Len is so intense and irrational that she violently tears into two halves a wedding photograph of the two, hoping by such a symbolic act to sever the bond between the couple. And to ensure the severance is final, she flings Lois's half away while retaining only Len. Her greatest sorrow seems to be the realisation of the loss of Margaret whom she had set her heart so much on as the wife for her son.

In Miss Aggy, therefore, one witnesses the same obsession for whiteness (white culture, white people) which Lestrade alludes to in *Dream on Monkey Mountain*. She, Lestrade and Makak share the same longing: to lose themselves in a mist of whiteness which they see as their only hope out of their black predicament. However, by presenting Miss Aggy as a comic character, Rhone invites the black audience to laugh at her and through her at themselves because she is their shadow or a projection of themselves. What one feels for Miss Aggy is in fact what one feels for:

Clowns and fools who express another shadow aspect of human nature: we are wise and circumspect; they are rash and silly: they can make all the mistakes and do all the childish things we might do if we were not forever straining to behave correctly and we can laugh with relief that another person falls - not ourselves (Fordham, 1961: 65).

In laughing at them, and by assuming that superior stance over them which is a hallmark of comedy, audience members are able to purge themselves of the tendency to behave like clowns and fools. But at the same time, the audience gets vicarious satisfaction from watching them act out their secret fantasies. If to accept inferiority and then struggle desperately to escape from their skins, as Miss Aggy does throughout the play, is foolish and laughable, then one must strive not to be like her even if one also feels the way she feels. This is a therapeutic function of comedy and one which Rhone exploits in *Old Story Time*.

Other black characters in the play are positive as they show no hang-ups about being black. Each in his or her own way tries to point out to Miss Aggy how wrong and foolish her attitude to her race and culture is. Pa Ben, the wise old storyteller, argues with her when it became known to both of them that Len had married Lois, a 'dutty black gal'. In spite of her hesitant acceptance of the validity of the old man's argument, she promptly explains it away with the justification that her son's interest was her only motivation. True as this is, she still pays so much for it, and she also pushes too hard because ever from childhood, poor Len had it drummed and sometimes beaten into him that he must marry fair skinned Margaret and not a black girl. It got to a point when he naïvely writes a love letter to the girl. Ironically, however, it is the letter and the humiliating treatment he got from George and his gang that set him free of his mother's projected white fixation. His humiliation forces him to recognise and accept the fact and implication of his skin colour, first for him and then for his mother's hope of social improvement through interracial marriage/miscegenation. It is, therefore, not surprising that by the time he returns home to start work, he had already begun to accept himself as a black person who is happy to be so. By the beginning of the play one can see Len's increasing impatience with his mother for her continued worship of white people. And as he tries to help her come out of her prison of inferiority, she, for her part, ironically, is convinced that her son is the one in need of deliverance from the bondage which he had unwittingly been placed in. For her, that bondage is Lois, the symbol of his acceptance of his black identity. Lois thus must be removed so that Len can become free. Miss Aggy's strong belief in the purity and rightness of whiteness makes her blind to the fact that George is a con man who had been financially duping many others besides herself. Try as hard as he does, Len can not penetrate his mother's closed mind. For her, being a white person is proof of George's goodness and integrity. Anyone who questions the truth and logic of this must be an evil person. Lois must have seemed so evil to her to have succeeded in turning Len's head to make him question her convictions and choice. Consulting and invoking *obeah* seems her only answer to this menace. It is both comic and ironic that in her moment of need, Miss Aggy should fall back on African-Caribbean magic art, she who before then had despised all things black. In the end, it needed a proof of George's fraudulence, combined with the re-enactment of his very sadistic torments of Len, and the scathing remarks about her made by George to convince Miss Aggy that she had been wrong all along. Only the restraining hands of Len, Lois and the dependable Pa Ben keep her from cleansing her hands with George's blood.

In realising that George was the 'evil wretch' while Lois and her late father were the good Samaritans who took care of her son when he ran away from school, Miss Aggy realises the full implication of the *obeah* which she had invoked on her innocent daughter-in-law. By the end of the play, it is a fully chastened and enlightened old woman, who is surrounded by her loved ones, Lois, Len and Pa Ben. The final image is similar to that of Rachel and her family together in love and understanding after their intense psychic tribulations in *An Echo in the Bone*. In Miss Aggy's case, it is doubly significant that Lois should be the one to begin the necessary chants to ward off the boomeranging wrath of the spirits which the ignorant woman had unleashed. Lois generously forgives her mother-in-law because she understands what her problem had been - a concern for the well-being of Len, their mutual love. Lois understands roots and the need to be in touch with one's culture. Education, the play argues, is no excuse for a person to deny their ancestral roots and identity, as Jean does in *Meetings* or as Len tries to when Pa Ben consulted him about the possibility of neutralising his mother's curse on his wife. Mervin Morris sums it up accurately when he writes that the educated blacks of Jamaica have come a long way in their journey up from slavery, but that,

> they are creatures of the past; they may remember hurts; the Ph.D. will acknowledge obeah; the roots go deep (1981: xvi).

Running away from one's roots is like running away from one's shadow; it is as futile as trying to escape from the castle of one's skin.

Walcott revisits and reworks the colonial myth of Crusoe and Friday in his play, *Pantomime* (in *Remembrance and Pantomime*, 1980). He has handled this theme in some of his poems and essays. But this time, he not only explodes the myth but also successfully transforms what originally is mythic into a creative liberating narrative. In the play, he

> takes that old enduring European myth of Crusoe and Friday and transforms it to bring Caribbean man a true confrontation with his freedom and history (Taylor, 1986: 170).

Here one is reminded of the Nigerian dramatist Femi Osofisan and his subversive use of history and myths in plays such as *The Chattering and the Song*, *Morontodun*, and *Nkrumah Ni, Africa Ni*. Walcott's purpose in *Pantomime*, as with other dramatists studied, is not to supplant one myth with another as might seem from a casual reading; rather he engages in a postcolonial counter-discursive re-reading of the Friday-Crusoe myth. Here, roles are swapped and Jackson, the black servant, plays Crusoe, while Harry, the white master, becomes Friday. Walcott's intention is to ridicule myths as being essentially fabrications which can be unpacked and rearranged to offer a different narrative point of view. It is obvious that replacing a white mythical concept with a black one is merely to avoid or to fail to confront reality in its totality. Myths, the play argues, are unreal and they only help those who construct them to escape facing the world by providing 'acceptable rationalisation for things'. And to show the audience that what is happening in the play is a joke, Walcott creates this very perceptive and cocky Negro servant who sees what they are doing as only a game of acting. Both he and Harry are playing roles in a mythical script, roles which he (Jackson) does not believe in, but which however are real for Harry. Jackson is, thus, master of the situation because of his ability to slip in and out of his roles, while Harry can not.

Harry is unable to switch roles because he is a 'classical' actor who wants the classical European myth of Friday and Crusoe to remain intact. But Jackson's 'creole' acting, on the other hand, is a postcolonial appropriation and interrogation of the myth in a creative process of liberation for both of them, and through them, all the colonisers and colonised peoples in the Caribbean. The creolisation which Jackson deploys here is a form of hybridisation, a revolutionary 'third space' and form that is designed to be both creative and liberating. Jackson's Creole acting, like the Creole language, is a revolutionary statement which involves an appropriation and domestication of the very instrument of colonial and slave negation to affirm a new image for the former slave and colonised populations of the Caribbean. Harry's problem is his implicit belief in the myth which explains why he vigorously resists any role change. But Jackson is strong-willed, and although playing 'the smiling nigger' he is at the same time challenging the stereotype through his style of acting. He knows his mind and is very protective of his pride and dignity as a man, and he expects respect in all his relationships with black, brown or white. He points out to Harry that serving in the latter's establishment did not give the latter any right to 'mama guy' him. And to show that his patience with or tolerance of people who insulted him or his race had limits, he tells this macabre story of his encounter with a nigger-baiter. The subtle threat in the telling of the story is obvious and Harry being no fool is quick to pick up the implied threat. True, Jackson is sensitive about his race and culture, but he does not reject or moan about it. What he can not stand is anyone making fun or putting him down because of it, as Harry and his racially prejudiced colonial parrot try to do. Jackson's summary execution of the offending bird is meant to give warning of how far he is prepared to go when riled. As far as he is concerned, the parrot is racist and the ideas which it had been fed are those from colonial times and so are out of date in a post-colonial Trinidad. Of the dead parrot, Jackson tells its distraught owner:

> Language is ideas, Mr Trew. And I think this precolonial parrot have the wrong ideas (*Remembrance and Pantomime*, p, 99).

These ideas, Jackson argues, are those of the parrot's owner. In effect, the play is arguing that racism is taught through upbringing, and a child who is indoctrinated into racist thinking, like the parrot was, would grow up to become a racist. And if it is learned, then it can be unlearned and this is the whole point of Walcott's ridiculing of the myths which justify white racism; and he also ridicules any attempt to create black counter-myths to replace them.

Walcott's Friday is not the blubbering cowed savage which Defoe created. Jackson is a match for Harry, both as a person, as an actor and as a character within their performance. Using the rehearsal which is the main action of the play, he begins to knock down all the values on which white Crusoe's superiority is based. He starts with a deft but powerful sally on Christianity, the bedrock of all Crusoe's civilising mission. The same cannibalism which the black native is accused of forms the pivot of the Christian myth of the sacred body of Christ. Christians 'eat' the body and drink the blood of Christ, and Jackson can not see why or how this is not cannibalism:

> Jackson: Supposing I wasn't a waiter, and instead of breakfast I was serving you communion, this Sunday morning on this tropical

island, and I turn to you, Friday, to teach you my faith, and I
tell you kneel down and eat this man. . . . What would you say,
eh? You, this white savage?

Harry: No, that's cannibalism.

Jackson: Is no more cannibalism than to eat a god . . .

(112).

Harry is truly afraid to face reality and so he clings to his myths
which he does not want exploded as Jackson's acting is threatening to do.
But the latter can not be stopped once he starts and he launches into his
theory of the shadow:

> I was your shadow. I did what you did . . . each movement you made
> your shadow copied . . . and you smiled at me as a child smiles at his
> shadow's helpless obedience . . . Mr Crusoe . . . . But after a while the
> child gets frightened of the shadow he make . . . . But the shadow don't
> stop, no matter if the child stop playing that pantomime, and the
> shadow does follow the child everywhere . . . . He cannot get rid of it, no
> matter, and that is the power and black magic of the shadow . . . until it
> is the shadow that start dominating the child . . . and that is the victory
> of the shadow. . . . In that sun that never set, they's your shadow, you
> can't shake them off (112-3).

The colonisers and civilisers set out to create shadows of themselves
out of the ignorant savage natives, and they succeeded, for Friday
became Crusoe's shadow, but he also becomes his eclipse. Friday and
Caliban are the creatures and shadows of Crusoe and Prospero
respectively, and even when they become tired of playing the master-
servant game, these shadows of themselves still follow and haunt them.
And to show that Man Friday can usurp the power and turn the tables, or
as Caliban tells Prospero that the language which he's been taught he
would use to curse his teacher, Man Friday begins to un-name and re-
name the world, precisely the same thing which Crusoe had done,
creating an identity through a process of naming, creating the world
through naming it. Friday is in the process also reclaiming his language
and through this, his lost identity.

What slavery and colonialism did was to wipe away the original
identity of the slaves and the colonised through a deliberate act of re-
naming. Through it, a man who surely had a name previously became
Man Friday, thus the creation and creature of another man, stamped with
an extra identity and role of slave or servant. And because he did not
wish his creature to escape from the confines of his new role and identity,

Crusoe insisted on being called master, and not by his own given name of Robinson or Crusoe. However, through his rebellious act of un-naming, Friday (Jackson) regains his original identity which had been erased by Crusoe's language. Crusoe (Harry) finds all of this rather threatening to the status quo, and at the same time much too serious as an ordinary pantomime. In Walcott's play, Harry sees reversing the roles as being a dangerous action whose seriousness would turn their show 'into a play' which the white audience of tourists was not likely to enjoy and which had the potential to make a black audience think. The mere thought of the implications of what Jackson is trying to do is enough to bring a fit of stammering in Harry. What his race had done for 'two thousand years' on the Negro race he was not prepared to endure for just the duration of the play. It was alright and normal to teach the African or Caribbean cannibal to unlearn his religion, to renounce his culture and civilisation which were presented as barbaric. If the pantomime goes along the lines of the old myths, the tourists would be entertained. But what Jackson is able to achieve here is to force Harry to judge and condemn himself and his race for the cultural devastation which was perpetrated on African and Caribbean peoples by colonialism. He is also able to show that deep down Harry is racist, in spite of the attempt to show himself off as a non-racist liberal. Jackson stubbornly insists on carrying on with the rehearsal and improvisation for their pantomime, and when Harry orders him to stop, he coolly answers with:

> Alright. Stay as you want. And if you say yes, it go have to be man to man, and none of this boss-and-Jackson business. It would be just me and you, all right? You see, two of we both acting a role here we ain't really believe in, you know. I ent think you strong enough to give people orders, and I know I ain't the kind who like taking them (138).

Jackson sees through the façade of the man-to-man that they had been playing, because deep down, Harry sees him as nothing more than a servant, a black person who is not his equal. What exposes the latter is his rage at Jackson's summary court-martial and execution of the offensive parrot. Harry really hit the roof, calling Jackson all sorts of stereotypical names. He unconsciously slips into a racist style of collective branding as he denigrates, not just the offending Jackson, but his entire race:

> You people create nothing. You imitate everything. It's all been done before, you see, Jackson. The parrot. Think that's something. You can't even be original, boy. That's the trouble with shadows, right? They can't

think for themselves . . . So you take it out on a parrot. Is that one of your African sacrifices, eh? (156).

Harry's emotional outbursts Jackson calmly dismisses as mere 'running of the mouth' because he knows he is nobody's shadow, and that if anyone had a problem, it was Harry himself. However, Walcott makes his point that those blacks 'who are not men but mimics' are nothing but the shadows of those they imitate, and that as shadows, they would always be hated and despised. Harry and Jackson, between them, demolish the myths and counter-myths of colonial racism. In the end, both men achieve respect for one another. They both have broken through the myth of Crusoe and Friday without creating another one in its place; that, for Walcott, is not the answer. Both blacks and whites should liberate themselves from the evils arising from the myth which hinders the free association of the different ethnicities and cultures in the Caribbean and for as long as the myths exist, for that long will the social harmony in the islands remain elusive.

Chapter 3

THEATRE AND AFFIRMATION OF HISTORY AND CULTURAL IDENTITIES

Recuperating African and African-Caribbean Histories

A significant number of African and African-Caribbean plays re-read history as part of their counter-discursive engagement with the colonial legacy of racial stereotyping of former colonised African peoples. African plays which do this include: Ola Rotimi's *Ovonramwen Nogbaisi*, *Kurunmi* and *Akassi You Mi*; Wale Ogunyemi's *Ijaye War*; Soyinka's *Death and the King's Horseman*; Ebrahim Hussein's *Kinjeketile*; Ngũgĩ wa Thiong'o and Micere Githae Mugo's *The Trial of Dedan Kimathi*; Cheik Ndao's *L'Exil d'Albouri*; Bernard Dadie's *Béatrice du Congo*; Thierno Ba's *Lat Dior: Le Chemin de l'honneur*; Abdu Anta Ka's *Les Amazoulous*; Ibrahima Sall's *Le Choix de Madior*; Herbert Dhlomo's *Cetsewayo*; and Jean Pliya's *Kondo le requin*. For the Caribbean dramatists, the most written about of African-Caribbean history is trans-Atlantic slavery and the story of the slave revolt in San Domingo led by Toussaint L'Overture, and later respectively by Jean Jacques Dessalines and Henri Christophé which led to the establishment of the independent Republic of Haiti; versions of this latter piece of Caribbean history is the subject of Aimé Césaire's *La Tragédie du roi Christophe*; Derek Walcott's trilogy of *Henri Christophe, Drums and Colours* and *Haitian Earth*; C. L. R. James's *The Black Jacobins*; and Edouard Glissant's *Monsieur Toussaint* and *Iles de Tempête* by Côte d' Ivoire dramatist, Bernard Dadie. Also worthy of note in this regard is Roger Mais's *George William Gordon*, a play about Gordon who was framed and subsequently hanged for the Morant Bay rebellion in Jamaica. In addition to these, Césaire also wrote *Une Saison au Congo* about the political troubles of Patrice Lumumba – the first democratically elected prime minister of independent Congo who was assassinated in 1963.

What these plays have in common is that they all deal with pivotal moments in African and Caribbean colonial and political histories, and they all try to re-interpret and re-present these histories, concentrating on major African and African-Caribbean historical figures. There is also a collective recuperation, re-instatement and reclamation of these historical figures whose images, in most cases, had been grossly misrepresented by colonial historiography. Of these texts, the book will concentrate on the following – *The Trial of Dedan Kimathi, Ovonramwen Nogbaisi, L'Exil d'Albouri, George William Gordon, Béatrice du Congo, Henri Christophé, La Tragédie du roi Christophé* and *The Black Jacobins;* the choice of these is because they provide a balanced distribution between Africa and the Caribbean, as well as being fairly representative of an even spread between Anglophone and Francophone. Occasional references will, however, be made to other plays when necessary.

Essentially, the plays share a concern with correcting the distorted facts of African and African-Caribbean histories. While the history of the slave era had completely dismissed Africa and Africans as being outside of history, colonial historiography, on the other hand, while acknowledging Africans had sought to favour European colonisers while denigrating and a-historicising the colonised Africans and peoples of African descent in the Caribbean. History was constituted by what Europeans did, and what Africans or other colonised peoples did was only seen and represented in the light of how these actions conformed to or deviated from the European ideas of human conduct. Thus, a momentous history changing event such as the Mau Mau revolt in Kenya during the colonial period, for instance, was consistently portrayed by colonial historians as the act of terrorists and a few disgruntled Africans, who were branded enemies of peace and progress (Ngũgĩ wa Thiong'o, 1972: 26-30).

The causes of the Kenya uprising were socio-economic as well as political. The Mau Mau arose in reaction to the economic exploitation, political and social repression of Kenyan peoples by the colonial British administration and its disproportionately privileged white settler population. These causes were of course not acceptable to the coloniser and neither could they be used to defend the colonial occupation of the country. There was therefore the need to create alternative narratives for the revolt. J. Carother's *The Psychology of Mau Mau* (1954), Louis Leahy's *Mau and the Kikuyu* (1952) and *Defeating Mau Mau* (1954) were products of this attempt to misrepresent what was happening by the colonial administration in Kenya. The ethno-psychiatrist Carothers, for instance, argues that Mau Mau was caused by some 'anxious conflictual situation' in a people who had 'lost the constraining and supportive influence of their own culture' but 'had not lost their magic modes of thinking'. These natives, he concludes, had therefore fallen prey to 'some sophisticated egotistic' who had exploited the inevitable lacuna to lead them into rebellion (1954: 30, also quoted in Maughan-Brown, 1985: 50). Leaky argues in a similar vein and paints Kikuyu politicians as megalomaniacs out to de-stabilise the colonial political order. Others were not as subtle in their attempts to explain the Mau Mau movement and the revolt it led. A British Parliamentary Delegation went to Kenya on behalf of the British government to investigate the revolt and returned to England in 1954 fully convinced that 'Mau Mau intentionally and deliberately sought to lead the Africans of Kenya back to the bush and savagery, not forward into progress' (Maughan-Brown, 49). The delegation was of course guided by the 'expert' advice of Carothers and Leaky who incidentally were both on the Emergency Commission set up to advise the colonial government in Kenya. Yet another account felt that 'in its very nature Mau Mau was a reversion to barbarism'(49) and Blundell saw in Mau Mau 'a collapse of the African mind in the face of pressure to which the modern world and its technology was subjecting it' (49). Of course, Mannoni in *Prospero and Caliban: the Psychology of Colonization* and Mason in his Preface to the same book can also be mentioned here since both agree that the movement was caused by a dependence complex and a concomitant abandonment-neurosis of the Kikuyu (1968: 11). Many other historians, psychologists and cultural anthropologists also explained the Mau Mau revolt against British occupation of Kenya, but what unites all of the pro-colonial discourse surrounding the Mau Mau is the fact that they were all dependent to an astonishing degree on the reproduction and constant reshuffling of the basic terms of the core myth of African primitivism, atavism, savagery, regression, and, of course, darkness (Maughan-Brown, 49) which formed the key tropes of the literature of colonialism. None of them acknowledged the real historical, political and economic reasons why the Mau Mau occurred.

In a similar manner, Oba Ovonramwen Nogbaisi has been painted in colonial history as the most cruel and sadistic king that ever ruled the Benin Empire. In fact, from all accounts given of his reign, the coming of the British was supposed to be a deliverance for the people of Benin from the clutches of this evil bloodthirsty king, just as the betrayal and eventual capture of Dedan Kimathi and the suppression of the revolt he led is made to appear in Ian Henderson's *The Hunt for Kimathi* (1958) as the restoration of peace, justice and order to a troubled Kenyan society on the brink of anarchy and disintegration, a view repudiated years later by the counter-discourse set up in *The Trial of Dedan Kimathi*.

When confronted with such distortions of history one begins to appreciate the value of these postcolonial re-readings in which the playwrights offer alternative interpretations and versions of the histories of Africa and African-Caribbean peoples. Rotimi makes this clear in the preface to *Ovonramwen Nogbaisi*:

> Ovonramwen Nogbaisi - a man long portrayed by the biases of Colonial History in the mien of the most abominable sadist, but in actuality, 'a man more sinned against [that] he ever sinned' (ix).

This misrepresentation is what Rotimi sets out to correct in the play. He approaches his material from the point of view of the king who he presents as an embattled leader wading through a series of political, religious and economic crises which threaten to tear his kingdom and his people apart. The play presents a multi-textured portrait of the monarch than that presented in previous pro-colonial historical texts; one witnesses his doubts, senses his motives and the actions he takes as he embraces the troubles that beset him. Rotimi allows the audience/reader full access into the psychic processes of this man-king as he grapples with the pitfalls of a doomed leadership, and in doing so the play makes his mistakes and successes understandable to the audience who can share in his humanity - something that colonial history denied him.

Ngũgĩ wa Thiong'o and Micere Mugo, like Rotimi in *Ovonramwen Nogbaisi*, also state their project of recuperating Dedan Kimathi and Mau Mau in *The Trial of Dedan Kimathi*, by recreating,

> . . . the same great man of courage, of commitment to the people as had been graphically described to us .... An even mĩore important spur was the realization that the war which Kimathi led was being waged with even greater vigour all over Africa and in all those parts of the world where imperialism still enslaved people and stole their wealth. It was crucial that all this was put together as one vision, stretching from the pre-colonial wars of resistance against European intrusion and European slavery, through the anti-colonial struggles for independence and democracy, to post-independence struggle against neo-colonialism (Prefatory Notes to the play).

The play paints a completely different picture of Dedan Kimathi and the Mau Mau from that which pro-colonial writers left behind in works such as Ian Henderson's *The Hunt for Kimathi* (1958), Robert Ruark's *Uhuru* (1962) and *Something of Value* (1955). In *The Trial of Dedan Kimathi*, Ngũgĩ and Mugo imaginatively recreate the collective will of the peasants and workers of Kenya who refused to break under the yoke of an oppressive and exploitative colonial rule. By recuperating the image of Kimathi and the peasants and restoring them to the status of heroes, the play demands the audience and present day Kenyan peoples to take pride in the grandeur and heroic deeds of resistance which these men and women represented. The play attempts, in the words of the playwrights, to 'recapture the heroism and determination of the people in that glorious moment of Kenya's history, a moment that was the culmination of struggles that were started by other national resistance heroes' (Ngũgĩ wa Thiong'o, 1981: 51).

Roger Mais's play, *George William Gordon* (1945, subtitled a historical play) performs a similar counter-discursive function of recuperating the image of the eponymous hero, George William Gordon, a mixed-race politician in mid-19th Century Jamaica who was 'legally murdered' by the colonial Governor Eyre on the trumped up charge of instigating and part-leading the Morant Bay rebellion of 1865. Gordon was tried without due process and executed as an insurgent on the orders of Eyre, while in reality Gordon's real crime for which he was hated by Eyre was that he fought tirelessly for the black and deprived people of Jamaica. It was not until much later in the 20th Century that Gordon and others were proclaimed Jamaican national heroes. It has also been suggested that Mais's play celebrating Gordon's nationalism, heroism and sacrifice for the poor and deprived parishioners of St Thomas contributed significantly to this national recognition and recuperation. Other African and African-Caribbean historical figures whose images are recuperated in the theatre are the Zulu warrior-kings Chaka (in Anta Ka's *Les Amazoulous*) and Cetsewayo (in Herbert Dhlomo's *Cetsewayo*); both defied colonial conquest until the end; Henri Christophé and Toussaint L'Overture (both heroes of the Haitian revolution) in plays such as Walcott's trilogy, James's *The Black Jacobins*, Glissant's *Monsieur Toussaint* and Césaire's *La Tragédie du Roi Christophé*; and among Francophone African writers, leaders celebrated include Albouri Ndiaye in Ndao's *L'Exil d'Albouri*, Dona Béatrice in Dadie's *Béatrice du Congo*, Lat-Dior in Thierno Ba's *Lat-Dior: Le Chemin de l'honneur*.

Writers dealing with history can do one of two things. First, they can report the historical facts as they are, with as much objective distance so the history in question can justify or condemn itself. Or, and which is the one we are concerned with because of the abuse to which African and Caribbean histories were subjected to by slave and colonial historiography, they can take the counter-narrative route by concentrating on the positive events of that history, especially those aspects which had hitherto been suppressed or denied by the biases of previous historians. Hayden White is his seminal work, *Metahistory: The*

Historical Imagination in the Nineteenth Century Europe (1973) talks about the 'fictions of factual representation', arguing that the history writer is engaged in as much selective and subjective ordering of the facts of history as the fictional writer. The fictional writers, however, are different because they are upfront about their subjective and creative intervention whereas the history writer denies their creative and selective tampering with the material. As postcolonial writers, African and Africa-Caribbean dramatists thus engage in a selective presentation of history; they create heroes of characters such as Oba Ovonramwen Nogbaisi, Toussaint L'Overture, George William Gordon, Dedan Kimathi and Woman, Chaka, Dona Béatrice, King Albouri, and it is telling that they choose especially those previously vilified in colonial history. This is not a falsification of history; rather, it is a careful selection of positive aspects from the lives and moments of these historical figures, similar to and a reversal of the elevation of Europeans and suppression of African and African-Caribbean heroism in colonial historiography. As David Cook and Okenimkpe point out in their study of Ngũgĩ wa Thiong'o's work:

> Selected images, events, speeches and individuals embody certain needs of a people. Myths draw upon history. But writers who develop national myths are using history as part of a continuing process which can help determine and shape the future by encouraging certain possibilities in society and perhaps discouraging others. To such writers history is not static, but is material out of which social and economic realities have created the present, providing various openings for the future (1983: 161).

Because the playwrights see Kimathi as a historical figure whose life must be properly understood in relation to the present in neo-colonial Kenya, they carefully select some of the positive aspects of his life, his vision, and especially his epic confrontation with the might of colonial authority. These positive aspects are intended to repudiate the distorted and negative portrait which colonial history had created for Dedan Kimathi and the resistance which he led. The same applies to other African and African-Caribbean historical figures, such as Ovonramwen Nogbaisi, Gordon, Chaka, Cetsewayo, Béatrice etc, who had been similarly misrepresented by colonial history. Dona Béatrice was consistently presented in colonial historical accounts as an evil witch who stood in the way of Christianity in the Congo, but in Dadie's play she is made to stand for Congolese culture, traditions and sovereignty under attack from the colonisers. Her defeat in the play signalled the defeat of the Congo which became fully taken over after her fall.

The reconstructed image is also designed to inspire the present generation into positive action for a better future. Thus, in *The Trial of Dedan Kimathi*, there is a re-interpretation of Kimathi's ideas in the light of present realities in Kenya. Because the cause for which he fought is made to reflect the neo-colonial exploitation which the people are still experiencing in Kenya, his story and life take on the quality of a national dream which cannot die, an idea which becomes in the minds of the people a symbol of their collective will to resist and survive oppression throughout their history. Through this technique, a bond of identification is created, and a new sense of pride is developed by Kenyans about significant moments in their collective history. Kimathi's image, and through him that of the Mau Mau, becomes a call to the present to realise that the struggle against oppression and exploitation is not over because the privileges of the white colonial oppressor has transferred to the native oppressor. The people are reminded through the actions of past heroes to shake off the yoke of oppression and to begin to participate as subjects in the process of their history. Plays like these aim to create a new awareness of self for African and Caribbean peoples of African descent through a creative and positive sense of history.

Rotimi, by presenting a more positive side of Oba Nogbaisi and his encounter with the colonisers in *Ovonwamren Nogbaisi*, shows a king whose concern is for the survival and sovereignty of his beleaguered kingdom. He emerges from this portrayal as a man betrayed because he tried to be diplomatically correct in his dealings with foreign visitors to his kingdom. The oba's attempt to establish friendship and mutual trust between him and the foreigners prevented him from taking appropriate action when this became necessary in order to protect his authority and his kingdom, doomed as the audience/readers already know he was because of the military superiority of the colonial forces massed against him.

In order to show the audience that these characters deserve to be celebrated as heroes of African history, the dramatists make clear that, contrary to the famed savagery of black and African peoples before they were 'kindly' rescued by the civilising act of colonisation, the first encounter between Africans and Europeans had been between equals. They had met as equal partners in trade as we see in *Ovonramwen Nogbaisi* and *Béatrice du Congo*, or as two opposing forces engaged in battle as in *The Trial of Dedan Kimathi*, *L'Exil d'Albouri* and *Une saison au*

Congo – in the latter play, a deeper political battle is being waged against a democratically elected Patrice Lumumba by an angered and meddling ex-colonial power, Belgium. The scene between Oba Ovonramwen, Hutton and Gallwey is typical of such encounters where Africa met Europe on equal terms. The oba first refuses to even touch the portrait of Queen Victoria which his guests present him as a gift because such an act is beneath him as a king. Besides, he sees his guests as being lesser mortals who are mere representatives of another sovereign like himself. Then he displays mild amusement at the fact that such a 'child-woman' is sole ruler over a people, and finally, his advice that the queen take another husband is almost a diplomatically worded but mild rebuke which he hopes would be passed on to her by her representatives:

> Let her take another husband from among her people. A woman without a man is like a rich farm-soil without the feel of roots. A beautiful woman without a man is a crab - over-protected by shells: selfish. Tell your queen that Ovonramwen Nogbaisi says she must have another man (*Ovonramwen Nogbaisi*, 18).

This short scene indicates clearly that Oba Ovonramwen sees the two men as traders who wish to enter into trade with his kingdom. But significantly, he also recognises them as ambassadors of another sovereign state and king, who therefore deserve the respect and hospitality, which he duly accords them in keeping with the 'law of nations'. He accepts the sovereignty of Victoria, but does not see her as superior by any chance.

Two other facts however emerge from this meeting. First is the oba's awareness of the significance of accepting to have Queen Victoria's portrait hung over his palace. Acceptance would have symbolised acceptance of her rule over Benin, the very implied intention of the bearers of the gift. The second is his refusal to even touch, let alone sign the treaty which was presented by his visitors. This act was to signify his intention that if trade was to take place between the two nations, it was he, the oba, who would determine the terms on which such trade is carried out. He refuses to fall for the hypocritical flattery from his visitors. In this regard, he is different from the Mani Congo in *Béatrice du Congo* who displays annoying naïveté and subservience to the foreign visitors to his court, and who also shows deference to another monarch. His conversion to Christianity and dependence on the foreigners is strongly critiqued by the playwright, while Béatrice's challenge is quietly praised. The oba emerges from this encounter as a man sure of himself and of his royal responsibilities and obligations to himself and his people. He is no simpleton, and in fact, he treats his guests with some royal condescension. The oba's actions are not those of the monster-king of colonial history, and the fact that he does not sign the treaty and his overall behaviour to his European visitors help to expose the hypocrisy of the British in their trade and colonising mission in Africa.

The scene is similar to the scenes between Kimathi and Henderson in *The Trial of Dedan Kimathi*. Henderson used to be Kimathi's childhood playmate, but is now judge and jury over him. Kimathi had always proved equal to and sometimes better than Henderson in all they did as children, and he had always refused to accept the latter's assumed superiority even though he was always physically the weaker. For instance, in their game of 'Horse and Rider', Henderson always insisted on playing 'rider' to Kimathi's 'horse'. For Henderson, it was his natural right because he was white; but Kimathi thought differently, questioned and rejected outright that 'natural' right of the other to play rider:

> Henderson: . . . . Don't you remember how we used to play together as children on the slopes of Mount Kenya? Remember the day we played Horse and Rider? We fell (*he laughs*).
> Kimathi: You mean I threw you off! And you went sniffing and crying to your mother.
> Henderson: You must admit you were rather nasty!
> Kimathi: You wanted me to play horse. And you the rider.
> Henderson: Well, my friend, there has to be a horse and a rider. What would be the point of the game?
> Kimathi: There must be a horse and rider, must there? Well, let me be Balaam's ass then (*chuckles*). Yes, the one who rejected his rider . . .
>
> (*The Trial of Dedan Kimathi*, p 34).

The act of throwing Henderson off his back is in itself symbolic as it was a forerunner to his act of orchestrating the throwing off of British colonial and settler yoke by the Mau Mau. And like Henderson, the colonial authority ran to the protective arm of mother Britain who threw in all her might to reinstate her threatened children. For Kimathi, if the game had to played, each player would have to play both horse and rider. It had to be played as equals or it would no longer be a game, a fact that seems to be completely lost on Henderson.

It is in the court room scene that Kimathi shows that he is more than a match for his white tormentors, in intelligence, wit and pride. Although chained and tortured, he remains defiant and his spirit indomitable. Here he exposes Henderson and colonial justice for what they are. Asked to plead guilty in court, he dismisses the whole judicial farce in just a few words:

> By what right dare you, a colonial judge, sit in judgement over me . . . .
> To a criminal judge, in a criminal court, set up by a criminal law: the law
> of oppression. I have no words (p, 25).

Kimathi in the scene savages the credibility of his persecutors by turning things around so that colonial justice and its agents are in the dock instead of him. Kimathi's response is a master stroke in the verbal play which constitutes the trial, and he comes out of it the winner.

The nameless Woman too is made to achieve the status of a universal symbol. In one respect, she is the mother of the revolution, yet in another she symbolises the mother of all oppressed boys and girls. And to make her suitable for her role, she is portrayed as a true heroine. The description of her is very detailed with highlights of her positive qualities brought to the fore. Her simplicity and rustic colour do not hide her mental and physical strength and maturity, as well as her sophistication and highly developed social perception. All these are qualities needed for the unique role, which had been assigned to her. As the mother of the revolution and therefore of the collective will of the people, she has dignity and is without fear. Her encounter with the colonial soldier helps to establish her depth of character, intelligence, courage and firm will to perform her role. In the end, the soldier comes out of the encounter looking infantile, weak, frivolous and above all, cowardly. The dramatists show no mercy for this bumbling, unintelligent agent of colonial power and repression. Similarly, in the encounters between Le Mani Congo and Diogo in *Béatrice du Congo*, although Dadie makes the African king very naïve and all too trusting of European sense of honour and the brotherhood of man, the encounters still represent a meeting of two sovereigns. However, Dadie goes a step further to highlight the hypocrisy and Machiavellianism of the European visitors whose sole interest is in laying their hands on the vast diamond and gold deposits of the Congo. Their greed is fore-grounded through revealing scenes in which they discuss motives and strategies among themselves. Although the king does not recognise this, Béatrice (the heroine) does and rebukes the king for his mental enslavement. She ultimately is more intellectually astute than she appears to the Europeans and earned the right to lead; and when it became obvious that the king was not going to do anything, she leads the rebellion against the foreign intruders.

Through creating such characters who prove their humanity, intelligence and equality in their encounters with their white opponents, the plays try to lay to rest the lie that European colonisers met only savages, or at best, benighted children when they first arrived in Africa. The Kingdom of Benin, with its coherent socio-political and cultural system, Kenya, filled with heroes who constantly opposed colonial oppression and exploitation, the Congo, with its complex socio-political organisation, the Zulu Kingdom with a mighty and efficient military and government structure, as well as the kingdoms of Cayor and Djolof (in *Lat-Dior* and *L'Exil* respectively), are testimonies from the past which audiences and readers are asked to examine and judge in the light of the previous images put forward on the pages of colonial history. If Africans and Europeans at some point in the past saw and treated each other as equals as the plays show, or if Africans had decided to challenge the assumed superiority and privileges of the Europeans, then it would be interesting to find out why, when and how the culture of dominance, inequality and oppression entered into the relationship between Africa and Europe.

The colonial powers, in order to justify their presence and project in Africa, created a plethora of myths about the inferiority, laziness, savagery and cannibalism of the colonised Africans; there were also myths about the dependency complex, abandonment neurosis and infantile tendencies of colonised peoples. These were put forward to convince the natives that but for colonialism they still would have been wallowing in darkness and that if the colonisers were to go away, the natives would naturally 'slip back into barbarism, degradation and bestiality'. Colonialism achieved this by what Fanon calls 'a kind of perverted logic' through which colonial historiography and literatures ' turned to the past of the colonised and oppressed peoples, distorted, disfigured and destroyed it' (Fanon, 1967b: 170). The need to put a stop to this kind of psychic disfigurement, historical and cultural erasure and to begin the process of re-educating his people are what, according to Kimathi, made him initiate the struggle against colonial occupation. Comparing the way of life of his people before and during colonialism had brought to him a realisation that colonialism was on the verge of destroying a viable culture and the people were being forced into a new kind of 'dance', a new kind of life of fear, silence and humiliation. Looking back, he remembered a tradition of strength, pride and wisdom passed on from generation to generation; these gave him strength and became his guides in the quest for freedom for his people. The people had a past, a culture which colonialism was trying to erase through its negative myths and revisionist histories. The native peoples had to be brought back on course, back into the historical process as active subjects. Kimathi's action should therefore be seen as a counter-force, an opposing ideological position which threatened the colonial apparatus and the myths that helped to sustain it. The two forces were therefore bound to collide and the product was the Mau Mau war. This is the theme of *The Trial of Dedan Kimathi*. A similar theme circulates through the other plays mentioned above, as each deploys postcolonial counter-narrative and counter-discursive strategies to dismantle colonial master narratives which peddled the notion of European intellectual and social superiority over colonised peoples. It is a point intended to counter the false and negative images of Kimathi and the revolt by apologists of colonialism and subsequent neo-colonial ideologues. And its success and effectiveness as a theatre for conscientisation is testified to by the fact that members of the audience took to the streets of Nairobi in celebration of their collective history after watching *The Trial of Dedan Kimathi*.

Once the audience begins to question one myth or one version of history it would be natural for it to question others as well, and this process is, as Fanon (1967b) says, '. . . responsible for an important change in the native'(170). The moment the natives begin to see that their past was not really one long night of savagery, cannibalism and darkness from which they were redeemed by the benevolent intervention of the Europeans; when they begin to see that there was nothing to be ashamed of about their past, and that what happened to them could have happened to any other group of people, then a new sense of pride in that past, and ultimately a new sense of self is born. This precisely is what the playwrights hope to achieve, to show African and African-Caribbean audiences alternative images of themselves and their cultures. It is to the credit of the dramatists that the events of the past are never idealised, nor are the actors in these events presented as flawless human beings. The African characters are portrayed with all their imperfections, with their glorious moments and their periods of weakness. Kimathi, for instance, tries to save his younger brother from paying for his treachery, and in doing so unwittingly sows the seeds of his own betrayal, capture and the eventual collapse of the movement. He has all his doubts, indecisions and errors of judgement, all of which are human, but what emerges from this portrayal of him is his integrity, courage and passionate and selfless commitment to the cause of liberating his people from domination and oppression. He is not made to appear in the image of a superhero, but rather as a humble instrument of his people's aspiration and their opposition to colonial domination. Likewise, King Albouri in his fight to avoid a humiliating defeat for his people is shown as considerate, occasionally indecisive and even weak; while Toussaint L'Overture, Dessalines and Henri Christophé, the three leaders of the Haitian revolution, come across in the five plays which explore this transformative period of black Caribbean history as essentially flawed heroes whose human weaknesses and imperfections occasionally led them to bad decisions. Even Toussaint, who from most historical accounts, is believed to be an almost perfect and selfless leader, is not such a figure in the plays, including even James's *The Black Jacobins* which greatly celebrates him.

The picture of Ovonramwen which emerges from Rotimi's play is that of a leader, competent, rash and stern, but capable of handling the myriad problems facing him. Like a true leader, he gives his full attention to all the problems and issues, sometimes attempting to solve or agonise over them simultaneously. Even in his one 'wicked' deed of executing the traitors, the oba seems justified in doing so. It was either them or him, and he had to save himself. His greatest problem from this portrayal, however, and perhaps the one weakness in his personality, was that he relied too much on the Oracle of Ife. By misinterpreting the injunction of the oracle for caution, Ovonramwen enervated himself and subsequently began to look like a man dominated by fear. There is no hint of his famed cruelty and sadism. In his dealings with the Europeans, all he asked for was respect for his authority over Benin Empire, respect for the traditions of the people, and a show of diplomatic integrity and trust from both sides. In spite of his doubts about the honesty and trustworthiness of the white visitors, he remains diplomatically polite to them. Even though he rejects their 'Trojan' gift, he remains hospitable, and when he refuses to sign the treaty, he merely does so because he was already given cause to doubt the sincerity of his guests who had broken every rule of friendship. In the end when he is defeated and forced into exile, the audience witness, as it were, the end of an important, if not so glorious an era in the history of a people. And in spite of his defeat, his honour and dignity remain intact. His final speech as he departs into exile is almost prophetic:

> Tell Queen Victoria that at last the big pot of corn has been toppled; now mother hen and her children may rejoice (*Ovonramwen Nogbaisi*, p, 78).

The speech leaves the audience/reader with a sad sense of the passing of an era in a people's history, but it was an era that passed with honour and the future after its 'barbaric' splendour looks gloomy as the people of Benin pass into a dark era of slavery under colonial rule. Oba Ovonramwen's kingdom fell, but not without a dignified struggle and the people therefore have nothing to be ashamed of about the lives and times of their ancestors. In the same way, the defeats of King Albouri and Dona Béatrice in Ndao's and Dadie's plays show African leaders who stood up to colonial power in the defence of their respective kingdoms and cultures.

Drama of Cultural Affirmation

Other African and Caribbean dramatists such as Soyinka, Walcott, Werewere Liking, Zadi Zaourou, Errol Hill, Scott, Efua Sutherland, Ngũgĩ wa Thiong'o, Ngũgĩ wa Mĩriĩ, Osofisan, Rotimi etc., approach the project of rehabilitating the damaged psyches of former slaves and colonised peoples by writing plays which reclaim and recuperate the denigrated and emasculated cultural systems and practices of Africans and African-Caribbean peoples. Plays of this type include *Death and the King's Horseman, La Puissance de Um (The Power of Um), I'll Marry When I Want, La Guerre des Femmes (The War of the Women), La Termitiér, Ti-Jean and his Brothers, The Marriage of Anansewa, An Echo in the Bone, Man Better Man*. However, the discussion will be based on *Death and the King's Horseman, An Echo in the Bone, The Power of Um* and *Man Better Man*. Two ways that the dramatists affirm African and African-Caribbean cultures are: extolling elements or aspects of these cultures, or using indigenous theatrical and art forms such as rituals, storytelling, *calinda* and carnival to structure their plays.

Soyinka's *Death and the King's Horseman* is definitely engaged in a re-interpretation of history, as well as investigating the tragic consequences for an individual mired in a cultural and psychological crisis. The underlying conflict in the play is within Elesin, the supposed 'human vehicle' of the regenerative process of the Yoruba world. However, the play also deals with a conflict and confrontation between two world views, two codes of honour and duty - the Yoruba and British. The latter is represented by the Prince of Wales who visits the colonies, at great personal risk, just to keep the flag of empire flying and by Simon who performs the thankless task of stopping Elesin Oba from performing his own 'barbaric' duty of committing ritual suicide. And on the Yoruba side, there is Elesin who must die as demanded by custom so as to accompany his dead king on the last journey to his ancestors, and Olunde who restores his family honour by dying when his father fails to do so. Soyinka challenges his audience, especially those more familiar with European codes to come to terms with the Yoruba world view, its metaphysics and its moral codes. He uses his Yoruba characters, especially Olunde in his discussions with the Pilkings, to put across the Yoruba view or to challenge some European philosophical assumptions.

The real conflict as pointed out earlier is within Elesin himself as he is torn between the need to perform his expected role of ritual suicide and a hedonistic desire to cling on to and taste one more time the bounties of his office. His desire to take leave of the material earth is as strong as his longing to linger a little longer, and it is the stagnation engendered by this opposing pull which plays into the 'rescuing' hands of Pilkings, the District Officer, and thereby threatening the survival of the Yoruba world the reins of which had been placed in the horseman's hands at a crucial point of the Yoruba regenerative cycle. Elesin's role is that of 'a carrier of a certain death for his community and as such, his failure is thus a communal catastrophe, evoking more anger than pity' (Moore, 1981: 127). The anger which Elesin's failure arouses stems from the cause of and the threat which his failure portends, rather than from a recognition of a trickster streak in Elesin, as Dan Izevbaye suggests in his study of the play (quoted by Moore, p, 119).

Although *Death and the King's Horseman* can be described as a play which dramatises the interruption of the 'psychic and cultural harmony' of traditional Yoruba society, partly due to external forces, it is not, strictly speaking, a conflict between Yoruba and European cultures. Soyinka's interest is not with the European presence, which he recognises as being merely circumstantial to the dilemma in which Elesin finds himself. The dramatist achieves this by deliberately making the king's horseman a major instrument of his own downfall, and thus tactfully leads the audience away from the usual ideas about conflict of cultures. The play is, in fact, an indictment of African peoples for having contributed significantly in their societies and views of the world being undermined by outsiders. The Europeans may have put the wedges into the cracks of the African world, but it was the Africans themselves who had created the cracks which weakened the texture of this world, and sometimes it was the Africans themselves who led the Europeans to the cracks. Without Elesin's internal conflict and weakness, Pilkings would not have been able to penetrate the Yoruba social order; Simon and the other Europeans in the play did not even understand what was going on in this world.

The colonial factor is there merely to help the playwright reinforce his thesis of the validity and immutability of the Yoruba world. His concern in the play is to present a people and their world on the stage, and the insensitive interference and blunderings of the district officer proved handy to help him achieve this purpose. To indicate his purpose, Soyinka cautions in his production note against the 'reductionist tendencies' which some plays that deal with the Africa-Europe encounter often fall prey to:

> The colonial factor is an incident, a catalytic incident merely. The confrontation in the play is largely metaphysical, contained in the human vehicle which is Elesin and the universe of the Yoruba mind . . . (*Death and the King's Horseman*, p, 6).

That is to say, that the Yoruba world carried on, following its own laws and internal rhythms, irrespective of the European imperial presence and its inevitable interference. This is successfully demonstrated in the end when, in spite of Pilkings' attempts to stop it, the ritual suicide goes ahead and the world that was nearly 'wrenched from its true course' is set right and the bond between the living and dead is completed as the 'horseman' joins his dead king. Olunde, the eventual surrogate horseman, is important in the play, even though the action in the main centres around his father. Olunde embodies the Yoruba concept of honour and duty which Soyinka is presenting as being as valid as the European one which sees the Prince visit West Africa at a very dangerous time. Elesin fails because of the lust for flesh which had drained him of the needed will to 'step into the passage' when the moment arrived and the drums called out to him. He thus fatally played into the 'saving' hands of Pilkings, and he becomes in the end a man 'who failed his master, his son, his people and himself' (Osofisan, 1978: 173). He failed in his honoured duty and therefore lost the respect and veneration of his people; Elesin's failure to perform his role is significant because it threatens the survival of the world he represents, and, by extension, the entire African world faced with a colonising Europe bent on its subjugation or devastation.

But despite his failure, Elesin remains, in my view, one of Soyinka's best characters - his personality and vitality is enormous and remarkable, and this makes his fall all the more sad. To understand him fully, his personality, his dilemma, one needs to refer to Femi Osofisan who sums up the play thus:

> In *Horseman* . . . we are concerned not with an exploration, but simply with a statement of which Elesin is the personification. He does not need to probe or question; he accepts; his dilemma is not born of inner rebellious Will, but from external sources and the confrontation unwinds itself not in physical or vertical lines, but horizontally in the collision of two different and equally valid communal ethos. It is undoubtedly this which explains both the mechanics of the play, as well as Elesin's singular personality (1978: 173).

The world personified by Elesin nearly collapsed, with the help of Europe but not because of it. His dance of passage could have gone on if he had not cast a lustful look back from the threshold of transition. Thus, in the confrontation with Europe, Africa became a victim not because Europe was stronger, but rather because of weaknesses within Africa's own socio-political fabric. The play suggests that these weaknesses could have been avoided, but that tragically African peoples, like Elesin, could not resist wallowing in them and thereby playing into the hands of their enemies. Elesin's exuberance and lust for life is the tragic flaw which leads to his downfall, except that his death in the end, unlike those of other tragic heroes, serves no useful purpose to anyone, and least of all to himself. Surprisingly however, one feels pity for him mixed with anger at his betrayal of a sacred communal trust. One pities him in his humiliation because apart from being a man with an infectious personality, he has the integrity to accept his culpability. As he acknowledges:

> . . . blame is a strange peace offering for a man to bring to a world he has deeply wronged, and to its innocent dwellers. . . . For I confess to you, daughter, my weakness came not merely from the abomination of the white man who came violently into my fading presence, there was also a weight of longing on my earth-held limbs (*Death and the King's Horseman*, p, 65).

Even his greatly disappointed son recognises this and allows the fallen father the honour of whispering the ritual message to guide the new human vehicle into the passage to begin the journey of accompanying the restless and wandering soul of the dead king. In the end, it is Elesin the man who failed, and not the world he previously represented.

Soyinka's concern, it seems, is to show the seeming immutability of the indigenous Yoruba traditional ethos. Perhaps, without meaning to,

Pilkings and the 'tawdry decadence of a far-flung but key imperial frontier' (*Death and the King's Horseman*, p, 45) are sacrificed to prove his point. Placed alongside the native Yoruba characters, such as Elesin, Iyaloja and Olunde, Simon, Jane and their servants and associates come across as shallow and one-dimensional. Simon's officious but ineffectual interventions which arise from an unsympathetic and typically colonial denigrating and dismissive attitude to the lives and cultures of the people in whose community he is working, all help to highlight the depth and solidity of these native characters. The vibrant energy and verve of Elesin, the highly philosophical disposition of his son, Olunde, and the dignified traditional wisdom and royal haughtiness of Iyaloja, all set Jane, Simon and the European culture which they represent at a great disadvantage. In all the encounters, the two Europeans, Simon in particular, emerge as blundering children who keep doing what they are not supposed to because they are ignorant of their surroundings. Iyaloja, in fact, adopts a maternal attitude to Simon in the prison scene when the latter, in a moment of utter confusion because he is unable to engage at the metaphysical level at which the Elesin drama is being played out, asks her in a resigned voice if the deaths of Elesin and Olunde were what she wanted. Her reply is like a mother reproaching an errant child:

> No child, it is what you brought to be, you who play with strangers' lives, who even usurp the vestments of our dead, yet believe that the stain of death will not cling to you. The gods demanded only the old expired plantain but you cut down the sap-laden shoot to feed your pride. There is your board, filled to overflowing. Feast on it (76).

And even with this accusation and reprimand, Simon blunders on in his mistaken and thankless act of duty and kindness. He almost commits the final sacrilege of closing Elesin's eyes, an act born out of an honest human bond with the dead man, but which in the circumstance is a usurpation of the 'vestments of the dead'. It is ironic that this one time when he abandons his official haughty aloofness for genuine feeling and understanding, he is in fact about to inflict the ultimate injury to the dead horseman.

Olunde's role in the play is important in two respects. First, he averts the catastrophe which his father's failure to carry out his duty would have brought about. Second, Soyinka uses him to put across the theme that Western education is not an excuse for one to turn their back on their culture and on the responsibilities which the culture demands of them. In this respect, Olunde contrasts sharply with Jean in *Meetings* who, because of her education, denies and denigrates her African-Caribbean cultural identity. Olunde, as soon as he got the message that the king was dead, came home to bury his father knowing what the king's death meant for his father and therefore for himself. And in spite of having received help from the Pilkings to get to England, he is the first to reproach them for their utter disregard for Yoruba traditional values and social practices. However, he shows neither shock nor indignation at their desecration of the ancestral mask; he offers only a mild rebuke:

Jane: Oh, so you are shocked after all. How disappointing.
Olunde: No, I am not shocked Mrs Pilkings. You forget that I have now
          spent four years among your people. I discovered that you have
          no respect for what you do not understand
(*Death and the King's Horseman*, p, 51).

Olunde knows that it is difficult to explain or make Jane understand that the Yoruba world which he, even with his medical education and exposure to Western culture, accepts, and which explains why he came home the moment he learned of the king's death and its implications for his father and therefore for himself, has meaning and validity for the Yoruba people. How could he make her understand that her husband's attempt to stop his father from committing ritual suicide was a great disrespect and threat to the lives of the people whose world view demands such a death? How could he explain to her that Elesin's suicide was a heroic and necessary act which would ensure the destiny and continuity of the Yoruba world and culture? But Jane, for her part, sees her husband's act only as a protection of the Elesin from an unnecessary barbaric waste of life, just as his sending Olunde to England was to help the latter to escape such an inherited fate. But Olunde sees his understanding and acceptance of the Yoruba world view and the ignorance of the Europeans differently:

How can I make you understand? He has protection. No one can undertake what he does tonight without the deepest protection the mind can conceive. What can you offer him in place of his peace of mind, in place of the honour and veneration of his own people?
(*Death and the King's Horseman*, p, 53).

Olunde sees his father's suicide as a social duty, in the same way that the Prince of Wales's highly risky visit in a time of war is a role demanded by his status and society. Therefore, to prevent Elesin from performing his duty, as Pilkings succeeds in doing in the end, was the greatest disservice anyone could have done to him as it only covered him in shame. The thrust of Olunde's argument is that Europe should see and accept Yoruba culture as another viable and self-contained mode of experiencing and dealing with the world. In view of that, Europe should therefore let other peoples live their own lives as they, Europeans, had no justification for assuming the role of the civilising race trying to bring benighted races out of primitivism. European wars, Olunde points out, have demonstrated that Europeans are as primitive as, if not more primitive than, the savage races they are trying to redeem. Europe has mastered the art of survival in spite of the blunders it has made which is the only reason why it has not destroyed itself:

> I have seen proof of that. By all logical and natural laws this war should end with all the white races wiping out one another, wiping out their so-called civilization for all time and reverting to a state of primitiveness the like of which has so far existed in your imagination when you thought of us. I thought all that at the beginning. Then I slowly realized that your greatest art is the art of survival. But at least have the humility to let others survive in their own way
> (*Death and the King's Horseman*, p, 53).

In the end, he is able to persuade Jane to accept the Yoruba and their world. This is possible only because she is slightly more perceptive and open-minded than her husband. She does not completely subscribe to all the prejudiced colonial notions on which Simon based his judgement and actions. Earlier in the play she had pointed out to Simon the possibility of their not really understanding the natives as they claim to do, whether the reputed 'babbling' of the natives did give much away to the foreigner. But Simon would not be convinced, and even when he realizes that she could be right in her argument about the Elesin affair which only they the whites knew nothing about, he dismisses it as the 'slyness and deviousness of the bastards'. And he remains obdurate till the end, moving from one blunder to another without the slightest understanding of his environment, its culture and its people. Jane, on the other hand, feels the need to understand the people and their ways. She realises that the feelings of the natives should be taken into account in any dealings or decisions about them. Simon's attitude is to put them down as infants or objects which have neither the right nor the ability to feel or express anything. His register when he talks about the indigenous population is replete with all the colonial tropes and phrases, such as 'yapping natives', 'sly devious bastards', 'they always find an excuse for making noise', 'when they get this way', and 'quite unlike them'. They are 'his natives' who he can read like a book. But Jane wants to know, at least, she asks to be enlightened about the complex and highly philosophical turn of mind of the average native; she wants to understand Olunde's stoic acceptance of his father' impending death. And when he does, she is finally able to learn and accept that the Yoruba firmly believe in their world and their view of it and that the European presence was not going to change this belief. For Olunde, education had nothing to do with an individual's relationship with their cultural roots and traditional responsibilities. His main concern on his way home from England, he explains to Jane, had been to ensure that he performed his ritual role properly:

> I kept my mind on my duties as the one who must perform the rites over his body. I went through it all again and again in my mind as he himself had taught me. I didn't want to do anything wrong, something which might jeopardize the welfare of my people.
> Jane: Thank you, I feel calmer. Don't let me keep you from your duties
> (*Death and the King's Horseman*, p, 57).

Jane's parting words are significant as they indicate an acceptance which the colonisers most often refused to accord to the native customs of the societies in which they worked. But despite colonial denials and suppression, the colonised went about their normal ways of life, kept their secrets among themselves. Colonialism could have avoided some of the confrontations or brushes with native ways if only its officials had tried to understand the people and the way they lived. Instead, the colonisers felt the need to wipe out what was not easily comprehensible to them or sometimes to put down as barbaric anything that could not be pertly reduced to European logic. At other times, they wanted to destroy any indigenous cultural practices which they perceived as a threat to the new social order which colonialism was hoping to establish – Simon always felt and behaved as if Elesin's position and power was a threat to his authority. This is a point which the play makes.

A key indicator of an alienated character of the post-slavery and post-colonial eras is the tendency to denounce one's cultural identity and roots as a measure of one's education and social status. This is represented by the uprooted mentality of Joseph in *Death and the King's Horseman*, the self-denigrating personalities of Jean and Miss Aggy in *Meetings* and *Old Story Time* respectively. Olunde sees neither contradiction nor conflict between his studying medicine in England and his duties as the Elesin's eldest son. He also does not think that education should mean accepting or allowing the European world view to disrupt or destroy the indigenous Yoruba cosmology. Olunde sees the Yoruba and British cultures as different but viable modes of experiencing the world, both serving the needs of their respective peoples. People and cultures fashion and modify their world view as they participate in the process of living. The harm which colonialism did, especially through Christianity, was trying to force colonised peoples to abandon a world view, a way of life which had been evolving all through their history. It is the instances where it succeeded that the problem of alienation arose.

Joseph, the Pilkings' man-servant, has completely surrendered his mind and identity to the notion of European superiority and infallibility. His comments about the *Egungun* and other indigenous customs reveal his enslavement to this belief in white superiority. Because Pilkings is a white man and a Christian to boot, 'black man juju can't touch him' even though he has desecrated a Yoruba ancestral mask Of course, Soyinka makes this slave of white culture look rather ridiculous in his misplaced Christian zealotry. Joseph ironically appears more Christian than the Christian-born Simon, and it is Joseph who is scandalised at Simon's gibe about the 'holy water nonsense' having wiped away Joseph's racial memory. The uneducated or not-so-educated can not, like Olunde, Hugh, Len or Kimathi, go deep enough, beyond what they are taught, to discover the inherent contradictions and weaknesses in the 'superior' culture which they seek. Joseph is so far gone and he measures his self-worth by the progress he has made along the road of the foreign culture; the further away he is from his Yoruba culture, the more accomplished he sees himself. He is very much like the soldier in the *The Trial of Dedan Kimathi* who sees the freedom fighters as 'bloody Mau Mau' terrorists, the exact terms used by the colonial authority to describe Kimathi and his fighters.

Another African character who is a slave of colonialism is Amusa, and he too suffers a conflict of identity. Although still dimly aware and respectful of the traditional way of life, he has to perform his duties as a colonial police sergeant. He must obey orders, especially those of the district officer. But he shows that he has not a mind and will of his own as demonstrated by his encounter with the young school girls - the latter succeed in bringing the police officers many pegs down. The girls through drilling the policemen show them to be just colonial dogs, always waiting on their "masters' voices". Structurally, apart from showing up the lack of inner strength of the black colonial officers, the mime scene between the girls and the policemen tactically delays and prevents the officers from disturbing Elesin's 'ritual journey into the passage' as Iyaloja had earlier on informed the fumbling Amusa:

> You ignorant man . . . it is his blood that says it. As it called out to his father before him, and will to his son after him. And that is in spite of everything your white men can do
> (*Death and the King's Horseman*, p, 35).

This statement proves rather prophetic because even though Pilkings succeeds in preventing Elesin from completing the ritual, Olunde takes on the responsibility and completes the process begun by his father. Soyinka is thus able to show in this act that the Yoruba world he is presenting is strong and its continuity unbreakable despite the forces of disruption represented by Elesin's weakness and Pilking's official interference. Olunde's contact with Western culture, and his experience of England had made him realise the strength of his own culture which he had carried within him when he left. And it is a culture and world which he is not prepared to give up, in spite of his education and social position.

Werewere Liking's *La Puissance de Um* and Scott's *An Echo in the Bone* are funerary rites which the dramatists use as a means of leading the present into the past and in the process to establish or provide answers to troubling questions of identity, status and social responsibilities for their respective communities. However, both plays significantly excavate indigenous African rites and use them as enabling performance aesthetic and in so doing reclaim a pride of place for what must have been dubbed barbaric practices under slavery (the Nine-Night ceremony in *An Echo in the Bone*) and colonialism (the *kiyi mbok* and Bassa funeral rites in *La Puissance de Um*). By using the rituals in these quests for knowledge from the past - in both plays the questions of who killed Master Charles and who killed Ntep Iliga are posed and the answers are only found through culture - indicating that knowledge is embedded in the cultural practices of each society. The point being made in the two plays, therefore, is that each locality's native culture is the source of knowledge as well as frameworks for living and exploring life's processes and uncertainties. The choice of using the rituals as structuring devices for their plays makes both Liking and Scott contributors to the project of restoring African and African-Caribbean identities through reviving erstwhile denigrated indigenous cultural forms and practices. In fact, in both plays through the use of ritual, the dramatists succeed in reclaiming an essential function of theatre in Africa which is to provide a context for society to interrogate itself, by also allowing the co-existence and interaction of the different worlds of the African and African-Caribbean universe - the dead, the living and the unborn, the past, present and the future.

The final play in this section which extols an indigenous aesthetic as a way of affirming its African-Caribbean cultural milieu and identity is Errol Hill's *Man Better Man*. In the play, Hill takes further his pledge to explore the potential of indigenous Caribbean performance forms – in particular carnival, calypso and storytelling - as the basis for developing a contemporary native Caribbean theatre aesthetic (see Hill, *The Trinidad Carnival: Mandate for a National Theatre*, 1972). In the introduction to *Plays for Today* which he edited, Hill in writing about the three plays that make up this collection highlights the fact that the,

> format of Scott's play is patterned on a death ritual during which the past is made manifest through communal submission to the power that resides in drum, word, song and gesture. The search for a West Indian theatrical idiom is then implicit in the plays presented here
> (1985: 3).

In *Man Better Man*, Hill, in appropriating indigenous forms such as carnival, calypso and *calinda* (stick-fighting believed to be of African origin and famous among the Zulu of South Africa), is able to set up a counter-dramaturgical (creole) style of playwriting and performance structure which foregrounds indigeneity while challenging European dramatic models, previously established as dominant dramatic styles under slavery and colonialism. As Hill, himself, again points out:

> In addition to its dramatic qualities, it is clear that *Man Better Man* was also written to celebrate certain aspects of the folk experience which, under colonial rule, were at one time denigrated and which nowadays provide the means for the emergence of a national culture. Thus, translating elements of native expression into theatrical form serves both to preserve them as art and to contribute towards establishing the identity of the people responsible for their creation
> (18).

Man Better Man tells the story of the flamboyant exponents of *calinda*, one of the few surviving African art forms and sport in the Caribbean; it extols their elevated and much celebrated status as folk heroes, especially their immortalisation in folk culture and mythology by the legendary calypsonians. In the play, Tim Briscoe, although of a renowned *calinda* pedigree, is a not very good or properly trained stick-fighter. But what Brisco lacks in skill or training, he makes up for in courage and he audaciously accepts the challenge of the charmed and highly-skilled Tiny Satan, the *calinda* champion. To many in the community except for Lily whose love had pushed him into this decision, this was a foolhardy and dangerous undertaking, one which could only have one outcome; Brisco's defeat and possible death at the hands of Tiny. Of course, despite his 'fortifying' himself with fake medicines from the *obeah* man and a valiant attempt, Tiny knocks Briscoe out with a single blow. But he is eventually nursed back to health by Lily, and the play ends with general reconciliation, even between Tiny and Briscoe and the latter winning the love of Lily for his bravery.

What is impressive, however, about the play is the manner in which Hill is able to recuperate the African-Caribbean cultural practices and forms through a celebration of them. He reclaims an African-Caribbean theatre and cultural identity by placing the folk forms at the centre of his dramaturgy. Under colonialism and slavery, such folk forms derived from Africa were comprehensively denigrated and concerted efforts were sometimes made to stamp them out as they posed a threat to the social order by forming rallying points for resistance and instruments of cultural affirmation for the slaves and their descendants. The play combines the artistry of the calypsonian in the person of Hannibal, with the chanting, singing, choruses, dancing, drumming and mimic dexterity of the stick-men. Even the dubious skill and effectiveness of the *obeahman* is brought into play, enabling Hill to present a social tapestry that captures the 'expressive elements that typify life as experienced ... in the Caribbean'. (p, 2) In doing so, he succeeds in creating a drama which in its form and structure is without doubt African-Caribbean in its power, fluidity, expansiveness and expressiveness.

This and the preceding chapter suggest that African and Caribbean playwrights are concerned with and committed to mending the damage which the two historical encounters with Europe had done to the individual and collective psyches of Africans in Africa and peoples of African descent in the Caribbean. The chapters also reveal that slavery and colonialism could only have happened because one race had assumed it to be its God-given right to feel superior to another race which it therefore had the right also to enslave or colonise. A similar conviction about the superiority and the desire of the Nazis to maintain the purity of the Aryan race had led to their attempt to exterminate European Jews, and Germany to finally declare war on the whole of Europe. Perhaps, it is

not a coincidence that Soyinka includes the Second World War and
Olunde's acerbic comment on it in *Death and the King's Horseman*.

What has emerged from the study thus far is that the enslavers and
colonisers, in order to justify their actions and to mask the economic
motive behind them, sought theories and myths to make these actions
seem right or divinely ordained. What these theories amount to is this,
that because African peoples are naturally inferior to Europeans, the
latter therefore had the incontrovertible right to dominate and exploit
them, while the former were expected to see this relationship as being for
their own good. Also, because African peoples were primitives, savages
and barbarians, they ought to be thankful that Europeans had undertaken
the thankless task of coming to bring them out of their darkness into
light. In these racist theories and myths, black peoples are assigned so
many psychological and physiological defects that their only hope of
salvation lay in their becoming white people, if not in body, at least in
mind through the adoption of European cultural values. Some of these
mythologised images which dominated trans-Atlantic and colonial
cartography did have some effect for it was not possible for the African
peoples so tagged to hide behind a wall of indifference. The negative
images succeeded in creating in some the sense of inferiority intended;
this process was helped, on the one hand, by the fact that the colonisers
controlled most instruments of representation, and reinforced, on the
other, by glaring inequalities between black people and white people in
both slave and colonial societies. The two societies had ensured that the
lowest white person was better than the average black person, and in
some cases, even better than the best black. The slave society of the New
World did not recognise the humanity of the African slave and so there
was no question of comparing a black to a white; one was a person and
the other a thing, someone else's property who featured in the economic
and social structure only as an element of production.

Because the process of conquering the minds of black people both in
Africa and in the diaspora had been achieved by all kinds of racist
literature and through the legitimisation by church doctrines, African and
African-Caribbean writers therefore employ the same instrument of
literature and theatre to help the affected minds to unlearn and to
critically evaluate the European cultural values which they have been fed.
The writers challenge enslaved black minds to break out of the prison of
European and colonial culture in which they have been placed all these
years. For the African playwrights and some Africa-Caribbean writers
such as Scott, the process of re-education has to be communal as we find

in *Ovonramwen Nogbaisi, The Trial of Dedan Kimathi, L'Exil d'Albouri, La Puissance de Um, Béatrice du Congo, An Echo in the Bone* etc. This is apparently because, unlike their Caribbean counterparts, African peoples in Africa had not been physically uprooted, they had never really taken leave of their culture and geographical location in a physical sense as is evident in *Death and the King's Horseman* or in most of the plays of Werewere Liking and Zadi Zaourou – the latter make extensive use of their native *kiyi-mbock* and *didiga* performance traditions respectively. What Africans suffered was a denial and inferiorisation of their African cultures and their humanity, as well as a distortion of their histories. What they needed therefore was to have these histories and cultures re-presented or reclaimed so that they can begin to take pride in them again. For the Caribbean dramatists, the search is mostly individual because the main problem for African-Caribbean peoples is one of crisis of identity; thus, the quest for identity seems to dominate Caribbean consciousness more than it does the African, and this explains why a majority of the characters in the plays are often individuals who are experiencing one form of psychic crisis or another. A lot of the Caribbean plays studied are often structured as journeys into the self which the characters make to gain understanding of who they are, and through that to an understanding of the society in which they live. The plays are like psycho-dramas that unfold at two levels and where the cure is both for the characters in the plays and the audience members who become vicarious participants. What the characters go through in the plays are similar to the problems and dilemmas members of the audience experience in their daily lives.

The slave experience had been a traumatic one for African-Caribbean peoples who are the descendants of the unfortunate African slaves and thus their memories of history and race are rather unpleasant. To fashion a new meaningful life and a new image of themselves as individuals and as a people in the land to which they have been uprooted and which they must now reluctantly accept as home, the children of slaves have to understand their history, their origins, the crossing which remains the dominant image in the collective unconscious of Caribbean peoples of African descent. *Dream on Monkey Mountain*, as Slade Hopkinson rightly argues, is:

> . . . in part, about West Indian man's rejection of his home, and therefore of himself. It is about the psychology of mental and cultural emigration . . . the psychology of the 'red' official who, in the play, is a mental and cultural emigrant to a Europe of the mind; the psychology of the black

bush recluse who is, in the play, a mental and cultural emigrant to an Africa of the mind . . . . Makak, crazed by loneliness, futility and longing for psychological status and self-respect, makes a dream escape from the prison of his island and condition and emigrates to a dream Africa (1977: 79).

It is because of this urge to escape from their present harsh condition, to find an anchor and a new meaning in their lives, that we find Caribbean characters in dreams or moments of trance or possession reaching back to slavery and to an Africa only dimly remembered. And the plays suggest that these unpleasant memories have to be retrieved, repossessed and understood for Caribbean peoples of African descent to move forward in their present home as is the case in *Dream on Monkey Mountain* where Makak 'within the dimensions of reality re-emigrates to an island where he has been freed from his prison'(79) of complexes. A physical return to Africa, the central idea of the Rastafarian movement, is shown to be a daydream, a mere escape from facing reality. Africa, therefore, while remaining in their dreams, must be acknowledged as a root which goes deep and which can provide them with an anchor. But ultimately the Caribbean is a home which they must accept because it alone is the reality they have. And it is a home fed from elements of many former homes, including Africa, the Caribbean and Europe.

Whatever approach to the quest for identity adopted, the dramatists are all involved in the one endeavour of helping alienated blacks or those who have strayed to see the signposts that would lead them back to the centre, the soul of race and the cultures of their ancestors. The plays show that black people have nothing to be ashamed of, nothing to feel inferior about with regard to their histories and cultures, or in themselves, as human beings. The plays echo in different ways Kimathi's assertion that:

Here in the forest armed in body
Mind and soul
We must kill the lie
That the black people never invented anything
Lay for ever to rest that inferiority
Complex
Implanted in our minds by centuries
of oppression
(*The Trial of Dedan Kimathi*, 68).

The plays therefore are plays of action, whether physical or mental, which would eventually lead to the liberation of enslaved minds. The dramatists do not recommend that black people should begin to prove or ask for equality with white people because that in itself, they believe, is a temptation as well as a trap. Rather, they advocate that African and Caribbean peoples should prove and celebrate their difference from European peoples, for ultimately it is the differences between blacks and whites which would command attention without pleading for respect. And by preaching the difference, the characters would by the same stroke announce their acceptance of the fact and irrevocability of their blackness. The plays are thus attempts to teach black people to be proud to be black – African and African-Caribbean.

Chapter 4

RACE, CLASS AND SOCIAL INEQUALITY IN AFRICAN AND AFRICAN-CARIBBEAN PLAYS

Race and Class Identity in Africa and the Caribbean

There is an affective correlation between race and class and the patterns of social inequality in African and Caribbean societies. These patterns of social relationships are reflected vividly in the theatre since they form the framework within which individuals live their lives; it is also out of these relationships that the dramatic conflicts develop, intensify and are resolved. Without these relationships there is no life and so no drama. It is important to understand fully the complex relationship between race and class in African and Caribbean societies.

On reading African and African-Caribbean plays, one notices that there is a difference in perception between playwrights from the two regions. For instance, whereas African dramatists perceive and present relations of social inequality in terms of class and status, their Caribbean counterparts tend to see these relationships as resulting mainly from race, and only occasionally from class. While the Africans see inequality as the result of the contradictions between the rich and the poor, or between the aristocrats and the commoners, the African-Caribbean writers see such social positions as a direct product of racial origins. One must, however, point out that South Africa under apartheid presented a different scenario from other African contexts. Apartheid as a political and social ideology and system of governance was essentially based on racial difference and segregation in which the white minority dominated and segregated against the majority African population. Therefore, a lot of the plays of this period in South Africa fore-grounded the significant factor of race as an indicator of social standing and privileges; plays such as *Sizwe Bansi is Dead* (Athol Fugard, John Kani and Winston Ntshona), *Woza Albert!* (Barney Simon, Percy Mtwa and Mbongeni Ngema), *The Pass* (Herbert Dhlomo) and *Banned* (Zakes Mda) illustrate this tendency.

It is not surprising that whereas the issue of class awareness and identity are present in most of the African plays, except for a play, such as Matura's *Meetings* in which there are clear intimations of class awareness on the part of the characters, most African-Caribbean plays are preoccupied with the issue of racial and cultural identity. In fact, *Meetings* carefully plays down the class dimension and concentrates on Hugh's quest for cultural/race retrieval. One can think of only one reason for this difference. African countries such as Kenya, Nigeria, Ghana, Senegal, the Congo, Cameroon, Côte d'Ivoire where the plays selected for this book are located, are no longer preoccupied with racial issues which understandably have lost currency with the demise of colonisation. Consequently, therefore, social inequality is seen purely as an economic condition in which different social classes or status groups contend with one another. Even a play such as *I'll Marry When I Want* (Ngũgĩ wa Thiong'o and Ngũgĩ wa Mĩriĩ, 1982) from Kenya which deals with a neo-colonial exploitative relationship between Africa and international Capitalism does so from the standpoint of class and capitalist economics. The poor marginalised peasants in the play see the African propertied class who expropriate their labour as belonging to the same class as the capitalists from America, Europe and Japan. For the peasants, poverty and marginalisation have nothing to do with race or their skin colour; the problem has nothing to do with race or their skin colour; it simply was a question of those who have and those who do not have. But not so in the Caribbean plays. The slave history of the Caribbean is a reality whose imprint is still seen and felt through the different strata of society. The social structure which slavery left behind is one which graded and still grades individuals along the social ladder from white, through brown down to black. Elsa Goveia explains the underlying principle and racial attitudes governing social stratification in the Caribbean when she writes that the West Indians

> belong to a universe in which it is the accepted thing that the upper class should be people of white or lighter complexion as the lower classes should be people of dark complexions.... This relationship of dominance of a light-skinned minority over the black majority is still one of the leading aims of the West Indian system ...
> (1970: 10).

Thus, identities in the Caribbean are based more on racial origins than they are on class affiliations or belonging – people perceive themselves as their 'race' as opposed to their class, and although this is gradually changing, it remains the key way people identify themselves. This underlying fact is responsible for the difference in social orientation and attitude between characters in the African texts and those in the Caribbean ones. For one thing, the themes in the plays are different. Virtually all the plays from the Caribbean explore the theme of survival in a harsh environment and the characters most often are engaged in a struggle to see to what extent they are able to rise above the limiting conditions imposed on them by their racial origin. And, in general, they go about overcoming this racial disadvantage through three means. Some do so through education or marriage as Len and his mother do in *Old Story Time*. Len's education finally elevates him above his racially ascribed social position, but not until after all kinds of put downs and racial discrimination at school and in his search for a job. Others, like Crew in *An Echo in the Bone*, try to improve their social standing by attacking and eliminating the barriers placed in front of them. Master Charles, the only white character in the play, and not surprisingly given the slave history of Caribbean societies, is the only rich person, owning the entire estate on whose periphery the majority of poor black characters dwell. He therefore belongs to a class apart, while the others constitute another and a lower class. However, this class divide is also a racial divide as is the pattern in post-slavery societies of the New World. By removing Charles who is the symbol of black subjugation and deprivation, Crew hopes to symbolically liberate his race from centuries of domination and poverty. Meanwhile, a third group is represented by Legion in Edgar White's *Redemption Song* (1985) and the Rastafarians in Walcott's other play, *O Babylon!* (1979). This group seeks to physically escape from a racially ascribed low status in their Caribbean society through the only other means; migration to Europe or North America, or sometimes in a longing to return 'home' to Africa. For all these characters, a sense of who they are is determined by their sense of a 'racialised' origin – as descendants of African slaves - and not by their social material conditions.

Whatever other reasons that may be given to explain the migratory tendency of Caribbean peoples, it is clear that they do so because the 'racialised' social structure of their island societies forces them to and also because, as David Lowenthal points out,

> . . . the West Indian who is poor and black crosses the ocean not only to make his fortune but to break out of a system that keeps him at the bottom
> (1972: 229).

Legion, the central character in *Redemption Song*, migrates from Redemption City because there is nothing for him to stay for, except the old house which his grandmother left him. He goes in search of greener pastures in England. White makes the theme of migration a central focus of his theatre as he follows the migrants through their tribulations, humiliations and disappointments in the equally racialised cities of Europe and North America. Similarly, the Rastafarians in *O' Babylon!* wait on the outskirts of Babylon for Emperor Haile Selassie of Ethiopia to come and save them from their long exile and lead them back home to Africa. Much as one recognises this longing to be a futile dream, one can not ignore the fact that an extremely difficult condition of life exists to give rise to such strong desire in individuals or a group to want to physically remove themselves from their homes in search of a new one. Hope must have died in many of these men and women whose only source of momentary escape and peace is in a fuzzy world of drugs while they wait for the dawn of the day of 'repatriation'. Even old Makak in *Dream on Monkey Mountain* seeks escape from his island home because of the poverty and humiliation he experiences because of his African ancestry. But for Walcott, escape is not the answer and so Makak, after a dream return to an African paradise, discovers that home is the Caribbean where he has to accept that fact of his African-Caribbean identity and its implication for where he is placed on the social ladder. Walcott's characters always fail to migrate at the last minute - Makak and his companions, and in the end the Rastafarians, stay to fight and make a life for themselves in their Caribbean homes. But for the number that stay, an equally significant number leave because the absence of hope directly equates to the lack of attachment which those who leave feel for their desolate island beaches.

However, as pointed out earlier, not all Caribbean plays use race as a marker of identity or as the reason for social inequality. A play such as *Meetings* has only characters of African-Caribbean descent, and so, like the African plays, issues of class and status are more to the fore. The relationship between Hugh, his wife, Jean and their domestic, Elsa, is based on economic capital on the one hand and cultural capital on the other - the couple possess economic capital and power and this places them in a higher social class than Elsa, while the latter possesses cultural capital in abundance which the former lack. Hugh wants to reclaim his African-Caribbean cultural capital, knowing that he needed both to have a rounded identity and is prepared to look for it. Elsa is comfortable and bases her identity mainly on her cultural roots, while Jean, on the other hand, rejects her culture opting instead to construct her identity entirely on her economic and thus class belonging. It is not surprising that Jean is the one who tragically loses in the end as her narrowly constructed identity does not equip her to negotiate the complex though still highly racialised tapestry of her Trinidadian society.

The Africa represented in this book by Nigeria, Côte d'Ivoire, Senegal, Cameroon, the Congo, Ghana and Kenya, having gone beyond the race issue with the demise of colonialism, on the other hand, produces plays that are not overly concerned with racialised identities and relationships. Only colonially focused plays such as *The Trial of Dedan Kimathi, Ovonramwen Nogbaisi, L'Exil d'Albouri, Béatrice du Congo,* and to some extent, *Death and the King's Horseman* do – but Soyinka in particular discourages any attempt to read a 'clash of cultures' theme into *Death* by pointing out that the colonial presence was merely coincidental to the main action of the Elesin's ritual suicide (see Author's Note to the play). The five plays all deal with the colonial situation which in the case of Africa and Europe was also a race issue with the inevitable tensions. Having said this, however, it would be inaccurate to say that all contemporary African plays deal with non-racialised relationships. There is poverty, oppression and exploitation, in fact, all manner of social inequality, but understandably these issues are in no way attributed to race. In fact, all of them emphasise the economic and political conflicts and tensions arising from colonisation. It would be incorrect though to say that all African plays see relations of inequality as class determined since a purely Marxist conception of class does not adequately explain African social structures. In analysing African societies, both pre-colonial and post-colonial, one needs also to take on board Max Weber's notion of social categories because only such a nuanced and integrated approach can adequately account for the peculiar African socio-structural systems which oftentimes defy or altogether elude Marxist classification. One must especially take into account Weber's distinction between classes and status groups, the latter which he sees as being constituted by functional relations and responsibilities within the political and social orders (for a differentiation in the Marxian and Weberian concepts of social categories and its relevance for African societies, see Katz, 1980).

African plays present societies that are distinctly graded and life is carried on within specific relations of social inequality. Plays that come to mind here are: Soyinka's *Kongi's Harvest* (1967), Femi Osofisan's The *Chattering and the Song* (1977), Ngũgĩ wa Thiong'o and Ngũgĩ wa Mĩriĩ's *I'll Marry When I Want*, Ama Ata Aidoo's *Anowa*, Cheikh Ndao's *L'Exil d'Albouri* and Bernard Dadie's *Monsieur Thôgô-gnini.* In fact, all African plays in which indigenous African social systems are in operation reveal varying patterns of social gradation based on privilege, domination and inequality. *The Chattering and the Song* and *L'Exil d'Albouri* contain an identical model of an indigenous African social system in which there is a divide between the aristocrats and the commoners, much in the same way that in *Kongi's Harvest*, Oba Danlola, Kongi, the Organising Secretary and other royals, including Daudu and Segi, belong to a political, economic and cultural elite that collectively constitutes the upper privileged class which is apart and different from the class of the Carpenter's Brigade, the Farmers' Cooperative, the habitués of Segi's bar, and the numerous royal attendants like Dende, the marginalia and scum of Isma.

The Chattering and the Song presents the audience with a view of two societies - one contemporary and the other historical/mythical - and it shows how the former, although slightly modified, is but a continuation of the latter. Osofisan uses the play-within-a-play device to make satiric comment on contemporary society which is the real concern of the play. The Abiodun-Latoye confrontation in the inner play is used to highlight the fact that class tyranny, oppression and exploitation have always been features of human society and history. Osofisan's most significant achievement in *The Chattering and the Song* is his audacious but creative use of the traditional folklore, myths and history of his Yoruba culture to offer new and startling insights into the often mystified reality of contemporary Nigerian society. What stands out most in his dramaturgy is, according to Sandra Richards (1987: 281) , 'his use of history, myth and other familiar performance modes in a dialectical, subversive manner which startles audiences into analysis' of hitherto veiled social realities. Osofisan seeks in his plays to offer his audience images and insights that suggest possibilities for social change and mass empowerment. But at a deeper level, he engages playfully with the flexibility and multi-layeredness of identity in an illuminating way. Each character in *The Chattering and the Song* is presented as a complex of disparate identities or masks assumed to suit whatever moment the character finds himself or herself or need to perform in - that is, the characters, in fact, almost play at being themselves or being what they need to be whenever necessary.

Osofisan subverts the original myth by tampering with sections of the Abiodun-Latoye confrontation in order to expose the class and exploitative nature of traditional Yoruba society. Abiodun and his royals and nobles do practically nothing, live a life of luxury, sanctified and sustained by an unwritten and unquestioned divine law, while the majority of the people toil and suffer to maintain the upper classes in their privileged positions. This is the immoral situation which Latoye challenges as he calls on the people to see beyond the smokescreen of the Alafin's sanctified position and privileges. It is similar to the sanctified role, which Oba Danlola cites as justification for his revered position and the privilege of eating the choicest portion of the communal harvest in *Kongi's Harvest*. The contest in the play-within-a-play in *The Chattering and the Song* is therefore meant to be an archetypal model of the contemporary one in the main play, which Sontiri and Leje are waging to radically alter the imbalance in the structure of social relations and opportunities. By altering the end of the myth through making Latoye victorious, the play is able to question the existing social arrangement which the aristocratic-cum-bourgeois class work hard and are determined to keep unchanged. The play achieves this by counter-posing two divergent views of the historical process, with the final outcome being a result of the collision between the two.

The first view, expressed by Latoye, holds that it is people who create their history and world by choosing and directing the course of events; people make themselves, they are not made and in making themselves they make history. This same view also underpins most postmodernist ideas of identity; people make or choose their identities as they engage with their world and with other people. All this of course has echoes of the historical materialism of Marxism. In the scene where Latoye joins battle with Alafin Abiodun, he calls on the people to intervene to stop a particular process of history that would only perpetuate their exploitation and poverty. What Latoye seeks is to awaken a consciousness of their social position and through that to make them realise the important role they have to play in the inevitable social struggle, which constitutes the dynamics, as well as the dialectics of their society. Moreover, he realises that he needs the masses in order to save himself from the powerful ruler, but in saving himself, he also saves the people by making them become active subjects in the historical process. Against this radical view that common people create history and society through their action, labour and confrontation with nature is an opposing conservative viewpoint which presents change as an aberration and a disruption of the natural order of the world. Olori, Alafin Abiodun's leading wife, not surprisingly espouses this view since it is in the interest of her social group that the world remains as it is and that the eyes of the people remain closed to the true cause of their poverty and the possibility of an alternative society. Olori, as she musters the women of the royal harem to form a protective shield round the beleaguered and vulnerable Alafin, argues:

The world is not of our own making. We inherited it. The world is as it
always has been. Will you turn it upside down?
(*The Chattering and the Song*, p, 43)

Using the struggle between the two viewpoints, Latoye is able to
expose the injustice, inequality and exploitation at the heart of Abiodun's
reign. He succeeds in proving that the structure of exploitative inequality
under which the people live is not natural and that the peasants, soldiers
and servants, in throwing Abiodun and his group out would, in fact, be
bringing history back to its natural course and remaking themselves in
the process.

Soyinka's *Kongi's Harvest* does not try to prove the existence of classes
in Isma; the play, however, leaves enough evidence to give a vivid
picture of the dynamics of class relations and patterns of social
stratification in the world of the play. Isma is a world in which status and
relations of inequality had always existed from the beginning. It was
present in the previous reign of Oba Danlola as it is in the extremely
repressive era of the power-crazed Kongi. The common people seem to
have merely changed masters with the ousting of Danlola and the nobles
by a new political elite led by Kongi. The basic class structure and
disparity in means and opportunities remain, and what has changed is
the fact that another group has moved up to replace the aristocrats and
Kongi's sado-masochistic rule now spreads extreme misery to everybody,
including members of his Reformed Aweri Confraternity. There is not
much to choose between Oba Danlola who claims a divine right to his
privileged position as compensation for his religious duties, and Kongi,
the upstart who has upstaged him and wants to push him completely out
of both religious and political reckoning. The conflict in the play is more
or less an intra-class struggle between an aristocracy on the brink of total
marginalisation and a new politico-technocratic elite which, though it
lacks any traditional or religious legitimacy, stakes its own claims to
leadership. The audience is thus made to perceive the action in the play
in the main through the already traumatised consciousness of a maimed
aristocracy.

It is unfortunate, however, that Soyinka, probably because he is more
interested in the intra-class strife of the upper class, does not give enough
attention and verve to the plebeians of Isma, and so they remain
throughout the play as mere backdrop to an internal upper class
confrontation. The audience does not learn much about them, what they
think and feel about their position in the scheme of things and the
alternatives open to them. Neither are their groans under the weight of

Kongiism heard. But silent as they are made to be, they remain eloquent testimony to the unequal social structure of Isma. Soyinka seems to be advocating that better the humane, benevolent and down-to-earth rule of Danlola, than the inhuman and insensitive tyranny of Kongi. Whichever view Soyinka or the readers hold of it, the play is a vivid illustration of the peculiar nature of social classification in most contemporary African societies where traditional values still play a part in complicating social class determination much further. African societies are unique in the sense that only in them is there the possibility of an aristocrat or a noble being also a member of the lower or working class. In the past belonging to the aristocracy guaranteed high social position, but not anymore because of the radical alteration of indigenous African social systems in response to imperial and global economics. This means that in Africa indigenous aristocratic power does not always translate into economic or political power, just as a high status in the indigenous system does not guarantee a high class position in the new social structure and vice versa.

I'll Marry When I Want, on the other hand, deals with a situation that illustrates the workings of global capitalism. In the play, one is looking at a society in which the occupation of a social position and the enjoyment of privileges arising there from are neither determined by race nor sanctified by any religious authority, but is simply a matter of economics. Because of its neo-colonial economic structure, the Kenyan situation as presented in the play is nearer the Marxist model of a capitalist mode of social classification. Kīoi, Ndugīre and Ikuua are all propertied men who therefore belong to the same class by virtue of their economic power; there is no racial difference between them and Kīgūūnda and Gīcaamba, and neither do the former perform any religious or political roles that allow them the privilege of owning so much and enjoying the good life which the latter have no access to. But Kīgūūnda and Gīcaamba are property-less and belong to the poor class and as such have fewer privileges. What the play shows is that Kenya is a class society divided along property lines; there are two groups - those who have and those who want. Wanja in Ngũgĩ wa Thiong'o's *Petals of Blood* puts it bluntly when she says:

> For to us did it matter who drove a Mercedes Benz? They were all of one tribe: the Mercedes Benz family; whether they came from the coast or Kisumu. We were another tribe; another family (1977: 98).

Interestingly, she uses the term 'tribe' to differentiate between the classes and this is a term that has very strong connotations of identity, of belonging and exclusion. Having or not having marks an individual out as either belonging or not belonging to a particular socio-economic group. But as far as relationships go, what there is between Kĩoi and Kiguunda is a master and servant, employer and employee, or an oppressor and oppressed relationship. And this in a society where an anti-colonial war of freedom had been fought so that a more egalitarian social order could be established. Kĩgũũnda, the former freedom fighter, is just a squatter on Kĩoi's large estate and his life and those of his family members depend entirely on the munificence of the latter who employs and pays them whatever he considers a good enough wage to ensure the regeneration of their labour power. Everyone in the play works for or is dependent on Kĩoi because he controls all levers of economic and social power in the world of *I'll Marry When I Want*; just as everything revolves around Master Charles in *An Echo in the Bone*.

It is obvious that societies represented in African and Caribbean plays, although they share remarkable similarities, differ in the way race and/or class are used as determinants of social structuring and relationships. Playwrights create characters and situations from their experiences of their societies and the plays are reflections of these differences in how race and class are perceived and how this affects relationships and positions on the social ladder. The Caribbean, because of its slave history, still has race as a dominant factor in the social placement of individual and also in the way individuals define themselves, whereas in Africa, despite the shift towards capitalist economics, traditions and culture still come into play in social identification and class determination in some societies so that class analysis becomes much more complex as a result.

Having now looked at the social background which informs the plays, this book will proceed to examine some African and African-Caribbean plays in detail to see how social inequality affects the characters and how they respond to it, and how this in turn affects or determines their sense of who they are. In fact, all the plays in the book deal with this problem and in most it is the central issue around which the dramatic action is built. To enable a thorough and insightful treatment of each play, some headings have been chosen so that plays that share common themes or use a similar approach to the exploration of class or race relations are analysed together. Inevitably, there will be overlaps and some plays will be discussed under more than one heading and this I feel should be useful ultimately. This chapter will concentrate on plays that look at poverty, oppressions and exploitation, the prey and predator relationship between the poor and the rich; while the next chapter will look at marginalisation, alienation and how the longing for utopia dominates the lives of the poor in Africa and the Caribbean.

Images of Poverty, Oppression and Exploitation.

What is common to all the plays grouped under this heading is that each sketches vivid images of the poverty, exploitation and oppression being experienced by the characters. The audience/reader is also offered glimpses of the misery which the poor and exploited majority experience in their daily lives. The plays make poignant indictments of the social systems that make possible the existence of such suffering and misery in African and Caribbean societies. One undeniable fact, however, is that whether discrimination is as a result of race or whether it is because of class, those who find themselves at the lower rungs of the social ladder are poor and hungry, and they are humiliated, oppressed and exploited by those at the top. The higher-placed live life to the full because they have all they need and sometimes more than they need, while those at the bottom in society have little or nothing. Four plays, Scott's *An Echo in the Bone*, Walcott's *Ti-Jean and His Brothers*, the two Ngũgĩ's *I'll Marry When I Want*, and Osofisan's *The Chattering and the Song* are good examples of plays in which situations of poverty, oppression and exploitation in Caribbean and African societies are explored. Others plays that have a similar theme and setting are Rotimi's *If ...*, Athol Fugard, John Kani and Winston Ntshona's *Sizwe Bansi is Dead*, Simon, Mtwa and Ngema's *Woza Albert!*, Soyinka's *The Road*, Walcott's *O Babylon!* and *Haitian Earth*, and Aimé Césaire' *La Tragédie du Roi Christophé*.

First, there are plays that deal with abject poverty, the kind of poverty that can force an individual to an extreme action because they have to find a way to survive and sometimes because the haunting spectre of their family slowly starving to death becomes an additional weight on their minds as they seek solutions. In four of the plays mentioned above, the major characters are faced with the difficult choice of either drifting along in penury or performing a decisive action to stave off the threat of total annihilation. What the characters have in common is their poverty and the precarious nature of their existence. It is not that other plays do not deal with poverty and exploitation, it is simply that these four highlight the problem more and they especially highlight the effects on the poor themselves. The plays do not romanticise the poor thereby calling upon the audience to pity them in their abject helplessness. Although there is sympathy for them, they are in equal measure admired because they try in their individual ways to rise above their material handicap and create some meaning and comfort out of their difficult lives. To the extent that they try to transcend the limitations imposed on them by either their racial or class backgrounds, to that extent do they earn respect; this I believe is one of the underlying messages which the plays relay.

Three of the plays, *An Echo in the Bone*, *I'll Marry When I Want* and *Ti-Jean and His Brothers* are similar as they present a world in which one individual as in *Ti-Jean* or *An Echo*, or a group of individuals as in *I'll Marry* has all the wealth, while the majority languish in abject poverty. Crucially, the problem is not just that inequality exists, but that the rich still do all within their power to widen the divide between them and the poor as Kĩoi and his group do in the Kenyan play, or to wipe the poor completely from the face of the earth as the Planter attempts to do in *Ti-Jean and his Brothers*, or do both as Master Charles nearly achieves in *An Echo in the Bone*. Whichever way it is presented, the existence of the poor stands as an eloquent condemnation of the immorality of the unequal and unjust distribution of wealth, social justice and material well-being in these societies.

An Echo in the Bone is a theatrically complex play with a sophisticated dramatic structure. It is a dialectically balanced piece in which Scott delves into the racial memory of Caribbean peoples of African descent to discover the reason for what on the surface appears to be Crew's mad and irrational violence against the white estate owner Charles. If the play says nothing else, it vividly makes the point that the poverty and squalor in which a majority of characters of African-Caribbean descent are in is but a continuation of the poverty and squalor of their African slave ancestors of many centuries ago. The setting for the play is a visual metaphor of this situation. Master Charles, who is the plantation owner of modern times, has the entire estate while the majority who are black are poor and have little or nothing, just barely enough to get by while living on the margins of Master Charles' large estate. The setting also restages slave times, yet it is a play about contemporary Caribbean societies in which nothing seems to have changed. Scott's play argues that the basic structures of dominance, oppression, exploitation created by slavery have remained untouched and still defines people. The farms and land, all the wealth still belong to just a few who are white or light-complexioned, and the majority who are black remain poor and as deprived as their slave forebears. P, one of the characters at the wake, expresses this:

> It is a terrible thing to go out like a fire that rain put out. This is what a man must live for, eh? You cut down the canes for a lifetime, every year you drag the sweetness out of the ground with you bare hands and pray the next season will be easy. Three hundred years crying into the white man's ground, to make the cane green, and nothing to show for it
> (*Plays for Today*, p, 86).

And to give a historical dimension and authority to what is happening in the play, Scott resurrects the slave scenes to enable the poor, suffering African-Caribbean peoples to understand the root of their predicament. They toil for a lifetime so that another person can grow fat on the sweat of their labour. And when they die, no one remembers them for what they gave to make the canes sweet and the rum strong.

Master Charles is the only white character in the play, and not surprisingly he owns the large estate, while the numerous black characters are consigned to the fringe of his immense holding. Not all black people are as lucky as Crew to have a tiny piece of land of their own, and these are therefore forced to find alternative means of escaping hunger - Stone, for instance, cultivates and sells 'grass'; Madam keeps shop; Dreamboat poaches game from the master's forests, and Crew's house and land are so small that one of his sons has to go into town to do menial jobs. All this while Charles owns a massive estate and lives alone in a big house that he can neither fully occupy nor utilise and which he contemplates turning into a museum. This is typical of the social structure and the kind of social relationships found in Caribbean plays. Charles could well have been the Planter in *Ti-Jean* or Mr Fowler in *Redemption Song*. But he could also have been Kīoi in *I'll Marry When I Want* or even Alafin Abiodun in *The Chattering and the Song*. The theme of poverty and the unequal and unjust relationship between the rich and the poor cuts across and unites African theatre and Caribbean theatre because inequality exists in both societies.

Crew acts in response to his disadvantaged position. The pressure of ensuring food, shelter and a future for his family forces him to go and beg for help from his enemy. But instead of the help he was seeking, Crew is further humiliated by Master Charles. Ultimately, the long suppressed anger explodes and he kills Charles. To Scott's credit, by outlining the long history of black oppression and humiliation by white people during slavery, he succeeds in transforming Crew's individual act into a symbolic confrontation between slave and master, between black and white, and not surprisingly between poor and rich. Crew's act - killing Master Charles and himself - rises above being a mere individualistic act of survival, as with that single blow he nullifies both races and classes; he symbolically in the context of the play, redresses the imbalance in the social relations between the descendants of European slave owners and those of African slaves, and between the white wealthy class and black poor working class. Crew (as the possessed Sonson) explains the spiritual as well as social significance of his action to his grieving wife, Rachel:

> Don't cry, Rachel, I had to do it. He was a bad man and the earth was calling out for his blood for what he do to us. (*Pause*) All of us . . .
> (*Plays for Today*, p, 87)

By the end of the play, the two symbols of white domination and black exploitation/oppression, Charles and Crew, are removed so that a new dispensation of social equality can begin. This, of course, is rather too optimistic a statement, but the play looks beyond the present to acknowledge that violence sometimes may be an inevitable consequence of the unjust situation which still exists between races and classes in the Caribbean.

The conflict in the play centres around the symbolic figures of the rich white landlord and the poor black peasant, and it is this which makes Crew's act of murder symbolic and as Errol Hill concludes, the killing

> is also an act of purification. It absolves the past record and looks hopefully towards the future. It typifies a cleavage between two dispensations, the old one of master-slave relationship and the new one of multi-racial brotherhood (*Plays for Today*, p. 13).

Ti-Jean and His Brothers, on the other hand, introduces a new dimension to the rich-poor relationship, although *An Echo in the Bone* and *I'll Marry When I Want* explore this dimension also, but at a much lower level. Where the rich oppressors and exploiters in the latter plays are content to allow the poor oppressed to live in their slums of poverty and despair, the white Planter in Walcott's play goes a step further; he actually sets out to physically annihilate the poor mother by depriving her of her sons who should be her support in her old age. His demand from her is ominously clear; he 'owns half of the world' and yet he envies the poor woman and her sons the only thing they own which is their humanity; this is the one thing which he has not got but is dying to have.

Whether this desire is out of greed or is born out of a general sense of loss is not clear, but the crucial point is that the poor family faces the threat of losing the single possession which it has, life. For the Planter to feel what it is to be human, the sons of the poor mother have to forfeit their humanness through the devious contests which he devises between him and them. The Planter, of course, is not prepared to play fair and subsequent events show this to be true. In reality, the contest is between the Devil and the poor woman whose three sons represent various qualities which she can call upon in her confrontation with him. Gros-Jean is raw strength without matching and controlling intelligence; Mi-Jean is vacuous intellectualism that is not firmly grounded in reality and practical experience; and T-Jean is cunning, wit and all the innate human instinct for survival. Together, these three can ensure success and survival in the world, but the first two are utterly useless without the third. The Planter is out to destroy these basic human necessities so that the poor mother would be left at his mercy. However, it is wit which defeats him in the end and saves her. In a sense, what the Planter is after is the mother's sense of herself, of who or what she is, all the things that constitute her being - her physiology and her psychology. His intention and tactic is, gradually through eliminating her sons, to reduce her to a weakened empty shell of herself and thereby bringing her under his control. An individual identity is a complex of many things which, working together, creates the whole; and in seeking to pare away the mother's constituent elements, the Planter was hoping to destroy her through absorbing her into himself by eating her sons.

Walcott in the play appropriates an old St Lucian folktale which he uses to reflect the unequal, predatory relationship which exists between the rich and the poor, between the oppressor and the oppressed, and between whites and blacks in his Caribbean society. In *Ti-Jean and His Brothers*, it is between the White Planter (who is also the Devil) and the poor black family who live on the fringe of his large estate. The disparity in their material condition is captured aptly by the poor mother as she tries to restore peace between her quarrelling children:

> My sons, do not quarrel,
> Here all of us are starving,
> While the Planter is eating,
> From plates painted golden,
> Forks with silver tongues,
> The brown flesh of birds,
> And the white flesh of fish (*Plays for Today*, p. 29)

101

The optimism of the play lies in the fact that Walcott is able to set out how the poor can get the better of their tormentors by matching and out-tricking them - i.e., if the rich set out to cheat the poor, the latter have to cheat the former first and if the rich are set on entrapping them, the poor should make the former get caught in their traps instead. The poor need their wits about them in their daily life and death struggle with adversity and abjection. They also need all the help they can get. Ti-Jean does not rely on his own powers alone in his encounter with the Devil. Every resource is pulled in - his innate and street-wise intelligence, his mother's and the bush creatures' advice and cooperation - all these are pulled together to defeat the enemy. In the end, Ti-Jean becomes, like Latoye in *The Chattering and the Song*, the liberator who in saving himself from the Devil is able to also save the Bolom (who in the play is a symbol of life trapped at a moment of development and held in bondage by the Devil). In Osofisan's play, Latoye is able to persuade the peasants to join forces with him against Alafin Abiodun, and using their support he is able to save himself but in doing so, he liberates the peasants from the long standing exploitative and repressive regime of the Alafin. Theodore Colson, in fact, sees the Bolom as symbolising 'all aborted human potential in a world of black mothers and white planters' (Colson, 1973: 83) while Kole Omotoso sees the play as Walcott's 'prescription for revolutionary praxis' (1982: 76). Ti-Jean is a revolutionary hero who refuses to play by the rules set by his opponent and in his confrontation with the white devil Walcott is able to weave a poignant parable of the black experience in the Caribbean. It is also a potent parable which points the way forward for the black underdogs to emerge victorious in their battle against exploitation and social marginalisation.

Ti-Jean and His Brothers opens with the bush creatures, who act as narrators and chorus, and Walcott openly admits his debt to the story telling tradition of his St Lucian childhood. However, it is a tradition which goes back to his African and slave ancestry:

> What was there too, but was too deep to be acknowledged, was the African art of the story-teller, a tradition which survived in my childhood through the figure of a magical, child enchanting aunt, the memories of firefly-pricked rain forests at dusk . . . and those skin-prickling chants whose words may change, but whose mode goes as far back and even past tribal memory (*Plays for Today*, p, 5).

The first image of the characters quickly establishes the sordid poverty in which they live. Frog begins the tale thus:

```
Frog:   Well one time it had a mother
        that mother had three sons . . .
Bird:   How poor their mother was?
        (sad music on flute)
Frog:   Oh, that was poverty, bird
        Old hands dried up like claws
        Heaping old sticks
        too weak to protect her nest . . .
        (Light shows hut)
        Lined in a little house
        Made up of wood and thatch
        On the forehead of the mountain
        Where night and day was rain
        Mist, cloud white as cotton
        Caught in the dripping branches
        Where sometimes it was so cold
        The frog would stop its singing
(Plays for Today, p, 26-7)
```

The audience is left in no doubt that this family's poverty is such that it can not protect itself from unkind elements, with not enough food to feed itself and not enough fire to keep out the cold. Neither does the family have a good roof to keep the rain out. Such a family, as pitiable and defenceless as it is, the Planter would not leave alone. In order to achieve his purpose, he devises a contest between himself and the three brothers; a contest designed to see who would get the other angry first. Anyone who succeeds in doing that wins and the prize to be won is: for the Planter, the opportunity to have human flesh for his dinner, and for the brothers, a promise of future wealth. The Planter sets the brothers very impossible tasks and he is always on hand to add annoyance to their frustrations as each brother struggles to accomplish that which is impossible to accomplish.

Gros-Jean, sheer brute force *sans* guiding common sense, is the oldest and the first to take on the Planter's challenge. He, as expected, fails and is promptly eaten. Mi-Jean is the second son and his excessive and vacuous intellectualism does not help him either and so, he goes the same way as his elder brother, to become a happy meal for the Devil. Both brothers were unable to stop the Devil because they tried to play by the rules which had been set by their adversary. But in Ti-Jean, the third and last son, the old man of the forest meets his match in devious intelligence and rebellious wit. Ti-Jean flouts all the rules and makes up his own in his battle with the Planter. Thus, instead of attempting the impossible task of tethering the Planter's obstreperous goat, he simplifies things for himself by first castrating and later killing the animal for his own dinner, an act which the owner did not find amusing at all. And again rather than waste time and effort counting innumerable cane stalks in the huge plantation, he just sets fire to the entire cane field. To crown it all, after he had helped himself generously to the goodies in the Planter's cellar and kitchen, he sets the house and the estate on fire. This ultimately gets to the Devil, who all along had been trying to control himself, but is forced to lose his temper and thus the contest. Accused by Ti-Jean of not smiling at the news that his house is on fire, the Devil finally explodes:

> Smiling? You expect me to smile? Listen to him . . . . You share my liquor, eat out my fridge, treat you like a guest, tell you my troubles. I invite you to my house and you burn it!

Ti-Jean [*Sings*]: Who with the devil tries to play fair
Weaves the net of his own despair
Oh smile; what's a house between drunkards?

Devil: I've been watching you you little nowhere nigger! You little squirt, you hackneyed cough between two immoralities, what do you think you are? You're dirt, and that's where you'll be when I'm finished with you. Burn my house, my receipts, all my papers, all my bloody triumphs.

Ti-Jean: [*To the Devils*] Does your master sound vexed to you?
(*Plays for Today*, p, 66-7)

Ti-Jean represents the only hope for the poor black person who hopes to turn the tables on their oppressor by changing the rules of the game. It is out of people like him, those who do not conform and who make new rules to act by, that revolutionaries are made.

The play is a vivid dramatisation of the unending confrontation between the forces of white oppression and tyranny and the poor and oppressed black peoples. Gros-Jean and Mi-Jean represent angry force and vacuous learning respectively and both qualities are shown to be inadequate in the struggle to liberate imprisoned black minds as in the encounter both carelessly play into the hands of the Devil. Ti-Jean, the youngest and the last hope, represents instinct, wisdom, conscience, commonsense, dare and good humour, and it is he who is able to match the Devil, trick for trick, and defeat him. In the play, Walcott fabricates a parable of hope for the poor and oppressed in the possibility of a future when the power of the oppressor could be neutralised and his yoke thrown off. It is a happy and triumphant Ti-Jean who returns to his home with his new found brother, the Bolom, at the end of the play to look after his ailing and weak mother:

> Come then, little brother. And you little creatures. Ti-Jean must go on. Here's a bundle of sticks that Old Wisdom has forgotten. Together they are strong. Apart, they are rotten. God look after the wise, and look after the strong. But the fool in his folly will always live long (*Plays for Today*, p, 70).

And as always, the play ends with unique hope and optimism, an ever present element in most Caribbean plays. It is the hope that together the various peoples, the rich and the poor, black, brown and white can make a peaceful home out of their Caribbean islands. They may have their different racialised and cultural identities, but what they all have in common is a shared Caribbean identity and home which they must all embrace. The same call which ends *Ti-Jean and His Brothers* is present in many other Caribbean plays, such as *An Echo in the Bone* and *Dream on Monkey Mountain*. The plays preach harmony in spite of the differences which currently come between the many ethnicities and identities in the Caribbean.

An Echo in the Bone, *Ti-Jean and His Brothers* and *I'll Marry When I Want* show the various tricks which the rich employ in their attempts to keep the poor and oppressed in continued poverty and oppression. In *An Echo* Charles diverts water from Crew's little farm in order to render the land unviable for farming and to thereby force Crew to move off or to get Rachel, his wife, to become a keeper in the big house. The Devil in *Ti-Jean* devises his sinister contest in order to trick the unsuspecting brothers to their deaths and so provide himself with his much desired supper of human flesh. In like manner, Kīoi in *I'll Marry* comes up with his equally sinister and devious idea of a 'proper church wedding' for Kīgūūnda and Wangeci, and through this he is able to trick the couple into mortgaging their only piece of land which is eventually auctioned off because Kiguunda defaults in the repayment of the loan.

I'll Marry When I Want dramatises the tricking of Kīgūūnda by Kīoi and his accomplices into forfeiting his small piece of land. However, in doing so, the play adopts a different approach in its handling of the unequal relationship between the rich and the poor. Instead of just cataloguing gross images of the poor in their hovels of poverty and misery, *I'll Marry When I Want* highlights the disparity and immorality by juxtaposing images of the poor and the rich. Unlike *An Echo* or *Ti-Jean*, *I'll*

Marry concentrates as much attention on the homes of the rich as it does on those of the poor. This technique of contrast achieved through montage creates powerful images that capture the relationship of exploitation and oppression leading to misery and penury that is the lot of the majority of people in contemporary Kenyan society. Ngũgĩ wa Thiong'o's earlier play with Micere Mugo, *The Trial of Dedan Kimathi*, helps a great deal in putting into perspective the situation being explored in the latter play The first play deals with the attempt of the Mau Mau leader, Dedan Kimathi, and his freedom fighters to win back land and rights which colonial authority had taken away from the masses of Kenyan peoples who, as a consequence, had become landless peasants, labourers and tenants in their own ancestral homelands. The play had presented Kenyan poverty as resulting from the racial oppression and exploitation of colonised Africans by European colonial authority and settlers. The vision from the play projects beyond the Mau Mau war to *uhuru*, to a more equitably ordered society in which a majority of Kenyans find fulfilment and happiness. This is the hope still remembered nostalgically by Njooki in the latter play when she laments:

> When we fought for freedom
> I'd thought that we the poor would milk grade cows
> In the past I used to eat wild spinach
> Today I am eating the same
> (p, 39)

This despair sums up the theme of the play, and it is a theme which has remained an abiding concern of Ngũgĩ wa Thiong'o's writings. This contrasts sharply with the ever present optimism found in the Caribbean plays. This is perhaps because the Caribbean peoples, in spite of their underlying identity problems, are not burdened by the disappointed hopes and disillusionment which seem to cast a cloud over much postcolonial theatre and literature from Africa. In addition to their fighting spirit, most of the African characters are disappointed, disillusioned and angry, unlike the Caribbean characters who feed on hope. The ironic truth which emerges from a play like *I'll Marry When I Want* is the fact that the freedom and the good life for all Kenyans which Dedan Kimathi and his men and women fought and some had died for have been subverted and it appears that only those who stayed home or betrayed the freedom cause have become beneficiaries, while the survivors of the struggle, men like Kiguunda and Gicaamba, are left to feed only on memories of a dream they once held. The land which they fought for and for which many had lost their lives and limbs is still not theirs because a select few had managed to buy up everything, and even the little that a person like Kiguunda could buy is being seriously coveted by the insatiable Kĩoi and his ilk, on behalf of their neo-colonial capitalist masters and partners. Ngũgĩ wa Thiong'o's summary of the play touches on the immorality of the unequal property relations in neo-colonial Kenya:

> *Ngaahika Ndeenda* [the original Gikuyu title of the play] depicts the proletarisation of the peasantry in a neo-colonial society. Concretely it shows the way the Kiguunda family, a poor family, who have to supplement their subsistence on their one and half acres with the sale of their labour is finally deprived of even the one-and-half acre by a multinational consortium of Japanese and Euro-American industrialists and bankers aided by the native comprador landlords and business men (*I'll Marry When I Want*, 1986: 44)

The Mau Mau revolt had not been staged so that the people would exchange white European masters for new black ones; rather, it had been staged to abolish both masters and servants created by the colonial relationship in Kenya. It had been staged so that each person in Kenya could receive according to their need. The fight had not been so that a few could step into the shoes of the former colonial masters and buy up all the land and bring into existence a new kind of unequal relationship: that of black tenants either squatting or labouring on vast estates owned by black landlords. This is precisely the relationship that exists between Kĩgũũnda and Gĩcaamba, on one hand, and Kĩoi, on the other. The independence which eventually came to Kenya did not change anything for the poor folks who had done the actual fighting in the forests, and all the ills which Kimathi talked about and which so many had died to prevent had come to be established in the new relationship between a shamelessly opulent land-grabbing, neo-colonial native bourgeoisie of the Kĩois, Ndugĩres and Ikuuas, and a still landless, labouring and starving peasant and proletariat class, represented by Kĩgũũnda and Gĩcaamba. Independence ironically had merely transferred property, wealth and power from the white colonial owners to a few black ones, while retaining all the socio-economic structures which colonialism had introduced to facilitate the massive exploitation and impoverishment of the native populations of the colonies. It operates in much the same way as the slave structures which have survived abolition and emancipation in the Caribbean, and are used today to ensure white domination of the black majority.

Most of the heroes of the Mau Mau war seem to have made little or nothing from independence. Kīgūūnda works in Kīoi's farm and owns just a miserable acre and half of arid land which the latter covets and schemes successfully to take away. Gīcaamba is a labourer in a shoe factory in the city. Their wives and children pick tea and coffee leaves in Kīoi's plantations, just as they did previously for the white farmers, and whatever little they receive as wage they give back as payment for a few items from shops not surprisingly owned by Kīoi and his associates. Independence did come indeed, but it did not bring economic and social freedom for all as hoped. The play highlights the disparity and unjustness in the property relations through presenting in detail the homes of the two representative families who stand in starkly contrasting positions - accusing and mocking each other respectively.

I'll Marry When I Want presents the audience with two very contrasting worlds. One is the world of the rich inhabited by Kīoi and people like him, and the other is the world of the poor and in which Kīgūūnda and people like him live. The first is a world of affluence and comfort, and the other that of deprivation and suffering. Kīgūūnda's miserable shack stands as an eloquent symbol which accuses the home-guards who had betrayed the freedom struggle and who are still betraying the hopes of independence. And on the other hand, Kīoi's superfluously furnished and lavishly provisioned mansion stands in mocking opposition to the extreme poverty of Kīgūūnda's home. The playwrights use this detailed description of the two homes to bring out the sharp contrast in the life styles of the two social groups in post-independence neo-colonial Kenya. Besides, it is this image of two separate worlds which the two homes stand for that captures and illustrates the enormity of the betrayal of the noble dream and hope of a better Kenya for all which the freedom fighters had cherished and some had perished for. The image is made all the more painful because it is those who betrayed or who did not fight in the forests and hills who have become the ultimate beneficiaries of *uhuru*, while those who sacrificed their lives and everything remain condemned to a life of unrelieved poverty. This is the indictment which a play like *I'll Marry When I Want* makes of present Kenyan society and its corrupt leaders, and no wonder that the two dramatists and many others who took part in making the play suffered all manner of official intimidation and violence for their effort.

Predator and Prey

Identity very often is a 'game' played in relation to - sometimes with and sometimes against - the 'other'. That is to say, one is what one is because one is not the other; and we know who we are by knowing who we are not. Identity therefore is a play of opposition and so far, the plays we have looked at in this chapter bear this out in the relationship between the rich and the poor, and between white and black peoples. Thus, another metaphor which captures this play of opposition in African and African-Caribbean theatre is that of predator and prey or the hunter and the hunted. This is the key image which the four plays in this section share – the image of a predator ominously stalking its prey. In the view of this study, this is a fitting metaphor for the relationship between the rich and the poor; a metaphor which proves the old saying that 'one person's gain is another's loss'. This means in effect that the deprivation and penury of the poor pay for the plenty and luxury which the rich enjoy. Poverty creates and sustains affluence and it is the hardship and suffering of the slave and colonised which pay for the privilege and comfort for the slave owner and the coloniser. This situation is achieved, as the plays suggest, through tricks and traps, the kind that Kīoi sets in his bid to rid Kīgūūnda of his only piece of land in *I'll Marry When I Want*; by Charles in order to drive Crew away from the latter's tiny piece of farm land in *An Echo in the Bone*; and by the Planter to ensnare and kill the three sons in *Ti-Jean and his Brothers*. The ploy is captured by Kīgūūnda's friend, Gīcaamba, in the warning proverb that:

> If you want to rob a monkey of a baby it is holding you must first throw
> it a handful of peanuts (*I'll Marry When I Want*, p, 33).

The monkey, in order to catch the peanuts, has to let go of her baby and this is all her enemy needs to take away her child. Unfortunately, this warning goes unheeded by Kīgūūnda as Kīoi succeeds eventually in tricking him into letting go of his precious title deed by pledging his one and half acres in order to secure a loan to finance an unnecessary wedding ceremony.

The multi-pronged assault which the Kīois launch on the Kīgūūndas is comparable to a scene in which a brood of hawks swoop down on a defenceless mother-hen and her innocent chicks. And by the time the assault is over, the Kīgūūnda family is totally brought to its knees and only the inconsolable mother-hen, Wangeci, is left clucking sadly at the desolation of her home – her husband becomes a drunk and wreck of a man after losing his land and job, while her innocent and lovelorn daughter, Gathoni, is left carrying an illegitimate child for John, Kīoi's philandering son.

Similarly, the moment the Planter swoops on the poor defenceless mother and her three sons in *Ti-Jean and His Brothers*, the audience senses that the family is in serious trouble, and by the time mother and sons realise what has been planned for them, the first two sons have already become dinner for the insatiable Devil/Planter. Like Kīoi, the Planter sets his trap in a sinister context/game of patience and reward between him and the three sons in which he was not planning to play fair. The first two sons play into his hands as they are naively blind to what or who they were up against. The contest between the first two sons – the strong but foolish Gros-Jean and the facetious Mi-Jean - and the Planter is like the game between a patient cat that toys with a doomed rat before pouncing to eat it. The Planter/Devil plays around with each until they tire and can offer him no more resistance and he then gobbles them up. But luckily, for his mother and himself, Ti-Jean refuses to be food for the Devil. From the outset he smells a rat since neither of his brothers had returned from their encounters with the Planter. His aim in the ensuing confrontation with the Planter is to beat the trap-setter by getting him caught in the trap.

The Planter's game plan is to always lure the unwary victim into his domain like a wily spider and by setting them extremely impossible tasks to accomplish leads them inevitably to their death. First, they are asked to tether his obstreperous goat. Then they are required to count all the cane leaves and stalks in the Planter's immense cane field. When these tasks begin to irritate and weary the victim, the old man is on hand to aggravate the situation by playing away unrelentingly at the already frayed nerves, tempers and other individual weaknesses of each victim. Either way, the two older brothers stood no chance of surviving the contest because they lacked the basic qualities which can come through such an ordeal; they did not have the natural instinct for survival which alone can provide the creative and stubborn determination needed for winning when the odds have been stacked heavily against the individual. Besides, they also lacked the commonsense, wit and cunning which could have guided their natural instincts and physical strength. Ti-Jean, their little brother, has all these qualities and it is these which enable him to finally turn the game around and instead of being the hunted, becomes the hunter, much to the chagrin of the Planter. Thus, the play's message is that it is possible for the prey to turn the table on the predator, a message very relevant in the Caribbean situation of racial and class oppression and exploitation. The play holds out a means and a hope for the black majority, who for four centuries have been besieged and hemmed in by an oppressive white minority, to take the initiative away from their oppressors and exploiters. In this way, they may place themselves in a position to help re-define the lines of social relationships and opportunity in the Caribbean.

Edgar White's *Redemption Song* recreates the predator-prey scenario found in the plays previously discussed. Like Kīoi and the other predators discussed so far, Fowler is the ubiquitous prowler in *Redemption Song*, and like Kīoi, Fowler too has his fingers deep in every available pie in Redemption City. His main concern in the play, it seems, is to destroy the Bramble family of father and son, and he succeeds in doing just that in the end. He attacks the family in three ways. First, he twists Bramble's arm and gets him to sell their home, his son Legion's only inheritance from his grandmother, an act which reduces the old man into a homeless wreck. Second, Fowler uses his money to 'purchase' Verity, Legion's childhood sweetheart. And finally, when the latter returns from his unsuccessful migration to England and tries to repossess all that was formerly his, Fowler arranges, with the help of his policeman son, Simon, to have Legion stoned to death. By the end of the play what is left is a broken and wretched Bramble who is good for nowhere else but the dung heap, while Fowler has the entire world of Redemption City as his private playground. The only thing he could not hold on to is Verity who discovers that her love is for the dead Legion and therefore refuses to return to Fowler's house.

Redemption Song handles a powerful theme which has remained dominant in much Caribbean theatre and literature - in the play White critically explores the theme of the famed migratory tendency of Caribbean peoples. Indeed, migration as an idea or a social phenomenon is ever present in the consciousness of most Caribbean men and women - and a great many of the characters in Caribbean plays exhibit in varying degrees this migratory inclination. Walcott's characters are always on the verge of migrating, but somehow they do not in the end. They remain because, for the dramatist, the Caribbean is the only home they have and it is for them therefore to stay and make it a home worth living in. The solution, in spite of the racially determined hierarchical structure of whites at the top and blacks at the bottom, lies not in running away, but rather in a determined and constructive utilisation of what is available, in staying back to help in the much needed fight to change the unjust social order, even if some like Legion die in the attempt. It is ironic however that Walcott too left for a while, and only returning from time to time, but time will tell whether his departure is temporary or permanent. White himself has lived abroad most of his adult life: the same goes for Matura, who is seen now in Europe more known now as a British playwright than a Trinidadian (Caribbean) one. The radical West Indian minds, it is claimed, never stay at home; they leave home to make their revolutions somewhere else.

What a play like *Redemption Song* illustrates is that the much touted migratory nature of Caribbean peoples should not be seen in isolation from the social pressure arising from the racial factors in the social structure which cause it. The characters in Caribbean plays and novels seek only to leave because there is nothing for them to stay for, and also because the outside world offers them a glimmer of hope that perhaps, they might be able to realise their innate potentials which the racially determined social arrangements of their former slave islands do not give them any opportunity for individual development. They leave, not because they do not love their island homes; they do so because that appears to be the only sensible thing to do and because the predators, who benefit immensely from the system as it is, would want them - the radical, ambitious, hot-headed and fearless ones - to leave. The predators, such as Fowler, do everything to force rebellious spirits, like Legion, out. Legion puts this well when he explains to Verity:

> You see this place, there is beauty, but we never see the fullness. Half the island is young but is only old men in control. And whom they can't control they drive out . . . . Like they did my mother (*Redemption Song*, p, 70)

In saying this, Legion also accuses his father whom he sees as having played a part in his dispossession. White implies here that the conservative spirit of the old generation is part of the problem plaguing the Caribbean nations for they are, as he says in the play, societies that 'eat their young' (70). It is also apparent that migration performs a 'useful' function of helping to maintain the stability and outlook of the Caribbean. As Lowenthal points out:

> Frequent migration . . . enhances local tolerance of colonial ties. Emigration continually drains away potential rebels, leaving behind those more prone to endure neo-colonialism. One of the reasons why the British West Indies have remained statically conservative, impoverished and without a revolutionary movement . . . 'is that all such radicals leave

home, like all other ambitious locals, and go off to make revolutions somewhere. The less ambitious stay-at-home is still more passive; the black West Indians are said to be the most conformist and accommodating people in the Caribbean (1972: 249).

This may well explain why a good number of the characters who remain do practically nothing to change the status quo. They are either conformists or conservatives. Those who challenge the system either die like Legion or they are forced to leave like his mother did. It is not surprising that a good number of the seminal minds and rebellious spirits of the Caribbean have lived or presently live abroad.

But, of course, those who migrate soon discover that it is not a bed of roses or a paradise of endless opportunities out there in North America and Western Europe. The humiliations, agonies and frustrations of Caribbean migrants as they trudge the often cold and unfriendly streets of North American and European cities have remained the abiding focus and theme of White's theatre in plays such as *Fun in Lethe, The Burghers of Calais, Lament for Rastafari, Like Them That Dream, That Generation*, among others. But returning as Legion does is a dangerous thing to do as his presence is perceived by those in charge as threatening the status quo; thus, he became a marked man from the moment he stepped foot on the shores of Redemption City and it was only a matter of time before they got rid of him.

Chapter 5

A HOME OF THEIR OWN: MARGINALISATION AND THE LONGING FOR UTOPIA

As Ikoli Harcourt Whyte tells Superintendent in *Hopes of the Living Dead*, all the lepers want is a place of their own, where they can grow their own food, look after themselves in their own way; where they can become free of their dependence on charity and government support. The Rastafarians in *O Babylon!* want to be allowed and supported to return 'home' to Africa with the Emperor Haile Selassie so they can live life on their own terms without any interference from Babylon. This is a reality the plays to be discussed here have in common; it is the reality of most urban centres in Africa and the Caribbean and goes to show how these plays are truly reflective and mirrors of their respective social and cultural contexts. Sometimes, however, the desire for Utopia can also manifest itself in the kind of radical transformation of existing society as the characters in Sowande's Babylon trilogy, *The Night Before*, *A Farewell to Babylon* and *Flamingo*, and Osofisan's *The Chattering and the Song* and *Morountodun* undertake. What both desires and approaches share is that both result from a judgment and rejection of a social order perceived to be unjust.

Characters on the Fringes

Sometimes the disparity and social distance between the rich and the poor is wide that one literally finds the latter consigned to the margins of mainstream society. In reality, it is not an unusual sight, especially on the outskirts of major urban centres of developing nations in Africa and the Caribbean, to see groups who have become economically and physically marginalised develop their own sub-cultures, usually of crime and violence, in their ever-widening slums of despair and hope. Characters from such settings and groups, depending on what the dominant ethos of the slum is, often live a life totally different from that of mainstream society. In some cases, as in Soyinka's *The Road*, the characters live, wait and hope for a chance to re-enter society and live healthy, normal and fulfilled lives. In other instances, as in Walcott's *O Babylon!*, marginalisation leads to the development of a counter-culture of drugs, violence and crime. Here the concern of the characters is not with not being allowed back into the society that rejected them and which they in turn have rejected. Their concern rather is with searching for an alternative to Babylon, a land far away and different from the present one that pushed them out. The slum setting in *The Road* is a society nourished on hope and in which the absence of despair lends vitality to the characters, while the slum setting in Walcott's play combines hope and despair in equal measure. Of course, the co-existence of hope and despair in the second brings with it a degree of inertia which is reflected in the inaction of the Rastafarians, who drift along waiting for the day of their miraculous release from exile in Babylon while they do nothing to change the situation.

The inequality in wealth distribution in Africa and the Caribbean makes it possible for one person or group of persons to have all the wealth, both land and other material resources. When this is the case as in the first three of the plays that will be discussed in this section, those who own nothing find themselves as tenants or squatters dwelling on the periphery or sometimes within, but usually in the backwoods of the immense holdings of their very affluent landlords or neighbours.

In *Ti-Jean and His Brothers* and *An Echo in the Bone*, all the characters, who incidentally are poor and black, are condemned to subsist on the little land left on the periphery of the large estates owned by single individuals like the Planter and Charles respectively. Scenes of such glaring inequality resemble life in the slave plantations of so many years ago. Besides, the inequitable distribution allows those who have wealth to play god to the poor marginalised group. The Planter, for instance, decides the fate of the poor mother and her three sons who have no hand or say in the contest that would determine their lives; while Charles decides to divert the natural flow of water away from Crew's farm so as to force the latter to make up his mind about staying on or moving out of his land, in the same way that Kĩoi decides what anybody gets or does not get in *I'll Marry When I Want*. These powerful demigods usually invade the abode of the poor at will, and each time it is to make life-threatening demands that usually leave the latter worse off than they were before the invasion.

Charles descends from his big mansion into Crew's little home because he feels it is his right to have Rachel, the latter's wife, whenever he desired. To get his way he is prepared to offer Rachel work in the main house as his personal housekeeper, which would remove her from poverty and misery but would of course place her at his beck and call as his mistress. When Crew refuses, Charles decides to play god by diverting water away from Crew's land, the family's only means and hope for subsistence. By doing this, Charles was hoping possibly to achieve two things. First, he was hoping to make life so unbearably hard for the Crew household that Rachel would eventually be forced into accepting his offer of a job as his housekeeper. Or, in the alternative should she refuse, to use the diversion of water to force Crew off the land and further into the woods to allow himself more land and therefore more clout to push everybody else around. But he underestimates Crew's pride and hot temper when the latter comes up to the house to ask for assistance. Instead of offering the help requested, Charles decides to inflict further insult on Crew and the latter's long held rage explodes leading him to kill Charles.

Each time the rich descend on the poor it is always to make demands that are never in the interest of those being visited. When the Planter sends the Bolom to make his request of the poor mother dwelling on the edge of the forest, the demand is not intended to be of any benefit to the suffering family. Rather, the Planter is out only to satisfy his desire for human flesh and in the process to eliminate the poor woman and her sons. The Bolom's message is direct in response to the mother's demand to know his mission:

Send the first of your sons for it
They must die in that order
And let the youngest
Return to the hut
(*Plays for Today*, p, 31)

So, in spite of claims to the contrary, and in spite of hiding his intentions behind the smoke-screen of a contest, the Planter's purpose is obvious - he must have the three sons for food. He owns all the forest and a big, beautiful and well provisioned house, while the mother and her sons have a tiny and ill-equipped home in a tiny corner, well outside this immense domain over which the Planter has absolute ownership and control. But even this little they have he envies them for and would destroy the whole family for it. The Planter (Devil) has everything but one, and that is, human feeling - he lacks the ability to feel emotions of anger, love, pain, sorrow etc. All these the mother and her sons possess and in order to experience these emotions, the devil has to kill and eat the three sons. Symbolically, by eating the sons he would be acquiring the various kinds of human endowment the sons represent. Also removing these possessions from the mother would mean reducing her to nothing, or more appropriately, to death. It is thus not surprising that once the first two brothers, Gros-Jean and Mi-Jean, die and are eaten, the mother begins to ail; and this picture of his mother is on Ti-Jean's mind as he goes into battle against the Devil in the final confrontation which was to decide whether she lived or died. Ti-Jean wins in the end and this is the radical message which the play offers to all oppressed and deprived peoples: that the oppressor can not win all the time and that the oppressed may sometimes, as Ti-Jean did, have to play outside the rules set by their oppressors in order to win.

The visits of the rich to the abodes of the poor, the three plays reveal, often highlight the abject poverty of those being visited and it is through these intrusions that the audience/reader gets a glimpse into the other world where life is fuller, freer and much happier. It is a world which is set out as a touchstone to measure the level of poverty, deprivation and oppression which exists in the society. It is also a measure of the level of social inequality which characterises human relationships. Charles in Crew's home, for instance, really brings out the poverty and the squalid degradation of the latter and Rachel accordingly feels uncomfortable in his presence. The rich always remind the poor of what they have not got, of all the things that are missing in their lives. Similarly, when the Kīoi family visit the Kiguunda family, the visitors' disdainful observations of their surroundings and fear of being infected by the all too visible squalor bring home to the very sensitive Kīgūūnda the sordidness of his existence.

When *Ti-Jean and His Brothers* is read as being made up of two antipodal worlds, the journey of the three brothers assumes a deeper significance. In the Devil's domain, the visiting brothers have all the obstacles and disadvantages placed on their way. Gros-Jean and Mi-Jean fail to negotiate these hurdles correctly and are therefore destroyed by them while their little brother survives because the basic human instinct for survival is alive in him, and also because he refuses to play by the rules of his enemy. Gros-Jean and Mi-Jean venture into the tantalizing and glamorous but treacherous world of the Planter/Devil and, like careless and naive outsiders, they are consumed by the wiles and glitter of this dream world. But Ti-Jean uses his wit, all the help he could get from the forest creatures who know the enemy territory very well, as well as the blessings of his mother. He rejects the rules of this new world, choosing instead to invent and play by his own. Ti-Jean observes the two worlds, sees the injustice and accepts the challenge of altering the rules that govern the oft one-sided game which the rich play with the poor.

An Echo in the Bone and *I'll Marry When I Want* demonstrate that the rich never pay innocent social calls on the poor, the grave mistake which Kīgūūnda and Wangeci make when Kīoi, Jezebel, Ndugire and Helen visit them so unexpectedly. And this is despite the warnings from their apparently more discerning friend and neighbour, Gīcaamba, that 'rich families marry from rich families' and 'the poor from the poor' (*I'll Marry When I Want*, p, 32). Wangeci's female instinct and counsel, however, prevail and the couple clutch at the hope that the visit was in connection with a possible wedding between their daughter, Gathoni, and John, the philandering son of Kīoi and Jezebel. But in real fact, the visit turned out to be part of an orchestrated plan to ruin the Kīgūūndas. Kīoi succeeds in tricking Kīgūūnda into borrowing money from his bank with the title deed as co-lateral, and when as expected, the latter defaults on the repayment of the loan, the deed is confiscated and sold off at auction. Kīoi, of course, buys the land. And while he is busy ensnaring the father, his son is also assaulting the family from another angle by exploiting the affection and hopes of Kīgūūnda's innocent and besotted daughter whom he finally abandons when she becomes pregnant.

On both scores, the intrusion of mainstream society into the poor world of the fringe culture brings with it shock and disaster for the poor and marginalised who, always, are the ultimate losers in all dealings with the rich. At the end of *I'll Marry When I Want*, Kīgūūnda becomes the village drunk, singing along the street as he staggers home from the auction of his land the same strains that the intoxicated Kamande had been singing at the beginning of the play. Kīgūūnda is a ruined man and his plea at the start for Wangeci to go easy on the broken Kamande now ironically applies to him:

> Was that not Kamande wa Munyui?
> Leave him alone
> And don't look down upon him
> He was a good man;
> He became the way he is now only after he lost his job . . .
> He was Kīoi's night watchman
> But one day Kīoi finds him dead asleep in the middle of the night
> From that moment Kamande lost his job
> (*I'll Marry When I Want*, p, 5).

It is doubly significant that it is the ubiquitous Kīoi who is responsible for the utter ruin of these two honest and hardworking men. Kīoi is very much like the Planter who appears everywhere in numerous guises to lure the sons to their death in *An Echo in the Bone*. However, unlike the Planter, Kīoi wears no masks and his actions, apart from being devoid of any sense of morality, are rather crude in their directness when compared to the Planter's sly games.

Soyinka's *The Road* (1965) and Walcott's *O Babylon!* are similar in many respects and they are different from the other three plays looked at so far in this section. The two deal with characters completely outside of society; unlike the characters in the other three plays, Professor and his hangers-on and Sufferer and the Rastafarian community are not marooned on another person's property and so they are not in reality solely dependent on external goodwill and kindness. They seek neither favours nor quarter from anyone and, therefore, in the eyes of 'legitimate' society they are lawbreakers. The two plays reflect the rather common feature of most urban centres of developing nations where poverty and unemployment combine to force a great many people from the countryside towards the cities that can neither accommodate nor provide an adequate means of life for them. The cities are totally ill-equipped to handle the influx into them because they had not been planned to, nor are the rural areas made attractive enough to retain their dwellers. These 'dispossessed of the earth' can not go back to their original homes because there usually is not anything for them to return to, or sometimes because there is not even a home to go back to. They therefore must find 'homes' on the outskirts of the urban societies while waiting for the day when they too will have their dreams fulfilled and good homes in the cities to call their own. This is the life of the lay-abouts who hang around Professor's Aksident Store in *The Road*, forming an ever ready congregation at Professor's daily twilight communion. This is also the life of members of the Rastafarian community in *O Babylon!* as they wait on the outskirts of Kingston, Jamaica while dreaming of escape to a never-never Africa where they would be given a chance to make a life and become the men and women of their dreams. Both plays present a community of the poor who live and dream of a better tomorrow.

Professor who is in charge of this fringe society in *The Road* is in disgrace from and disagreement with mainstream society because of his past activities in the church. He has therefore established his own alternative society; first, to take care of other rejects like himself; and second, as a base from which he can keep a watchful eye on the goings-on in the enemy territory. He and his habitués are supposed to be of mutual benefit to each other; he provides them with a home and the evening communion, while he expects them to provide him with the material and information he needs in his metaphysical quest for the elusive Word. It is hugely ironic that the lay-abouts all pin their hopes on Professor for their elevation into mainstream society, while he, on his part, pins his hopes on them for a fuller understanding of life and death and for his own rehabilitation. Either way, it is a 'cycle of futility' for neither is able to lift the other and so both at the end of the play remain where and who they were at the beginning, rejects of and on the road of society and still on the outside.

Professor forges driving licences; he also occasionally tampers with road signs to ensure and/or to quicken the periodic harvest on the roads that would lead to the ultimate revelation that he is seeking. Salubi waits patiently for him to forge him a driving licence to enable him to land a job as a chauffeur. The others wait around for the jobs of thuggery that people like Chief-in-Town throw their way from time to time. This type of existence typifies the humdrum life of the murky fringe, a world of petty crimes, theft, marijuana smoking and a host of other little illegalities. It is a world that serves as a pool of ready hands for those who have money whenever any dirty or unpleasant task, like destroying property or roughing up political or business opponents needed to be carried out. However, this abuse of human potential infuriates Professor because, for him, it is a mere waste and not worth his retaining and ministering unto the lay-abouts for. Still, what unites them all, Professor included, is the shadow-like dream-like nature of their existence. Some of them do not have proper names; they are just persons or faces. Most do not have any histories and thus no identities of any type; they simply represent a mass of nameless faceless underclass living on the margins of mainstream society. And like the other group of twilight figures in *O Babylon!*, they all are sleeping or floating through life. Hope seems to be the only palpable element of their lives and it is this alone which redeems them as it offers them purpose at least. They are thus best understood as liminal characters patiently waiting for the moment of transition into the world of their dreams. And as with all who dwell on hope, the characters sometimes in moments of intense feeling or ecstasy get carried away on the wings of their dreams, and it is at such moments that they begin to live the dreams. One such moment occurs in *The Road* when Samson and Salubi give the audience snippets of the men they would love to become in the mimed scene of the millionaire. Through mime the histrionically resourceful pair gives the audience an insight into the flamboyant, vulgar and corrupt world of the rich, the world that they too would like to enter. It is the world of people who can and know how 'to chop life'; people who sit astride society doling out rewards and favours like gods.

This world of the rich is starkly different from and materially better than the murky one which Professor and his group inhabit. It is a world of beautiful cars, nice houses, of beautiful and elegantly dressed women (of course, there are no women at all in the hovel where Professor and his companions live), money and all the good things in life. It is possible that Soyinka uses the mime scene to question the immorality of such gross inequality and injustice in the distribution and enjoyment of life opportunities. He also uses the scene to launch a vitriolic attack on the corrupt and opulent lifestyle of the rich who use the world and the poor as their play things. Despite the light-hearted tone which he employs, his anger at the very existence of such a class differential and its implication in the lives of individuals is obvious. Besides, the loving care and the *joie de vivre* which he bestows on the enigmatic but roguish Professor, on the delightfully salubrious pair of Salubi and Samson, and on the no-gun-in-the-hip cowboy, Say Tokyo Kid, are indicators of where the playwright's sympathy lies. His portrayal of them suggests that he views them as men who may be poor, rejected and marginalised by society, but who are still fully human, lovable and intelligent; and that the corruption and little crimes they commit as they try to scratch a living out of a difficult life situation are not the result of any innate inclination to be evil or lawlessness. Rather, the play asks that these acts be seen as products of extremely hard and near intolerable circumstances. These characters therefore lay claim to the audience's sympathy and are admired even in their comic naïveté. They are naïve because the audience is well aware, as the characters themselves are not, that while they wait and hope for the day they would become part of mainstream society that that possibility is hardly ever likely to happen. They must therefore remain lively but 'sad comedians of the road' that leads to nowhere (Ngũgĩ wa Thiong'o, 1972: 65).

But while the characters in *The Road* wait and hope for a chance to enter into mainstream society, those in *O Babylon!* seek escape from the penury and pain of their marginal existence. Like the Devil in *Ti-Jean and His Brothers*, the oppressor class does not even allow the poor the luxury of some peace in their slum of poverty. The all-devouring Zion Construction Company, under the guidance of another ubiquitous rich man, Deacon Doxy, wants the very land upon which stand the miserable shacks of the Rastafarians in order to develop a tourist resort. The latter are expected to either vanish or at least to move further into the mountains, completely away and out of sight of the society of the wealthy. This scenario reminds one of Charles in *An Echo in Bone* as he schemes and pressurizes Crew to drive him away from his little piece of land, and Kĩoi in *I'll Marry When I Want* who bounces Kĩgũũnda out of his one and half acres of land. It is ironic that the Rastafarians actually believe that it is they who had broken links with mainstream society which had been oppressing them and they hope to set sail for far away Ethiopia (Africa), the perceived land of their ancestors. They see their settlement on the outskirts of Kingston as a temporary abode before their mass repatriation to a dream African homeland. The Rastafarians claim to have judged and denounced Babylon, and have therefore established a temporary Zion as the opposite. But the audience, of course, recognises that none of this is true, for it is in fact Babylon which has relegated the Rastafarians to the periphery, having made no provision for them in mainstream society.

It is hardly surprising that the leaders of the Rastafarian community in the play - Sufferer, Aaron and Samuel - are or had been petty criminals and marijuana sellers and smokers. However, Walcott uses this fact to accuse mainstream society and its unjust structures of social inequality as the main cause of criminality among the poor. A similar statement made by Soyinka in *The Road* is succinctly articulated by Aaron's defence lawyer during the arson trial:

> The crime of poverty to which the world is a witness
> We do not have, we do not have a witness
> to the history of injustice
> Of the world outside these windows
> Therefore, your honour, our defense is simply this:
> Oh who in his heart has not wanted to burn
> the unjust city
> The ghettos, the slums, the barrios, the dunghills
> the shanty-towns . . .
> Who has not raged like a fire
> when all a great fires needs
> is one spark of pity?
> Who would not have the city of our desire
> instead of these dunghills of shame . . .
> We are all murderers
> We are all destroyers;
> the criminals that we defend
> and the criminals that defend us, the lawyers
> (*The Joker of Serville and O Babylon!: Two Plays*, p, 253-4)

Goldstein's defence is sympathetic but, it also is a strong indictment of the rich for the injustice and deprivation which pushes the poor to commit crimes so that lawyers and magistrates can make more money defending or convicting them. He sees the crimes of these poor people as their only means of protesting against an unjust social order. And in this respect, the play is demanding a reordering of society so that every person can be accommodated and given a purpose and a contribution to make. Crew's killing of Charles in *An Echo in the Bone* must also be seen in this light because its violence, like Aaron's attempts to burn Babylon down, acquires an ennobling and liberating quality since it is in the context of the play the only option open to the oppressed but angry Rastafarian community keen to hang on to their humanity threatened on all sides by the powerful forces of Babylon. What members of the community want is not charity from Babylon, but the right to fair treatment, the right to exist and be themselves.

But having said that, Walcott is not wholly sympathetic to the doctrine of 'love and peace', of the hope for migration back to Africa central to Rastafarian philosophy - a doctrine which Sufferer actively preaches to his group. The playwright shows his anger at what he sees as an inexcusable collective impotence and inertia of the people in the Rasta commune as they dreamily sit by the desolate plains of Babylon and weep while their besotted gaze is cast towards a never-never Africa. This is an anger and frustration which Walcott expresses more openly in his essay, 'What the Twilight Says':

> The West Indian mind historically hung-over, exhausted prefers to take its revenge in nostalgia, to narrow its eyelids in schizophrenic daydream of an Eden that existed before its exile. Its fixation is for the breast of a nourishing mother . . . (in *Dream on Monkey Mountain and Other Plays*, p, 19-20).

There is a sense among members of the Rastafarian community of being Zion's children in captivity in Babylon which creates the two worlds that the play is about. The Rastafarians refuse to see themselves as members of Jamaican society; they are outside and would wish to remain so until the day of repatriation. It appears then that, in a way, they welcome their marginalisation. But one must not fail to recognise this attitude for what it truly is: a mere rationalisation so that the misfortune can be made a little bit more bearable; plus, it also excuses their inaction in confronting the social structure responsible for creating so much misery in their society. The rationalisation is also a means of making temporal the poverty and suffering which the community is experiencing. This ultimately is a negative attitude because what Sufferer and the community do is simply avoid confronting their passivity and thereby the need to seek a solution. What one finds in them therefore is not the noble and liberating rage of Crew, but rather a paralysing anguish which in some of them reveals itself to be self-destructive. The only person who eventually feels and acts out of self-righteous anger is Aaron, but Sufferer concentrates all his teaching of 'love and peace' on keeping Aaron in check. He succeeds only for a while to keep this rebellious spirit under control. Only Aaron, of all the community members, acts when he realises that the dream of a return to Africa was not going to happen.

The idea of utopia is also explored in Ola Rotimi's *Hopes of the Living Dead* – a play published in 1987 but first performed to national acclaim in Nigeria in 1985-6. The play deals with another group of rejected and marginalised individuals who like the Rastafarians, dream of a new world of their own where they can be responsible, useful and respected as integral members of the society. But unlike the Rastafarians, Rotimi's lepers take steps to make their dream come true. The playwright's introductory description of the inmates of the leper Wards G and H is filled with indicting comments and powerful images of poverty, rejection and marginalisation. These images dominate the play and haunt the audience's imagination throughout. A good example of this is the graphic description of the grim setting and wretched characters inhabiting this dreary landscape:

> A number of slender iron-frame beds, overlaid with blankets - some beds spruced up with pillows, others without - introduce the setting as the ward of a hospital. To be expected, this ward is stark, drearily ungarnished as any hospital ward can customarily be. The inmates are just as spartan as their assorted clothes. Some are clad in the traditional, white, apron-style, tunics; others in more personalised wear depicting a brazen melange of homely, Nigerian cuts in competition with borrowings from Europe. All the clothes have one common texture, however. They are aged, wear-chafed, and submissively weather rattled. But they are **by no means** filthy. . . (*Hopes of the Living Dead*, p 3-4)

These men and women are not only poor, they are sick as well; they are suffering from the dreaded leprosy disease which on its own in Africa traditionally consigns the unfortunate victim to some place outside of mainstream society. Even very close relatives and friends tend to treat the stricken with tolerance and much distance. Rotimi's powerful metaphor of leprosy and its associated infectiousness, unwholesomeness and exclusion is significant. It is not difficult to see his veiled reference to the infectious social malaise affecting independent Nigeria's social fabric in the years around when the play was written. One can also extend this metaphorical allusion to the Rastafarians in *O Babylon!* who in a manner of speaking are social lepers too because the intruders from mainstream society seem afraid of becoming contaminated by close contact with members of the community. No one desires to be seen in close contact with them, including erstwhile close friends like Dolly. The Kĩgũũndas in *I'll Marry When I Want* are treated in a similar manner by the Kĩois who refuse any food and water when they visit the former in their home - the visitors treat their hosts as if they were contaminated or carried a disease of some kind. All through their stay the visitors behave as if genuinely afraid of contracting some disease from their hosts or having to live in squalid conditions. In all respects, the two groups are separate peoples with separate values and ambitions, in spite of their sharing the same ethnic identity. The protagonists in *Hopes of the Living Dead* are, in fact, in double quarantine. First, they are real lepers. And second, their poverty is an eyesore to the rest of society and so they are shut away from public gaze. The lepers have built a community of their own with their own codes of behaviour which gives them a sense of belonging, which mainstream had denied them because of their infirmity. But the patients ask for neither pity nor charity; all they want is the opportunity to build and live in a society of their own where they can order their lives the way they choose since the parent society has made no provision for them. This aspiration, they are share with the characters in *O Babylon!*. It is always the one hope of the poor and oppressed to be given a chance to establish or inherit a society where they can become 'somebodies' with meaningful lives.

Hopes of the Living Dead celebrates the process of struggle to achieve this aspiration and also the vision and tenacity of the champions of the struggle. As Rotimi tells the reader, the play 'salutes the example of an Ikoli Harcourt Whyte, a hero of a people in struggle' against poverty, rejection and living death (Profile Notes to *Hopes of the Living Dead*, 1987: iv). But above all, the play salutes the courage, the spirit of love and unity on the part of those who have been cast aside to live forever as unwanted and unacknowledged ghosts on the fringes of society. This is a thoroughly researched play and Rotimi displays great artistic and emotional sincerity in his handling of his material, even as he squeezes out the intense dramatic possibilities which the Ikoli-led lepers' revolt contains. What he succeeds in creating is a very powerful parable capable of emotionally moving and disturbing audiences, especially with its electrifying atmosphere and energy in performance - this writer watched one of its premiere performances at the Arts Theatre, University of Nigeria, Nsukka in 1986. It is able to do so because the sentiments it expresses are hauntingly true and real. The dramatic action and the thematically appropriate songs touch and haunt the mind long afterwards. There is total belief in and an unqualified admiration for these men and women and what they believe in and fight religiously for. Rotimi's love for these unfortunate but determined patients is never in doubt for a moment, yet he manages to retain enough artistic and emotional distance to make the subjects objectively convincing and dramatically powerful. One hardly hears the dramatist's voice as the vitality of the characters takes over, commanding the attention and respect of the audience.

The play deals with the struggle of the inmates of two leper observatory wards in the General Hospital in Port Harcourt against an insensitive government that would rather have them either begging on the streets or depending on government and/or missionary charity, while all the patients want is a piece of land set aside for them so they would find rehabilitation, dignity and fulfilment in thinking and acting for themselves. The patients have been rejected and cast out, and this they accept and they ask for neither pity from nor readmission into mainstream society which does not want them. Their leader, Harcourt Whyte (a historical figure), states simply the collective desire of the inmates when he confronts the intransigent Superintendent of Police, the symbol of the uncaring government:

> . . . do not fling us apart like corn, one head from another head of the same stem, without caring wherever we fall - beard and all. Drop us with feeling into one basket. . . . Let the government give us a place, a place we can call our own, where we can keep ourselves to ourselves, feed ourselves, work for ourselves. . . . Give us the chance and leave the rest to our glory or our shame (*Hopes of the Living Dead*, p, 47)

This is a plea for the shared bond and sense of belonging which the inmates have developed among themselves; they are a group identified by their disability, but still a collective asking to be allowed to nurture this identity in their own way. It is a plea, but also a challenge. The government, however, is not prepared to entertain this plea and the Superintendent in an off-handed manner dismisses it as a modern daydream of Canaan that no sensible government was ever going to support. But it is a challenge and, in the end, it becomes a confrontation of will and might - the will of the marginalised patients who are seeking a decent life of their own against the might of an irresponsible and totally insensitive government that does not care about the deepest yearnings of a section of its population. The message of the play, it seems to me, is that no government, no matter how uncompromising it is, can suppress the united and indomitable will of its people. To the Superintendent's order and threat that they vacate the hospital premises on the order of the government (very similar in many respects to the order of the Zion Construction Company for the Rastafarian community to move further into the mountains in *O Babylon!* and Charles's scheme to force Crew to go away from his land in *An Echo in the Bone*), a threat that is quite intimidating:

> Now you listen to me! By the powers conferred on me by the laws of the land, I hereby again order you and all patients in the Leprosy Wards, within 24 hours to clear out of the premises of the General Hospital of Port Harcourt, and from the environs of Port Harcourt! (*Hopes of the Living Dead*, p, 49)

To which Harcourt counters with an equally vehement:

> And by the powers conferred on me by our suffering people, I say: give us a chance to live like human beings, or we shall remain bones in your selfish throats forever! (49).

And from this moment on in the play the battle is joined and in the end it is the united will of the lepers that triumphs as they get officially relocated to Uzuakoli, a colony/society of their own to manage and live in as they wish.

All the plays discussed in this section suggest that it is the rich who create poverty and the many slums of despair that dot and besmirch the outskirts of most urban centres in developing countries. The rich in order to purge their conscience of guilt try everything they can to push the poor out of sight, completely away from the borders of mainstream society. But as Harcourt Whyte says, the suffering masses would always remain within sight to torment the conscience of the rich and the mainstream as long as the cycle of poverty and oppression exists. The leper patients in *Hopes of the Living Dead* get their wish in the end and happily depart to Uzuakoli to begin a new life on their own terms; Crew in *An Echo in the Bone* refuses to give up his land and in righteous anger kills his tormentor, Master Charles; and Aaron burns part of Babylon to register his protest against an unjust social order and against the inhuman and oppressive machine of the Zion Construction Company in *O Babylon!*. It is to the credit of these rejects that they refuse to give in to the life designed for them by their oppressors; they fight for their right to be and by doing this, they win respect and admiration because of their stubborn refusal and resistance.

Longing for Utopia

Poverty, deprivation and inequality in the social system are the grim realities of most societies in the world, and the societies portrayed in African and African-Caribbean plays are no exception. In fact, in these highly underdeveloped postcolonial societies, the reality is grimmer and more pronounced. It is thus not surprising that in African and African-Caribbean plays the reader often comes across individuals or sometimes a group who find themselves at the bottom end of the social ladder experiencing extreme hardship resulting from unjust social arrangements and who, completely fed up with their lot, begin to seek or long for alternatives, a kind of Utopia where life would be more fulfilling. The idea of Utopia is used here not to suggest just a wild unattainable dream which enables a person or group to avoid facing up to reality. Rather the term denotes here an anti-thesis of a social structure based on oppression, exploitation, deprivation and mass poverty. Utopia does not necessarily have to be a separate place far away from existing society which those seeking it would have to physically relocate to; it could just mean any change that sweeps away any unjust and inhuman geo-social reality and replace it with a more humane and egalitarian one – as Bode Sowande explores in his Babylon trilogy, *The Night Before* (1979), *Farewell to Babylon* (1979) and *Flamingo* (1986).

The desire to escape from poverty, injustice and deprivation based on race is at the root of Caribbean migration and it is this desire which some plays from Africa and those from the Caribbean Diaspora have in common. Plays in this category include Rotimi's *Hopes of the Living Dead*, Sowande's *Farewell to Babylon*, Walcott's *O Babylon!*, White's *Redemption Song* and Osifisan's *The Chattering and the Song* and *Morountodun* (1982). Other plays that may be regarded as sharing the dream of utopia are Ama Ata Aidoo's *Anowa* (1987), and to some degree Soyinka's *Kongi's Harvest* (1967). However, the discussion will be restricted to only the first four but with occasional reference to others when necessary. In all these plays there is a central utopian dialectic of denouncing and announcing at work; there is an act of judgment which is followed by a journey of hope. Utopia often involves judging and denouncing a present reality and announcing and hoping for a future that would be the opposite and a better one than the present. In this respect, utopia is a form of social critique since it sets up a model by which one reality is compared to and judged by another.

Very often, utopias are not realisable in their entirety, but the hope for utopia is still positive in the sense that it helps propel human society and history forward to progressively better and better states. However, White in *Redemption Song,* and to some extent Walcott in *O Babylon!,* deliberately puncture a communal utopian dream of migration to Africa, Europe and North America held by underprivileged peoples of African descent in the Caribbean. Legion, the migrant in White's play, returns home disillusioned because of the terrible experience which he had had abroad. The land of hope and limitless opportunities had turned out to be a hell where, as he says, 'they put you in any darkness and then charge you for merely being alive' and 'where they lift you up by your class' or race (*Redemption Song,* p, 47). Legion ended up in prison instead of the high hopes and dream of making a successful life in England, and once out of prison he realised that home was where the soul must rest and that it was much better to suffer the hardship at home than face the insults, unfriendliness and humiliation of a foreign place. In doing this, the play takes a different approach to the theme of migration by concentrating on the life and death of a failed migrant who returns to his native Caribbean. Legion returns to Redemption City when his dream was smashed by the harsh realties in England, and in coming home he naively pinned his hopes on repossessing all that belonged to him before he went away. Having failed to find salvation in a foreign land, all he had left was what little his poor island could offer. The central conflict in the play, however, is that that little is not there waiting for him to repossess because Fowler had got on to it first, so Legion has to fight to get his inheritance back. Fowler, of course, is not prepared to give any of it up, and with tragic consequences for Legion. A key question which the play sets up through Legion's return and eventual death is whether in going away, he had given up his right to return, as well as his right to claim any inheritance. And his death suggests this to be the case; Caribbean migration of the period was a one way journey, and in returning Legion had broken a code and so had to die.

What emerges from White's new handling of the theme is that he exposes the often ignored fact that some people actually benefit greatly when poverty and a bleak future force the ambitious and the non-conformists to depart from the islands for greener pastures elsewhere. Fowler and people like him stay back and buy up the little land and property left by those who are leaving. They thus become richer on the misery of the poor wretches like Bramble who can not afford to go and who have resigned themselves to a miserable life at home. Bramble is not only poor he is also a no-hoper which makes him an easy prey for Fowler who forces him to sell his son's only inheritance. People like Bramble have no more hopes or dreams left to feed on or to spur them to redemptive action. Such people stay and merely go through the motions of life while they wait for death to release them from their misery. Unlike in most other Caribbean plays, the issue of social inequality in *Redemption Song* is not a matter of race since the have-nots (Bramble, Legion, Sores, Mad Anne and Miss B) and the haves (Fowler, Verity and Simon) are all of African-Caribbean descent. Thus, inequality in the play is a matter of economics, and so Verity, who previously belonged with Legion (as his girlfriend) to the class of have-nots, is now in the other camp after marrying the wealthy Fowler. And so while the characters share the same 'racialised' African-Caribbean identity, they have different class identities; in the same way that Kīgũũnda, Wangeci, Njooki and Gīcaamba share the same racialised identity as Kīoi, his wife, Jezebel, Ikuua wa Nditika, Samuel Ndugīre and Helen, his wife, while belonging to two opposing economic classes.

Both Fowler and Bramble did not expect Legion to return, and empty-handed at that! This is seen by everyone in Redemption City as an unusual thing to do; it is a silly thing to do and those close to Legion, such as Bramble and Verity, are shamed by it. It is even perceived by them as a defeat and failure worse than the inaction of those who never tried at all. There was no place for a failed migrant. It is therefore not surprising that as soon as Legion arrives back to Redemption City, Fowler begins to feel threatened because he knows the injustice he had done to him, and he is also aware that Legion is one of the restless ones who would not accept dispossession tamely without putting up a fight. To protect himself and his ill-gotten acquisitions, Fowler had taken the extra insurance of sewing up the police force in the person of his son, Simon. The latter's job is to protect his father's wealth by coercing people into a silent acceptance of the status quo. The play is a vivid dramatisation of the internal workings of a capitalist-exploitative set up in which the capitalist class would like to own everything with nothing left for the underclass. Charles had done something similar in *An Echo in the Bone*, by cornering the flow of water so as to force Crew off the land and in the process to force Rachel into his employ. Kīoi also succeeds in taking away Kīgũũnda's little piece of land to add to the immense holding which he already had, thereby forcing the latter into debt and ruin. And Legion is without land, no home and no love because one person has taken all and has the force and protection of the law to help him keep them. The play is about Legion's fight to get back what was his, what had been taken away from him by Fowler.

His fight, however, is doomed to failure because he does not have a programme of action to enable him achieve his aims. Legion's claim on his return from England of wanting to reclaim his inheritance sounds rather half-hearted and convinces nobody, least of all himself. Legion remains very much the dreamer and is almost afraid to open his eyes because he wants to hang on to the dream. Verity, ever the realist, tries desperately to rouse him, but he stubbornly clings on:

Legion: Me I need more. I want to come into a kingdom.
Verity: (*Laughing*) No kingdom coming again, man. Time for Kingdom done.
Legion: So you never dream?
Verity: Dream . . . no. Nothing come from dream. Don't worry tell me 'bout dream
(*Redemption Song*, p, 70-1)

Legion stubbornly refuses to see that he has to sit up if he is to seriously challenge Fowler's dominance. But one also recognises that he is powerless because he lacks any solid base from which to launch an attack, Fowler having literarily taken the ground from under his feet while he was away. The only thing he is able to regain from his foe is Verity, and this not because of what he does but rather because he had never lost her love for him. However, White's concern in the play is not with the seriousness or the success of Legion's bid to repossess his lost inheritance as much as it is with a desire to show that migration is beneficial to a particular group in Caribbean society, and that this group has the wealth and power with which to deal with anybody who dared to return to challenge their authority or threaten the 'smooth-flowing' order of things as Legion tried to do in Redemption City. Bramble presciently forewarns his son of the dangerous ground he was treading on by challenging Fowler. He refers to the tussle between the two as an ill-advised and ill-equipped attempt to steal a bull's genitals. Anyone who tries to do so without first killing the bull will only have living daylights kicked out of them by the enraged animal. This precisely is what happens to Legion because Fowler could not just stand by and watch the latter mess up or take away the things he had so painstakingly put together over the years.

So, at home or away, the poor, oppressed Caribbean person has all the odds stacked against her or him and on their own they can never achieve anything unless they are prepared to bend to the powerful prevailing winds of the ruling and moneyed class. Those who have a stubborn will and a rebellious spirit, such as Legion's mother, have no place or hope in the Caribbean. But conformists like Bramble and Verity stay and live compromised lives.

In the end, the play makes the point that those who have left should not bother to come back, unless, of course, they would be prepared to tow the line or be disposed of in the same way that Legion is. This view is hardly surprising coming from White who himself has lived outside his native Monsterrat for a very long time and who, perhaps, uses the play to come to terms with his own exile. It is significant that he dedicates the play to his country, a dedication which reinforces the impression that the play is a kind of atonement for the betrayal of a beloved homeland still remembered with nostalgia, but a land that was not likely to be a home to return to and live in. The play also warns that those who have wealth also have the power which they are prepared to use ruthlessly against those who challenge them. To fight such people as an individual is thus very dangerous and ultimately futile because the lone individual would simply be eliminated as the odds are usually highly stacked against them. Legion's only convert to his cause is Verity, but her not so much because of his power of persuasion as because of her love for him. His father and his aunt, Miss B, are not convinced about what he is doing. The struggle for social equality and redress has to be raised to the level of a class war because the issues at stake can only be resolved at the level of superstructures inherited from slavery and colonialism that have created relations of inequality between those mainly of European descent (descendants of former slave owners) and those predominantly of African descent (descendants of African slaves), and not at the individual level as Legion tried to do.

A key question about Caribbean society such as Redemption City raised in the play is this: what, for instance, are the structures that cause the extreme poverty which forces some to depart from home thereby leaving the way open for a few rich people to appropriate everything? Only at the level of superstructures can issues and questions arising from it be identified, tackled and resolved. But because he pursues a personal revenge, Legion becomes a mere ripple in the pond of Redemption City which returns to its indifferent calm once the ripples have passed and their cause is quickly forgotten. Crew in *An Echo in the Bone*, on the other hand, achieves more even though his own action is also an individual one, but the difference is that Scott manages to make both Crew and his victim, Charles, representative symbols of two contesting socio-economic and racial groups. Through this he is able to elevate Crew's act of killing into both a class and race confrontation which ultimately leads to the abolition of both forms of social division. There is a Lukacsian (1971) sense in which the proletariat in changing society abolishes itself by the same stroke. The victory of the oppressed class is designed to bring about the end of classes in society, not just the supplanting of one by another, in the same way that the issue of race disappears from the world of the play with the removal of both Crew and Charles. The act was also meant to signal the cancelling out of poverty or wealth, inequality or social injustice.

Scott's vision is definitely utopian, but, as Oscar Wilde writes:

A map of the world that does not include Utopia is not worth even glancing at, for it leaves out one country at which Humanity is always landing. And when Humanity lands there, it looks out, and seeing a better country, sets sail. Progress is the realisation of Utopias (Wilde, 1966: 1081).

Utopia is a positive notion which helps to keep human society in motion as individuals and groups in their quest for it grope towards the ideal state. Aesthetically, the vision which *An Echo in the Bone* holds out is a satisfactory resolution to an action that had built up to a high point where something had to give, and in doing so leads to a neutralisation of the contending social forces: the elimination of the two representative symbols of the master-slave or white-black relationship which characterises Caribbean society. But *Redemption Song*, on the other hand, leaves the reader rather frustrated because Legion's death suggests a waste of a life full of potential and in his words Redemption City succeeds in eating another of its young while the old conservatives are left in complete control. Thus, while *An Echo in the Bone* ends on an optimistic note, *Redemption Song* offers only pessimism and stasis.

Rejection and marginalisation bring in their wake a desire to escape, preferably to an utopian alternative where the rejects can hopefully be accepted as is the case with the Rastafarians in *O Babylon!*, or where they can at least have the opportunity to direct their lives like the farmers in Sowande's *Farewell to Babylon* or the lepers in *Hopes of the Living Dead*.

Walcott and Sowande employ the Rastafarian opposition between Babylon and Zion as the powerful metaphor with which to explore the quest for an alternative society where a greater number of people would find happiness and fulfilment. The concept of Babylon and its relationship to Zion in Rastafarian philosophy needs further clarification here since it has a significant bearing on the understanding of the two plays, especially Walcott's.

Underpinning the philosophy of Rastafarianism is a Manichean principle of the cosmos in which for every good there is a corresponding evil and the two opposing forces are eternally locked in battle. Based on this, Babylon is evil and opposed to it is Zion (personal interviews in Leeds and Sheffield 1988). Any society or social order that is a source of human misery, poverty, oppression, repression, moral decadence, or any form of social injustice, is considered to be Babylon. And conversely, therefore, wherever a Rastafarian community is set up, there is 'holy ground', a Zion where all can cast away their sorrow, and where all can find acceptance, peace and freedom. Guided by this Manichean dualism, the Rastafarians are always to be found moving away or seeking to move away from or out of Babylon toward Zion; this is what the characters in the two plays, *O Babylon!* and *Farewell to Babylon* are doing, looking for alternatives to societies which they have judged and rejected. It is also in the light of this notion and quest for an alternative society that the study will look at Rotimi's *Hopes of the Living Dead* because it also is about the quest for Utopia, even if it does not do so using the same Babylonian metaphor.

The titles of the three plays are in fact very suggestive of the spirit which underpins their respective dramatic actions. The titles also capture the attitudinal dispositions and behaviours of the characters. Sowande's is entitled *Farewell to Babylon* and thematically it is 'a farewell' to Babylon as the major characters are, in various ways, involved in the search for a means to put an end to the unjust society that Babylon is. The central character, Moniran, in his own words, is in the mouth of hell, 'but ... only to fetch fire' with which to burn Babylon (*Farewell to Babylon*, p, 65). These characters all reject Babylon and therefore are working to eliminate what they perceive to be the source of poverty and misery. Their wish is more realistic than that of the Rastafarians because they seek utopia within a familiar terrain - that is to say, they seek to change an existing social order in which they too live. Theirs is not a wide off the mark wish to run away from their lived reality to a completely new place like the Rastafarians in *O Babylon!*, with their dreamy fixation for an idealised

135

African homeland. Walcott's title, on the other hand, is almost a cry of despair: 'O Babylon!'. One gets the impression from this cry that Babylon is so strong and unassailable. Appropriately, the characters, instead of looking for ways to bring the walls of Babylon down, the city of their rejection and oppression, turn their backs on it and begin to feed themselves on dreams of escape to an idyllic Africa, whose outlines have since become dim and blurred in their collective racial memory. As a psychic journey into the centre of being, such as the one undertaken by Makak and his companions in *Dream on Monkey Mountain*, the longing for Africa is fine, in fact, necessary, but a physical return which the Rastafarians hope for is not possible. This they fail to realise or accept.

Walcott does not hide his anger at the escapist inertia of Sufferer and his doctrine of 'peace and love' while what is needed is for them to work to help pull Babylon down. Walcott uses Mrs Power to very strongly criticise the community's drugged dream of Zion which provides a protective cloak that the Rastafarians wrap round themselves to help them hide from contributing towards transforming Babylon into a New Jerusalem. The brief scene below illustrates an instance of such an attack on the indulgent dream of Zion:

> Mrs Power: It's time to cut the umbilical cord that joins them to Zion .
> . . . If they want to build Jerusalem, let them get off their
> arses and lift a bloody shovel.
> Deacon Doxy: (*Sings*) Don't tell me about Zion,
> I've got work to do . . . . The Zion I'm building
> is schools for their children . . . a place in this world.
> Dewes: In the ideal republic there's no need for visions and what
> are their visions?
> A junkie's dream!
> Mrs Power: Surrealist nightmares with no place for decisions. In a
> country that's all prophets, look, someone must quit
> prophesying and just for once
> mix Jerusalem's mortar and build the roof beam
> (*O Babylon!*, p, 262-3).

Walcott here attacks the escapist attitude of the Rastafarians, even though he also does not agree with the Machiavellianism of those who criticise them. Granted, it is the dream and the doctrine which make the Rastafarians wallow in squalid poverty while doing absolutely nothing to help themselves. The play therefore is an effective dramatisation of what Walcott argues passionately in his evocative essay, 'What the Twilight Says', in which he writes that sometimes it is necessary to stir the poor into bitterness and rage and then, perhaps, into action for the last thing the poor need is:

> idealisation of their poverty. No play could be paced to the repetitive and untheatrical patience of hunger and unemployment. Hunger produces enervation of the will and knows one necessity. . . . Hunger induces its delirium, and it is this fever for heroic examples that can produce the glorification of revenge (*Dream on Monkey Mountain*, p, 19).

Thus, what the poor need is a presentation of poverty in its most sordid, most revolting and humiliating aspects and hopefully, the revulsion arising from it would spur them into rethinking their situation and seeking ways to change it. And, by the end of the play awareness dawns on Aaron as he realises that not all of them were going to be chosen to return to Africa with the Emperor Haile Selassie. Home, he realises painfully, is Jamaica and that it was for them to convert it into a place decent and viable to live in. In this play, therefore, Walcott gives a severe tongue-lashing to the two sides of the Babylon scenario; the Rastafarians for their escapism and indolence, and the agents of Babylon for their insensitive Machiavellian materialism.

The last play to be discussed in this chapter is Rotimi's *Hopes of the Living Dead*, which also deals with a collective dream and the struggle by a group of leper patients in a general hospital ward to escape from an insensitive society that does not want them. Unlike the Rastafarians in *O Babylon!*, Harcourt Whyte and his fellow inmates know what they want and where they want to relocate to. They are also sure in their minds about what they were going to do with themselves once they got to the place of their dreams. They are not dreaming of a land flowing with milk and honey in the biblical sense of Canaan, and neither do they expect any manna to drop from heaven while their arms are folded. They recognise that they are poor, yet they neither give in to despair nor do they want to surrender their dignity by submitting themselves to charity. All they want is the chance to experiment with and realise their own ideas within a social framework of their own creation. And for this dream, they fight the government and hospital authorities all the way, like the farmers in Sowande's play, totally rejecting the demeaning charity which the government and other agencies had lined up for them. They are quite right because charity degrades and demoralises, and as Wilde again points out:

> We are often told that the poor are grateful for charity. Some of them are, but the best among the poor are never grateful. They are ungrateful,

discontented, disobedient, and rebellious. They are quite right to be. Charity they feel to be a ridiculous, inadequate mode of partial restitution or sentimental dole, usually accompanied by some impertinent attempt on the part of the sentimentalist to tyrannise over their private lives (1966:1081).

Thus, Harcourt and his comrades refuse to have anything to do with charity because they know that it has in-built traps and besides, it can never go on forever. Besides, charity never alleviates poverty or destitution so those who want to transcend poverty reject charity. The inmates are therefore prepared in spite of their physical handicaps to struggle together for themselves for only then can they begin to think of themselves as truly independent human beings worthy of respect. Significantly, the only help the lepers would accept is a gift of hoes, cutlasses and other farm implements with which they hope to achieve self-sufficiency in their food needs. Rotimi also uses this play as a critical parable for independent Nigeria, and maybe other decolonised countries and peoples who refuse to break with the umbilical cord that ties them to the goodwill and charity of their former colonial 'mothers'. He takes a swipe at a neo-colonial situation which encourages a relationship of dependence between the developed and the not-so developed nations. The inmates of the leper wards forbid any form of begging from among their ranks and they are determined to grow whatever food they require. To his colleagues, Harcourt decrees thus:

> Henceforth, nobody, and that means nobody. No one leaves here without permission, and no one goes out to beg. From today, we grow our own food (*Hopes of the Living Dead*, p, 106).

It is through this strong collective determination to be their own masters and servants that their self-respect and humanity are best expressed and validated. This is a challenge to, but also an accusation thrown at African leaders who feel no shame in scouring the capitals of Western Europe, North America and Japan begging for aid instead of finding ways of eliminating poverty and underdevelopment in their countries. *Hopes of the Living Dead* is a play of struggle and it holds out hope for those, as Harcourt says, 'who are dead' but who struggle to live. It is a powerful play whose emotional impact on audiences, especially in performance, is enormous given the enthusiastic response the play enjoyed during its premiere run in Nigeria.

The action in the play centres on the conflict between the patients and the government; between the formers' determined struggle to be allowed to move to Uzuakoli, the place of their dreams, and the government's intransigence in wanting to disperse them to their respective former homes. The play suggests that once a people are united, tenacious, and with good and honest leadership, they can be guaranteed success in their struggle for a better future. The success of the lepers contrasts sharply with the failure of the Rastafarians who did not work to realise their dream and who chose to run away from their reality instead of confronting it as the lepers do theirs. Even the partial success of the farmers in Sowande's *Farewell to Babylon* is an eloquent testament to the fact that without effort there can be no success. But the three plays collectively argue that Utopia is not a bad thing because it provides the imagination with a desirable possibility to aim for, and in striving for the ideal state human society and history are propelled to better and better conditions. In this respect therefore, the notion of Utopia and progress gives history and society a dialectical dimension because Utopia will remain a challenge for humanity and the quest for it an unending process.

All the evidence in this chapter suggests that patterns and determinants of social inequality in Africa and the Caribbean differ. It also became obvious that the way social inequality is perceived, both by the playwrights and by the characters, differs as a consequence of the first. The plays are therefore good reflections of the social realities which the patterns engender, and at the same time they are comments on the patterns as well as on the characters who act in response to them. African and Caribbean societies are similar in many respects, yet they are quite unlike each other in many other respects. And the most significant area of difference seems to be in the criteria for individual placement on the social ladder and the consequences of occupying such positions, especially in the construction and performance of their corresponding identities.

The question of race and its impact on individual position in the social hierarchy seems to be a distinct area of difference between African and Caribbean societies. Whereas the issue of race no longer plays a significant part in determining social relationships and positions in Africa (except to some extent in former apartheid South Africa as in plays such as *Sizwe Bansi is Dead*, *Woza Albert!* and other township/workshop plays), race still plays a major role in a person's position in the Caribbean. As a result of this however, one finds in Caribbean plays black characters who are mainly concerned with finding ways of escaping from the limiting conditions imposed on them by the colour of their skin. They hardly ever question or attempt to attack the social structure responsible for keeping one race down while another enjoys unlimited freedom and luxury. The African plays, on the other hand, are peopled with characters whose view of the world is not clouded by racial considerations. They tend to see being poor, not as resulting from their being black or whatever colour, but as a situation in which the deprivation and misery of one group ensures abundance and happiness for another. The African characters are therefore angrier than their Caribbean counterparts because they feel that they too have as much right as their wealthy neighbours to a decent life. They also characteristically avoid playing the victim which a majority of their Caribbean counterparts understandably fall into. Appropriately, a significant number of African characters are either rebelling, fighting the government or their oppressors, railing at authority or society, even the physically handicapped lepers in *Hopes of the Living Dead* are dogged fighters until they prevail in the end. The Caribbean characters start from a position of inferiority and thus they are more on the defensive and sometimes diffident towards authority and those in privileged positions in relation to themselves - there are exceptions such as a fiery spirit like Crew who is unusual, but even then he seems to implicitly accept Charles' superiority and right to so much while he and other blacks have little or nothing. Superiority or inferiority does not feature in the consciousness of the African characters. *Redemption Song* and *Man Better Man* are different in this regard as in the two race is not an issue at all in social relations; most of the characters are of African-Caribbean descent - in fact, only Joe Portager in Hill's play is of European stock, but this fact is only mentioned but is of no consequence in the dramatic action. However, there is also no attempt to explore the economic nature or basis of the relationships in the two plays as one finds, for instance, in *I'll Marry When I Want* or *Kongi's Harvest*.

Modes of perception affect modes of reflection and this holds true for African and African-Caribbean plays, in which it seems that although they are all concerned with showing patterns of social inequality, the images are varying reflections of the same phenomenon. It appears, for instance, that those who perceive inequality as a factor of race show it through compelling images of black poverty, oppression and exploitation as in *An Echo in the Bone* and *Ti-Jean and His Brothers* (other plays that do the same are Rhone's *Old Story Time* and *Two Can Play, Man Better Man* etc), and in doing so, perhaps they hope to confront the human conscience with the immorality of the unjust social structures which are responsible for the existence of such human misery. Others like Walcott in *O Babylon!*, Ngũgĩ wa Thiong'o and Ngũgĩ wa Mĩriĩ in *I'll Marry When I Want*, Soyinka in *The Road*, Rotimi in *Hopes of the Living Dead*, as well as Scott, feel that relations of social inequality are best captured by the image of a group of members of the society who have become marginalised through deprivation and extreme poverty. Such characters are consigned to the periphery of mainstream society, and are a unifying and unflattering feature of most urban centres of developing nations in Africa and the Caribbean. They are eloquent testimonies to the existence of poverty and the injustice of the unequal distribution of life opportunities. And yet, there is a third group of dramatists who express their perceptions in the very powerful image of predators and their unsuspecting victims. This third image aptly captures the underlying nature of the relationship between the poor and the rich, and between the oppressed and the oppressor. This image of an often defenceless prey facing relentless assault from an uncompromising predator testifies to the inequities in social relations in society, and the plays in drawing these images are questioning and bearing witness to such unequal relations. And finally, a last group of playwrights are more concerned with exploring situations where, because of the extreme hardship and poverty of the present, the poor and racially oppressed and marginalised begin to build dreams of Utopia, a place where they can escape to and where they can hopefully find happiness and fulfilment. The desire for Utopia, the chapter has revealed, takes different forms. For some, it is a dream which can be actualised through hard work, either by changing the existing society or by founding another one. For others, it is a mental escape from confronting a present that is harsh and daunting. But, in both instances, the existence of desire is proof of the existence of a system which can drive a section of its population to long for an alternative, in whatever form or place. The existence of such unkind social systems is the central focus of the African and Caribbean plays mentioned above.

In all, the plays are accurate reflections of the societies from which they sprung and in their various ways, they reveal to the reader or audience the internal workings of similar and yet differing social systems and what each does to its people. Sometimes, as some of the plays do, the dramatists analyse and make suggestions for alternatives, and at other times, they merely reflect the society as they see it and leave judgment to the reader or audience and to history.

Chapter 6

FORM AND CONTENT IN AFRICAN AND AFRICAN-CARIBBEAN THEATRE

A Shared Cosmology

Colonialism's first form of attack often is to berate and denigrate the native/colonised culture, and postcolonial playwrights by seeking to recuperate their cultures and histories through destabilising and assimilating into their own cultural forms, the dramatic models of the coloniser effectively carry out decolonisation and re-colonisation. This study, however, argues that beyond their acts of recuperation, postcolonial playwrights, through domestication and hybridisation, create what Homi Bhabha (1994, 1997) refers to as a 'third space' (location) from where they enunciate their respective national and shared postcolonial identities.

Africa is the original home of most black peoples in the world and based on that, it is true to say that a shared cosmology unites all black people in Africa and in the African diasporas. But having said that, one needs also to acknowledge that the cultural traits which make up this system have in some instances in the diasporas become attenuated by historical and geographical interventions. Yet, overall, these traits have remained and are referred to as 'African survivals' in the Caribbean or 'Africanisms' and 'neo-Africanisms' in the United States of America. Walcott (1989) acknowledges the ancestral connection between Africa and the Caribbean when he says that 'life in the archipelago is a mirror of the one on the other side'. The source of these enduring traits can be traced back to trans-Atlantic slavery and to the original African homeland of the slaves.

The slaves may have crossed the Atlantic empty-handed, but definitely not empty-minded. Each carried within them their own portion of Africa and as much as possible, in spite of the sustained cultural emasculation by the slave owners, these bits of Africa survived in the slaves: in the songs, dances, story-telling and those surreptitious acts of worship which helped them to retain their humanity in the face of the harsh conditions of New World slavery. William DuBois (1965) traces the origins of African-American folk culture to the slave ancestors who transmitted what they could of Africa through songs and tales. Of the music, he writes:

> They are the music of an unhappy people, of the children of disappointment . . . The songs are indeed the siftings of centuries; the music is far more ancient than the words, and in it we can trace here and there signs of development. My grandfather's grandmother was seized by an evil Dutch trader two centuries ago; and coming to the valleys of the Hudson and Husatonic, black, little and lithe, she shivered and shrank in the harsh north winds, looking longingly at the hills, and often crooned a heathen melody to the child between her knees. . . . The child sang it to his children and they to their children's children, and so two hundred years it has travelled down to us and we sing it to our children, knowing as little as our fathers what its words mean but knowing well the meaning of its music. This was primitive African music . . . the voice of exile (162-3).

And recently, Emmanuel Obiechina (1986) repeats this sentiment about Africa and her children in the diasporas when he says that Africa somehow managed to survive and in fact still survives in the souls of her dispersed children. This may well explain the persistent soul journeys which characterise the drama and literature of the Caribbean African diaspora. These works suggest that deep in the souls of peoples of African descent in the Caribbean is an Africa that has not died, an Africa within that they must acknowledge for a fuller understanding of themselves. The psychic journeys are never easy and to represent them in literature or theatre demands new techniques and new forms.

Because of the survival of Africa in her children in the diaspora, there is a remarkable similarity in how reality is perceived by Africans and peoples of African descent in the Caribbean. The study believes that this similarity exists because the same cosmology, in what ever form of purity or attenuation it is found in the Caribbean, generates and sustains modes of perception of the universe on both sides of the Atlantic. It is this shared way of seeing the world which distinguishes black African peoples from other peoples of the world. This African worldview has created its own peculiar mode of perception, cultural practices and forms of expression and little wonder there are striking similarities between the dances, songs, folktales and theatre of black peoples around the world. Even within specific genres of cultural expression, the black African worldview also engenders its own types and genres, like tragedy, comedy, musical and dance forms which are unique and different from the tragedies, comedies, musics and dances from other cultures. Specifically, the influence of the black African cosmology on the forms and modes of cultural expression and how this relates to issues of identity politics on both sides of the Atlantic will be the focus of the chapter.

Africa is made up of different peoples and each group has its own way of perceiving and dealing with the world, as well as its own modes of cultural expression. But diverse as these cultures and modes of perception are, there are common characteristics and it is to these cultural and perceptual constants that we owe what today can be loosely referred to as the African world and cosmological system. The African cosmology is predicated upon the notion of life as an experience of totality. This means that the African, no matter which part of the African continent he or she comes from, tends to perceive the universe as a total structure made up of a complex system of interlocking relationships and mutual affectivity. That is to say, that all phenomena or experience are seen as constituting a system and that no part of this interlocking cosmic structure can be fully comprehended without recourse to the other parts. Perhaps, the best description of the African cosmology is by Soyinka:

> I would like to speak of the African world view in terms of three orbs floating within infinite space; the world of the living, the world of the unborn, and the world of the ancestor . . . a cyclic world view . . . . The continuity between the worlds of the ancestor, the living and the unborn is not really unique to the African except in one respect and that is the way it is permanently affective in the consciousness and activity of the living . . . . What is it that dominates man's ideas . . . . It is the constant relating habit of the world of the dead, the world of the deities, the world of the living and the world of the future . . . . What constitutes also his sense of strife, of conflict and resolution, what constitutes the source of his energies, of coping even with the contemporary world . . . is always related to his experience of passing from one world to another . . . he represents it by the area of transition, between one area of existence and another . . . (in Ketu Katrak, 1986: 43).

Soyinka here uses the Yoruba universe as a paradigm and with just slight modifications, this model can be applied to understanding other African cultures. Here is a cosmology that assumes a mutual dependency and affectivity between the three realms of existence and between the three time schemes of past, present and future. The three realms and schemes co-exist, and 'life, present life contains within it manifestations of ancestor, the living and the unborn' (Soyinka, 1976: 144).

Thus within the African universe is a unique ontology upon which the cosmological system hangs enabling Africans to explain their special relationship with their ancestors, their gods and all other supra-human forces they deal with in their confrontations with an immense and often chaotic universe. The ontology also enables them to establish their position and significance within the universal chain. Basically, Africans see life as a continuous movement from one state of being to another along a chain of existence. The movement represents a progression from the state of being unborn, through being born, and into becoming an ancestor. Movement from one state to another often demands a rite of passage and the pacification or taming of the gulf of transition. This process incidentally forms the central drama in plays such as *A Dance of the Forests, The Road, An Echo in the Bone, Singuè Mura* and *La Puissance de Um (The Power of Um)*.

At the apex of being are the gods; they are followed by the spirits and other nature forces. After these come the ancestors whose closeness to the gods and spirits explains their pride of place in the African world - their high position and nearness to the gods makes it easier for them to communicate with the latter on behalf of the living. Next to the ancestors are the living who are then followed by the unborn. The living are central to and in the chain because it is the one group in touch with all the other groups. It is for and because of them that the other groups exist. The ancestors, despite being near to the gods, are not very far away from the living and that is why it is ever so easy to summon them as masquerades at festivals and other special occasions when the human world has need for their help. This is an idea explored in *A Dance of the Forests* and *An Echo in the Bone*. The ancestors are also important in the African universe because they constitute the basis of moral and legal thought, a function which,

> raises them above the transitory human level and invests them with sacred significance. Superior and powerful, beyond all human challenge, the rights and duties sanctioned by the ancestors both define and regulate basic social and political relations (Ray, 1976: 147).

This clearly indicates the importance of the ancestors in African life and thought. But their power, it should be added, is limited in its application because, although the ancestors can govern rules relating to politics and social morality, they can not influence how individuals conduct their lives. Even the gods themselves in African thinking do not completely control human behaviour; humans are seen as free agents and not the toys or tools of the gods of Greek and Christian thought. This is responsible for the difference between the African concept of tragedy and the Greek and Western European one. Human tragedy for Africans is human-made, and so even when the gods will it, humans can refuse to comply. The principle of culpable inevitability which impels Oedipus in Sophocles's *Oedipus Rex* to fulfil the unfair ordinance of Apollo does not apply to either Elesin Oba in *Death and the King's Horseman* or Professor in *The Road*. This may perhaps explain why African tragic characters such as Zifa and Tonye in John Pepper Clark's *Song of a Goat* and Shanka in Tsegaye Gabre-Medhin's *Oda-Oak Oracle* who are cast in this mould of tragic inevitability come out rather weak as they refuse to challenge or act to change the will of the gods. African tragedy is rather the tragedy of acting men and women who have to pay for their transgressions of moral codes either by their pride or their excesses in the exercise of their free wills. The gods and ancestors therefore exist and function to help humans realise their potentials, but the ultimate choice to act or not to act belongs to humans, and they can work each to alter their destiny; but they also each must accept full responsibility for their actions.

A Dance of the Forests, more than any other play studied here, illustrates this proximity between the worlds of the gods, the spirits and ancestors to the world of the living, as well as the possibility of movement between them. *An Echo in the Bone, The Road, Old Story Time, Death and the King's Horseman, Ti-Jean and His Brothers, La Puissance de Um* and *Singuè Mura* also explore this special relationship between humans and their dead, and also between them and the other forces of their universe. *A Dance of the Forests, An Echo in the Bone* and *Singuè Mura*, for instance, involve a summoning of the dead and spirits, a key aspect of indigenous African life and theatre. The masked figures which feature in the masquerade theatre are believed to constitute a community of the dead who can be summoned for communion with the living at required periods. This, of course, explains the religious underpinning of the indigenous theatres and performances of Africa, a religiosity which has not disappeared altogether from the contemporary conceptions of theatre in Africa. The same religious conception underpins much African-Caribbean theatre, especially in function and relevance. Theatre in both contexts is not just entertainment; rather, it is a communal act, a kind of ritual which enables the human community to explore and come to terms with itself, helps humans to explore and navigate those regions of their universe which lie hidden or beyond the everyday experience. It is thus not surprising that action in most of the plays is situated within zones of transition - almost all of Soyinka's plays are concerned with exploring the gulf and process of transition; so also are Scott's *An Echo in the Bone* and

Walcott's *Dream on Monkey Mountain*, both centred within the gulf and their characters are essentially processual beings caught at various stages of rites of passage. The same can be said of Liking's *Singuè Mura* which explores death and return to life of the central character - the process and period between dying and moving on into the ancestral world. Liking's other play, *La Puissance de Um*, also uses the transitional period between the death of Ntep Iliga and his burial and the rites in-between as a space and time to explore communal and individual histories, tensions and wrongs which need to be understood and redressed for healing to occur for all those involved.

For African peoples, no point of existence is terminal, finished or permanent. The living die and become ancestors; the unborn are born to become the living; while the ancestors can revert to being the unborn. This is a universe in perpetual flux, and the idea of onto-mobility between the realms is fully explored in many of the African plays. *The Road*, for example, handles the theme of death and the process of transition from life to death, and from death to the dissolution of flesh. The Yoruba refer to this period as *agemo,* a stage frozen by Professor in his irreverent imprisonment of Murano. Both *Singuè Mura* and *La Puissance de Um* freeze the period but not in the selfish manner that Professor does but as a chance to remedy past wrongs by the mother-in-law and the entire community who had treated Singuè Mura badly, or for the wife to absolve herself of any guilt in her husband's death. In the three plays, death is not perceived as terminal or the end of life; rather, it is a rite of passage, a process and journey into knowledge of life. For Professor, knowledge of life comes only through knowledge of death; as he tells his 'disciples': 'the word may be found companion not to life, but Death' (Soyinka, 1965: 11). And for Singué Mura and the Mother-in-law, death can be negotiated with and life is not over until all sides agree it is; for the community in *La Puissance de Um*, death is a path to knowledge and a moment for communal soul-searching.

An Echo in the Bone also sees and treats death as an elevating phase in the over-all chain of being - the newly dead Crew is remembered and he returns to help his family understand the reason behind his killing of Master Charles and his own subsequent suicide. *A Dance of the Forests*, on the other hand, handles a complex of ideas: the unborn becoming born, the dead coming back, and the general movement between the realms of existence in the African world. Obaneji, a god, disguises himself in order to lead the three unsuspecting human protagonists to the 'dance of welcome for the dead'; at this 'dance', gods, spirits, ancestors, the living and the unborn meet and coexist in the same ritualised time and space. The dance has been laid on by the gods to quieten the ghosts of the restless and wandering dead so they can finally be accepted as ancestors. It is customary for the living to consecrate the dead so that their wandering souls may find peace in the ancestral world. This is a central tenet underpinning and realised through the elaborate funerary rites which are so much part of African life - this rite is the context in *An Echo in the Bone*. However, the living in *A Dance of the Forests* refuse to perform the rites for the dead whom they had helped to kill; the latter, of course, have been sent back by the gods to be accusers at the 'Feast of the Gathering of the Tribes'. Walcott's *Ti-Jean and His Brothers* explores the idea of the unborn and the interdependent relationship between them and the living. The play also acknowledges a unity of being, association and mutual dependence between all forms of life in the universe - between humans, spirits, animals, insects and the elements.

Because of its continuous state of flux, its persistent striving for totality and unity of being and experience, the African world often appears immense. Its seeming immensity arises from the fact that it contains a whole universe of contraries and harmonies, a universe of multiple existences. This world functions on the principle of inclusion and mediation. Its expansiveness thus demands an equally expansive mode of representation. The oral traditions of Africa provide the best forms for representing the African world in all its numinous complexity. The two forms most suited for the task are the folk tale and the folk theatre. The structures and internal dynamics of these two genres are elastic enough to cope with an expansive world which traditional African arts and literature seek to express. The folk theatre, because of its rootedness in religion, proves to be the best form for exploring the inter-relationship between the various realms of existence, and it is able to do so because within its often symbolic matrix the realms can be brought together to coexist, both ideationally and physically.

The contemporary theatre in Africa has not completely lost its sense of religion. And the same applies to the theatre of Caribbean peoples of African descent. Even though the links to and inspiration from religion have become attenuated, and this is despite contact with foreign cultures and theatre forms, African peoples continue to perceive the universe in much the same way as their ancestors did. And the greatest challenge for the creative minds on the continent has been to express an African world and experience, from an African perspective, and in forms that are African. Some artists succeed in borrowing from existing indigenous forms, adapting these forms to suit changed materials and circumstances. Even those attempts to express Africa through African eyes but using non-African forms only succeed in creating artistic hybrids or forms of transition. What unites all these efforts is their deliberateness - the dramatists seek to create theatre that is quintessentially African or African-Caribbean in the way it appropriates and domesticates foreign elements, and in the way it updates indigenous forms.

The persistent search for appropriate theatrical forms to best express the African experience has led inevitably to a healthy explosion of experiments with dramatic structures and modes. Of significance is the fact that the experiments have been tending more and more toward borrowing and reshaping the indigenous forms. A good example will suffice to illustrate this tendency. Storytelling, a very flexible form, is employed by a good number of African and Caribbean dramatists as they seek to represent African and African-Caribbean realities. Soyinka modifies it in *A Dance of the Forests*. Efua Sutherland bases her popular play, *The Marriage of Anansewa,* on the *anansegoro* tradition of the Akan of Ghana. Ngũgĩ wa Thiong'o and Mĩcere Mugo adapt some elements of storytelling in *The Trial of Dedan Kimathi,* especially when they resurrect the past as a background and commentary on the present. Liking also deploys elements of narrative and ritual in *Singuè Mura* with commentaries running alongside the action. Storytelling is also adopted effectively by Walcott in *Ti-Jean and His Brothers,* and by Trevor Rhone in *Old Story Time* - the second play being faithful to the storytelling genre to the point of creating within the theatre a real storytelling session. Both Walcott and Rhone observe the key conventions of the tradition as still found in villages all over Africa. Rhone's play is the perfect example and Pa Ben is the typical storyteller become actor, director and stage manager of storytelling theatre in Africa.

Others in attempting to appropriate the folk theatre form experiment with a ritual-dream structure. Indigenous African theatre most often is episodic and works more by a process of cumulative association rather than a linear continuum of events. The episodic mode is best achieved by plays which use the dream technique or operate within a ritual framework. Some of the plays combine both structures since rituals have a liminal phase similar to a dream. Examples of plays which have the ritual-dream structure are *Dream on Monkey Mountain, An Echo in the Bone, Singuè Mura* and *La Puissance de Um*. Even a play like *The Road* has the qualities of a dream, especially the somnambulant demeanour of many of the characters is rather reflective of the dream state. The dream form in particular is flexible and can be easily manipulated by a dramatist wishing to throw in many ideas and characters in their play, no matter how contradictory or widely divergent these ideas and characters are to one another. Walcott does this effectively in *Dream on Monkey Mountain*, as do Soyinka in *A Dance of the Forests* and Liking in *La Puissance de Um* and *Singuè Mura* respectively. The dramatic situations in *An Echo in the Bone* and the languid existence and disparate actions of the characters in *The Road* are as illogical as only those in dreams can be.

The dream allows the dreamer to witness or partake of events, sequentially or disjointedly, and on waking these events can be remembered and reordered so that the apparent chaos of the dream is restructured into a coherent and meaningful experience or message. This takes one back to the principle of totality central to the African cosmological system in which action and events acquire meaning only in relation to other actions and events, and only when everything has been seen or experienced. This is also how indigenous African theatre and performances work (see Gotrick, 1982; Okagbue, 1987; and Ottenberg 1975); a good number of contemporary African plays are best approached this way. This manner of or approach to perceiving and representing the world accounts for the seeming absence of linear plots in most African and African-Caribbean plays. The same is also true of African-American plays which have been described as typically "anti well-made" with plots [that] "meander in circuitous association, returning at key moments to the centre . . . of the action"(Hatch, 1980: 27). Hatch may well be describing African and African-Caribbean plays as all of them share an African continuum of sensibilities which manifests itself not only in content, but also in form and style.

Both the storytelling and the ritual-dream forms impose a cyclic structure on reality which reflects the African mode of perception. From an African perspective, life follows a circular pattern - that is to say that all life returns to an original source; put another way, what is, has been and will be again. The implication of this for theatre influenced by this mode of seeing the world is that its action can start from one point, cover a lot of ground, but usually returns to its starting point. This kind of dramatic structure is again described by Hatch as resembling the courtship dance of a male pigeon which:

> circles the female, doubles back, walks away, plumes himself, pecks at the earth, struts back, circles her again, all the while burbling, cooing, clucking various songs in a slowly developed dance, which for all its apparent diversions still has but one purpose to be fulfilled when the

female is ready . . . . This style of writing is quite different from the straight line, built-to-a-crisis at the end of scene, Western formula (1980: 27).

This analogy captures the main structural features of African and African-Caribbean plays which exhibit a tendency to begin in the present, wander off into the past, stray occasionally into the future, but always doubling back to the present at critical moments and then taking off once more. Only when the drama makes the final return to the present does the audience take stock of their experience and draw meaning out of the disparate events. Meaning from a typical African or African-Caribbean play therefore is the product of a process of cumulative experiencing. This is the structure of Walcott's *Dream on Monkey Mountain*, as well as Soyinka's *A Dance of the Forests*, Scott's *An Echo in the Bone*, *The Trial of Dedan Kimathi* by Ngũgĩ and Mugo, Rhone's *Old Story Time* and Liking's *Singuè Mura* and *La Puissance de Um*. This structure enables the playwrights to effectively show the contiguity of the different time schemes and realms of existence which underpins the African cosmological system.

The dream technique operates best within a ritual framework and this is because of the liminal phase in the ritual process. This phase is truly like a dream in which normal time is suspended temporarily and the mind is free to go beyond time and space to experience other realms of existence. But once out of it, the participant or dreamer can sit back and restructure what initially must have been a chaotic experience.

Understanding the two forms enables a deeper engagement with the plays being studied. Principally, the study will be unpicking the architecture of each play to see how the structural pattern serves as an index to meaning. This is more so because, as the preceding pages suggest, African and African-Caribbean plays, despite having stories to tell, elect not to tell them linearly or on the principle of causality. Because of the non-linear plots, the dramatic actions are not arranged consequentially. Rather, the stories unfold in bits that are contiguous, but which at the same time have hidden structural patterns. The rest of this chapter will look at the hidden patterns in the plays and how each structure helps in the understanding of the play. The chapter also argues that the choice of structure each dramatist has made is very much influenced by the cultural codes and modes of artistic expression of the place of origin of the play - that is that form and content are symbiotically meshed together. The structural models already identified combine in many ways in some of the plays, with the result that a storyteller can sometimes be telling their dream, while the dreamer sometimes is actually caught up in a ritual process. For one thing, this ability to marry the different patterns is a testimony to the versatility of the playwrights, as well as the flexibility of the African and African-Caribbean theatre sensibilities.

Structure and Meaning.

Structurally, two features can be identified as being common to all the plays. The first is that in all of them the drama follows a cyclic pattern. The second is that within the cyclic structure created by this, situations do not unfold in any discernible linearity, rather they are random camera shots with certain key shots or images repeated and always kept in focus; meaning thus comes through a process of cumulative association, that is to say, meaning emerges from total and final experience.

These plays are structured as rituals, and to understand them one has to understand the nature and structure of rituals; in particular one has to understand ritual's complex and symbolic mode of signification. Arnold van Gennep and Victor Turner's analyses of ritual and the complex symbolic idiom which a ritual employs help in the appreciation of the structure-meaning relationship of the plays, especially *The Road* and *Dream on Monkey Mountain*. Of particular relevance is Turner's concept of liminality which applies in great measure to the plays being studied because in them all significant dramatic actions take place within the liminal phase. In rituals, and this includes all rites of passage and pilgrimages, the liminal phase is the stage of the symbolic death and rebirth of the protagonist leading to new knowledge and heightened awareness.

In *Dream on Monkey Mountain*, Makak begins his journey from his cell and into the heart of the forest which is the liminal zone in this pilgrimage. In the forest he encounters and grapples with human and non-human forces. Finally, he emerges from his 'journey to Africa', reborn to himself and to his community. Action in *The Road* takes place within the liminal zone - the setting is a shack along a road to and from nowhere. There is an overwhelming feeling of indeterminacy and in-betweenness surrounding character, setting and action in the play which is a quality of liminality. Professor is unwilling to step fully into the abyss of transition and yet he hopes to pluck from it the jealously guarded mysteries of life and death. And so, unlike Makak, he disintegrates when finally he is pushed unwillingly into the abyss by the frightened Say

Tokyo Kid. He, however, receives knowledge because, though reluctant, he finally sleeps 'beyond the portals of secrets' to pierce 'the guard of eternity to unearth the Word' (Soyinka, 1965: 44). Unfortunately, he can not reveal what he has learnt because, like Murano, the 'golden nugget' hangs heavily on his tongue and he too must forever remain silenced.

The central action in *A Dance of the Forests*, the dance of welcome for the returning dead, takes place deep inside the forest - similar to the forest in *Dream on Monkey Mountain*. Most initiations in African cultures take place in the forest. From the moment Forest Head (disguised as Obaneji) begins to lead the three unsuspecting humans deeper and deeper into the forest, one senses the commencement of a ritual process. Appropriately at the end of the extraordinary series of events, Demoke, Rola and Adenebi emerge from their ordeal subdued but properly chastened but significantly wiser. Equally, in *An Echo in the Bone* the fact of the ritual wake consecrates the barn and immediately alters normal time and space conceptions as the characters step into the liminal zone where past and present meet in a kaleidoscopic concatenation of events that makes possible the simultaneous existence and experience of sacred and profane realities. For the duration of the wake, the characters as a group wade through the abyss as they grope towards the light which they find when they return to the barn. The journey takes them to Africa and back, and like a group of initiates after an intense night of ordeals, they emerge more enlightened than they were before the initiation began. The journey to Africa is a symbolic one and a reminder for the Caribbean peoples of African descent of the need to go into the self to discover what lies hidden within and which has to be unearthed as a first stage on the long road to psychic recovery. It is thus not surprising that *An Echo in the Bone, Dream on Monkey Mountain* and a host of other African-Caribbean plays contain this very symbolic journey.

Having looked at the ritual structure of the plays, and also having noted the centrality of liminality in the events, the book will now examine the complex mode of symbolic interaction in each play. *The Road* and *Dream on Monkey Mountain* are two structurally complex plays which on the surface seem convoluted and illogical. Because Walcott's play is conceived as a dream, it has all the illogical expansiveness of dreams; in fact, it is a mélange of events and characters, and its world is accommodating yet contradictory like the liminal world of rituals. The play is like an epic narrative - a quality which it shares with *A Dance of the Forests* and *An Echo in the Bone*. It traverses an expanse of space and time, beginning in the Caribbean in the present, roams to Africa of centuries ago, and then back to the Caribbean of the present, with glimpses of the future thrown in occasionally. But this world is illogical only to a mind trapped within the rigid frame of normal time. As with the other ritual plays, *Dream on Monkey Mountain* embraces the world of anti-structure which is possible only through the freedom of liminality and communitas (Turner, 1969: 80-118). It is only within such a zone of neither-nor that Makak's dream or new moon hallucination, Professor's crazed search for the elusive Word in *The Road*, the group of wake-keepers' tortured search for the reason behind Crew's killing of Master Charles in *An Echo in the Bone*, the nightmarish groping and experiences of the three humans in *A Dance of the Forests* and the in-between dead-and-alive world of Liking's *Singué Mura* and *Puissance de Um* have meaning. These plays, in spite of their disjointed and tortuous structures, are in fact far from being illogical or meaningless. The key to understanding what is happening is in a careful deciphering of the metaphoric and symbolic idiom and universe in which each operates. The plays speak in metaphors and symbols, and understanding the patterns of symbolic associations is crucial in understanding each play.

Two kinds of symbols can be found in a ritual context/structure: dominant and subordinate symbols. In a ritual, according to Evans Zuesse, 'the dominant symbol provides the orientation for the ceremony, while the subordinate symbols supply their own inner range of associations and give a context' (1979: 140). This means that the subordinate symbols help to define and extend the meaning of the dominant symbol in the ritual, but that each symbol, whether dominant or subordinate, still retains its own depth and polysemous web of associations and meaning. The arrangement of symbols in a ritual is such that 'each dominant symbol has a fan or spectrum of referents and these are interlinked by what is often a simple mode of association, its simplicity enabling it to interconnect a wide variety of significata'(Turner, 1967: 50).

The liminal phase is the central phase in a ritual process and it is within it that the complex pattern of symbolic interaction on which depend the meaning and therefore the significance of the ritual ceremony are found. A ritual, more often than not, has more than one symbol, and these are deployed in a specific pattern within the ritual context. As they interact, each symbol yields its meaning while extending or modifying the meaning of the other symbols present. Within the phase, the symbols converge, merge and then explode in an ever-spreading fan of meaning, and in this sense, a ritual is a configuration of symbols, a kind of 'musical score in which symbols are the notes' (Turner, 1967: 48). The plays function or are structured in much the same way. All contain a complex array of symbols, and their esoteric idioms depend largely on the complex patterns of symbolic associations which provide the architecture of their dramatic structures.

The Road and *Dream on Monkey Mountain* both have a mask as a central symbol. In the former, it is the mask of Ogun, the Yoruba god of the road, metal and drivers, while in the latter it is the mask of the White Goddess. In both, the mask is overtly polysemous, and it is the spreading out and coming together of each mask's broad fan of signification that guides the audience to the central issue in the play. Of the mask in *Dream on Monkey Mountain*, Walcott helps by highlighting its multi-vocality - at different points in the play it is the Apparition, the moon, the muse, and the White Goddess. Each symbolic referent has its own inner range of associations, while together they all refer back to the mask which ultimately is Makak's obsessive, debilitating and denigrating desire for a white culture that he can never belong to. His desire to lose himself in the 'white mist of the moon' is the root cause of his psychosis. The play is thus a ritual designed to purge him of this desire so that he can find himself by coming to terms with his African, black and Caribbean identities. The meaning of the play is revealed through the manner in which subordinate symbols progress and associate with each other throughout the play. In the heart of the forest they all merge into the white woman who Makak has to ritually behead so as to truly free himself of his alienation and spiritual death.

Within the play, however, there are other symbols which do not directly refer back to the mask, but which still help to define or modify it. These are mainly the human symbols such as Basil, the black-and-white painted coffin maker who in the play symbolises death; the spider and its ensnaring web which by association has similar qualities as the moon and the goddess as purveyors of death. As the spider spins its web and lies in wait for its unsuspecting victims, so does the white diablese woman of great seductiveness who lures men to their deaths. With the exception of Makak, all the other major characters in *Dream on Monkey Mountain* are symbols of one kind or another. Lestrade and Moustique represent aspects of Makak. Lestrade (the mulatto), for instance, symbolises his dream union of black and white; and the impossibility of achieving this desire is responsible for his psychic problem. Moustique, on the other hand, represents the black hating side of Makak's personality which itself is also a product of his all-consuming love of whiteness which has given rise to hatred of himself as a black person. The play creates meaning through a subtle process of reconciliation and or disposal of the symbols and their individual associations with the central character, Makak, the primary initiate in this rite of passage. The negative symbols, such as the Apparition and the black-hating Moustique, are eliminated through ritual executions. Only Lestrade, finally purged of his black-hating and nigger-bashing tendencies, is left as Makak's sole alter ego. What makes *Dream on Monkey Mountain* even more complex is the fact that most of the subordinate symbols are not just objects, but rather human impulses which Makak anthropomorphises to assist him in acting out his fantasy. And seen in this light, the play ceases to be the contradictory and disjointed dream which, on the surface, it appears to be.

A mask is also the central symbol around which other symbols configure and associate in Soyinka's similarly complex play, *The Road*. However, there is a difference in the way the mask concept is used in the two plays. Firstly, the mask as used by Walcott lacks the mystical depth which Soyinka, working from his Yoruba background, imbues his with. Soyinka has, as Walcott probably does not, an intimate acquaintance with the other-worldly aura and association which the mask has in African contexts. Walcott's mask has no life beyond itself as a symbolic object, whereas Ogun's mask suggests a trapped metaphysical energy waiting for a moment of actualisation. For the former, the mask is dead, a museum piece even if it is a symbol of Makak's longing for white culture. On the other hand, the mask in Soyinka's play is a felt presence, one that broods over the action from the moment the audience becomes aware of it. The difference arises mainly from Walcott's inability to realise and exploit the primary dualism which the mask embodies in traditional African thought. For the African, the mask contains both diachronic and synchronic principles and in *Dream on Monkey Mountain* the mask of the White Goddess is simply a static object, whereas in *The Road*, the Ogun mask exists in both the diachronic and synchronic states. That is to say, it is an object that stands for something else, but also as the god, Ogun, waiting to come to life. This is the most significant difference between the symbolism of the masks in *The Road* and *Dream on Monkey Mountain*.

Central to the *The Road* is the festival of Ogun. Murano was wearing Ogun's mask at the festival when he was knocked down. This fact alone sets up a complex chain of symbolic associations. Murano at the moment of his death was the 'god-apparent' because the transforming power of the mask had made him that and the wily Professor is therefore right when he boasts that he 'held a god captive' by appropriating the liminal

Murano, a being of transition, who straddles two worlds. The mask links Murano to Ogun and to the world of gods and spirits; it also links him to the drivers; while the dead masked dancer links him finally to Kotonou, Samson and Professor. They all are in turn linked to the all-powerful and all-pervading road which in the play functions at one level as a passage between points and places and at another as a passage from life to death. The ubiquitous spider which Samson never tires of calling attention to links the mask to the road which, like the spider, lies in wait patiently for its unwary victims. The spider in *The Road* performs a function similar to that which it performs in *Dream on Monkey Mountain* - as a patient agent of death and in both plays it refers to bigger agents and symbols. Thus, the two plays not only share structural similarity, they also use virtually similar symbols for, as well as pursuing the theme of death.

As action progresses in *The Road*, the spider, the road and the mask merge into a single symbol whose most recognisable quality is mystery and danger. And Murano is all of that. Professor's search for the mysterious, dangerous and elusive essence of death is carried out in the rituals of Ogun. Professor is uncannily perceptive in choosing Murano because, as Soyinka points out, the latter is the closest to the mystery which Professor seeks to penetrate as he embodies *agemo*, the cultic arrest of the death process. Murano in the play is the sole inhabitant of the gulf of transition and the silenced container of its mysteries. Professor stands on the edge, as it were, sacrilegiously probing this dark and deep child of transition. All the other symbols in the play are thus important in regard to how each helps to define, modify or extend the ritual arena in which the mask-Murano-Ogun complete its interrupted dance of transition. Viewed from this angle, there is nothing crazy about Professor, nor is anything illogical about the events in the play if one accepts them as constituting a temporary arrest and eventual completion of the dance of the masked figure which sinks into a lifeless heap of cloth on the floor at the end of the play.

The dance of welcome for the returning dead is the central event in *A Dance of the Forests* - the play's inspiration as pointed out earlier comes from the indigenous masquerade theatre of Africa. In traditional African societies, periodically, and sometimes in times of communal crisis, the dead are called up by the living for a communion, to bring back ancient wisdom, or give advice to guide the living. This theatre is part ritual and part entertainment and it relies a lot on the metaphorical idiom of the mask. The dead pair who break surface at the beginning of the play are practically masquerades or ancestors who have been invited by the human community. Normally, their arrival would have been greeted with joy, but instead an ironic situation develops leading to dramatic conflict. The conflict arises because, through Aroni's intervention, what was intended by the living to be a joyous reunion with their 'illustrious ancestors' turns into a tense confrontation between hosts and guests. Aroni has sent, instead of the illustrious ancestors requested by the human community, a pair of the restless dead who have come back to accuse the living of crimes from the past. This is a conflict which only the gods and the forest dwellers can resolve and hence the dance which also becomes a court in which the living are tried for present crimes and those from centuries ago. The play's ritual frame is intended to help absolve the living of guilt and to also purge them of the propensity for future crimes.

Unlike the previous two plays, *A Dance of the Forests* concentrates most of its symbols in the forest scene when the masks appear and it is the interaction between them that brings out the conflict as well as its resolution. The mask here acts as a signifier and this goes to show its value and importance as a useful and versatile metaphor for dramatic action in indigenous African masquerade theatre. Soyinka's deft manipulation of the mask metaphor here is worth noting as it is more complex than in *The Road*. In *A Dance of the Forests*, the mask does not just represent death or the dead, it rather becomes what it has always been in traditional African society and thought – otherworldly and spirit forces which the human community wants to bring itself into contact with.

Once the masks appear in *A Dance of the Forests*, the ritual becomes a complex dance of symbols. Each mask as it appears is an idea or a force and one witnesses from this point on an interplay of harmony and opposition, of good and evil, as the sides jostle for the fate of the future symbolised by the Half-Child. At a crucial point in this ritual to secure the future of the human community, the Half-Child becomes a focus of all action culminating in the 'dance of the Half-Child' when Eshuoro and his forces of revenge toss the defeated child dangerously between themselves. Into this dance steps Demoke who with Ogun's help makes the symbolic intervention to rescue the child from those intent on doing it harm. This is the climactic point of the play, when all action and characters freeze, breadth held, waiting for Demoke's to decide the child's fate. He finally chooses to return the child to its mother, an act which symbolically represents returning the future to the dead, although no longer the restless past. However, Demoke's act is as good as saying that the child had to wait for a better time to be born. The implication of this symbolic statement for the emerging Nigerian nation (the play was commissioned for Nigeria's independence celebrations in 1960) on the eve of independence could not have been better put because Soyinka uses the symbols to make the point that the present and the future have to come to terms with the past. Temporarily, the forces of discord in the play are in the ascendancy and claim Demoke, at which point his 'dance of the Unwilling Sacrifice' commences and concludes with the burning of the offending totem, the source of his crime against Eshuoro. The totem is the symbol of the divine ire between the two gods, Ogun and Eshuoro. It is also a symbol for the gathering tribes, however, it is a unity built on strife and bloodshed. When one identifies these symbols, what each signifies and the complex interplay between them, *A Dance of the Forests* becomes quite a stimulating play to read and probably to watch. The dead couple symbolise the crime which the living committed and which they are required to atone for. The couple begat the Half-Child, who is an extension of themselves, but at the same time, represents life throttled by the crimes of yester years. In this subtle manner, the playwright shows the relationship between the past, the present and the future, and thus at a symbolic level, *A Dance of the Forests* is quite a powerful play.

Scott's play, *An Echo in the Bone*, works in a slightly different way from the other plays; it relies on trance and possession more than it does on conventional symbolic interaction. In fact, the possessed mediums in the play function more or less like masked figures, in which case they too are symbols, and like symbols, they act as or represent entities other than themselves. *An Echo in the Bone*, like *A Dance of the Forests*, incorporates the principle of masking because it involves an invocation of the dead by the living for a communion. Through the ritual of the Nine-night wake, characters that are long dead and gone are called upon, but unlike masquerades they do not come in the flesh. Their spirits arrive and pass into live humans who become them for the duration they are needed.

The nearest model of African performance that comes to mind in relation to the technique employed in this play is spirit-mediumship found in many indigenous African cultures. *Bori* trance and possession ritual performances of the Hausa help to explain the nine-night ceremony, the central ritual in *An Echo in the Bone*. The Nine-nights is of African origin and has been modified to suit the new Caribbean setting of the African slaves. Similar rituals of African origin can be found in Haiti, Brazil and Cuba. Scott, in fact, uses Nago and Mahi (Yoruba) drum music to induce trance and possession in some of the characters, in the same way that music (*kirari*) is used to invite the spirits in *Bori*.

Bori is a cult of spirit-mediumship in which possession and trance are the predominant modes of communication between possessing spirits, through mediums and the audience. Members of the cult - collectively called *masu bori* (children of *bori*) - provide a ready pool of vehicles or 'horses' (*doki*) which the spirits mount when they arrive (for more on *Bori* see Okagbue, 2007, 2008). A similar principle is at work in *An Echo in the Bone*; structurally, the play develops as a series of possession and trance episodes. Situations develop, either through possession as when Crew arrives and 'mounts' Dreamboat and later Sonson, or when the music induces a state of trance on Rachel so that she could propel the action back into the past to supply the missing link in the narrative. Dreamboat's possession is very much like a *Bori* scene:

[Dream, *in the silence, pants loud and fast. The others watch him motionless. His head begins to swivel on his neck, slowly till the whole body is weaving on the spot. His feet slightly shuffle a little, then . . .*]

[Rattler *crouches over the drum, picks up the beat softly, moaning a little with concentration.*] . . .

[Dream *moves in a circle around the drum.* Rattler *turns on his heels so as to be always facing him*]

Rattler [*In a high voice*] Ah ah ah ah ah . . .

Stone [*At the door, panting, a paper in his hand*]: Crew, show yourself!

P: Crew? Where?

Stone: Jesus! Dream, what happen?

P: The spirit take him, just so, and him start to dance.

Stone: Then is him I see!

P: Who?

Stone: Is the dead man walking in the air. Is Crew! From the bottom of the road I see this man walking and I say that is Crew, I would know that walk anywhere . . .

(*Plays for Today*, p, 80-1)

It is worth pointing out that there are two kinds of possession used in the play. There is the involuntary one as described above when Dreamboat is suddenly seized without any conscious preparation on his part. Then there is planned possession as experienced by Sonson - who moves to one side to prepare himself. This is similar to the scene in *The Road* when Samson consciously begins to play Sergeant Burma after stepping into the uniform of the dead soldier. These scenes have all the transforming elements of the masquerade theatre where the actor once they put on the appropriate costume are transformed into the character they are playing.

The group of ten gathered for the wake are like the *masu bori* - potential mediums who eventually play so many roles before the night is over, and Rachel, Crew's wife, acts as the *magajiya* or *Bori* mother in whose compound the session is taking place. Rachel also acts as the priestess of the rites as she sets the ritual tone for the evening with her chant with which the scene and play opens. Early in the play it is made obvious the play will be dealing with the other worldly as the house becomes consecrated in the words of Rachel herself into 'a house for the dead'. Once the consecration is done, the spirit of Crew announces itself by possessing Dreamboat who becomes the dead man for a while. With his presence announced and acknowledged, the ritual begins and the audience and characters are taken into a constantly changing world of trance and possession sequences, and through these the play's action travels back in time into African-Caribbean history to uncover the reason behind Crew's savage deed. In referring to the very flexible dramatic structure of the play, Errol Hill (1985: 1-2) concludes that:

> The entire action is subsumed in a single evening's performance of the traditional Nine-Night ceremony . . . in honour of the spirit of a departed loved one. By re-enacting, with the aid of ritual possession, the central event that led to the murder of a white estate owner by a black peasant farmer who then drowns in a river while attempting to escape, understanding is shared and atonement made.

Of more theatrical significance is the economic use which Scott makes of the ritual framework and the technique of possession-trance which enables him to present such a complex and wide-ranging story. What he succeeds in doing in *An Echo in the Bone*, and this is a success shared by other playwrights as well, is the ability to allow the content of his play to determine its form, and naturally, the structure of the events and the characters is the best guide to the meaning of the play. By throwing the past and the present into constant contrapuntal collision, both realities and time frames become better revealed as constituting a continuous pattern of character and situational evolvement.

Although *An Echo in the Bone*, as pointed out earlier, is structured like a ritual, it does not use symbols in the conventional manner. As in *Dream on Monkey Mountain* it is the characters that end up becoming signifiers who have to be decoded first before one can fully understand their individual significance and of the actions they are involved in. The only conventional symbol in *An Echo in the Bone* is the very conspicuously placed metal chain which hangs over the action and characters for the duration of the play. And it is not until Crew kills Charles that he is able to finally climb over the chain in his bid to escape. Once within the ritual ambience of the play, the characters through their multiple role-playing become, as it were, mobile symbols that acquire higher significance as the action progresses. They become ideas, other personas, social forces and groups in contention, and, as in *A Dance of the Forests,* the interaction between them becomes a veritable interplay of symbols and images which culminates in the final act of Crew killing Charles.

At one level, the two men are just themselves - two men who have a misunderstanding over land and a woman. But when Scott symbolically establishes a recognisable pattern of confrontations through history and place, these two are transformed into representative symbols of opposing historical, cultural and social forces. They become symbols of oppressor and oppressed, master and slave, rich and poor, and white and black. And through being witnesses to the unchanged pattern of slavery, exploitation, oppression and racism which began in the slave ships to the doorstep when Crew raises his machete to kill Charles, the audience no longer perceives the killing as the act of one angry individual against another. Crew's action rather becomes the explosion of the long suppressed rage of one group of people who could no longer contain an unrelieved history of pain, injustice and humiliation. Similarly, when Crew (Sonson) climbs over the intimidating chain after killing Charles, it is, symbolically speaking, the whole African-Caribbean community that has risen above the chains of many centuries of enslavement. Crew is the ritual protagonist-cum-tragic hero who at the climactic moment of the tragic action becomes spokesperson for his group. To fully understand the tragic significance of Crew's action, there is a need to understand the Yoruba concept of tragedy which, Soyinka points out, largely arises out of,

> the protagonist's confrontation with inimical forces, which results in the 'disintegration of the self' . . . . Whether the protagonist is alive or dead at the conclusion of the drama, his tragic experience is profitable both for his self-knowledge and for his people. Society benefits in different ways - the hero can bring the community to a new knowledge of itself, or he can display an exemplary moral courage in the face of social injustice. . . . The goal of Yoruba tragedy is to energise the community at the conclusion. . . . The resolution lies not in the protagonist's death but in his bringing new strength into the communal life-blood (in Katrak, 1986: 19).

This is what Crew achieves, for what he did he did as much for himself as for his community. Those left behind draw strength and a new awareness from his singular act of courage. The structure which Scott has chosen for his play works well for the theme which he explores. By having mediums perform the roles the structure enables him to lead his characters and actors on the journey into the communal psyche 'to relieve the past, not just the immediate past, but the history of an oppressed people in order to find meaning in madness' (Hill, 1985: 10).

Ritual-Dream Plays

The five plays to be discussed here are: *A Dance of the Forests, An Echo in the Bone, The Road, Singuè Mura* and *Dream on Monkey Mountain*. The ritual nature of these plays means that action and character are situated firmly within the liminal phase or zone of transition, a fact which has both thematic and structural implications.

A key advantage of the ritual-dream structure is that its liminal phase creates an environment of unlimited possibilities and unrestricted boundaries for both dramatist and character. Each of the five plays is based on some form of ritual ceremony. *An Echo in the Bone* focuses on the Nine-Night wake for the dead Crew, and within this ritual matrix, Scott is able to 'explode sequential time in a series of dreamlike episodes'(Hill, 1985: 1) which reveal pivotal moments of African-Caribbean history, beginning in Africa, through the middle passage, to the plantations, and up to the present. *Dream on Monkey Mountain* is a pilgrimage-cum-rite of passage for Makak and his companions. Theirs is a journey into the knowledge of the self which begins in the present in the Caribbean, travels back in time to Africa of pre-slavery, and finally, like cleansed and enlightened pilgrims, they return to the present and their island home. In each of the two plays, the ritual format enables each playwright to theatrically present 'what is essentially an episodic and panoramic view of history in the most economic way imaginable' (Hill, 1985: 11). *A Dance of the Forests* is centred on the ritual 'dance of welcome' for the returning dead which has been organised by the forest dwellers. And as in the previous two plays, once within the forest which is the liminal space and phase of the ritual, normal time schemes are discarded and action moves effortlessly through the present, past and future. The audience is also presented with characters from different realms of existence coexisting within a single environment of action. *The Road* is concerned with the ritual of *agemo* which Professor has irreverently and sacrilegiously interrupted in his morbid desire to study the death process. *Singuè Mura* is based on a similar ritual in which the death process is temporarily frozen to enable the healing process - of soul searching and communal cleansing - to happen for those close to the dead woman. The knowledge from this ritual is communal and useful whereas no one knows what Professor found out in his quest to understand the death process in *The Road* and there is no suggestion that anyone or the community is enriched by his experience.

Some factors are common to these works, and these stem from the shared ritual framework within which their dramatic actions are set. The first common factor which applies to all the plays is that action, events and characters are very symbolic. The second is that within the ritual structures created, each playwright has the freedom to bring in the past, the present and the future to exist in harmonious simultaneity. It also enables them to bring characters from the various realms - gods, spirits, ancestors, humans, the dead and the unborn - to interact within the same milieu. By the end of each ritual/play, both characters and audiences achieve a special understanding of the seemingly chaotic events they'd witnessed or participated in. *A Dance of the Forests*, for instance, brings together in a single dramatic envelop humans, gods, the dead, ancestors, the unborn and other nature forces and spirits, and each is dramatically at home in the company of the others.

Theatrically, these plays demand to be understood using a new set of aesthetic rubrics, an African derived set. They are episodic in structure and panoramic in their sweep, events and characters develop through a process of cumulative association and not by the principle of linearity of Western European or North American theatre and narrative traditions. Above all, the dramatic actions trace circular patterns, always returning to their originating points. This is a deliberate attempt by the playwrights to use a structural representation of an essentially African-generated world view and sensibility to assert distinct African and African-Caribbean identities. Significantly also, all the plays make use of specific African or African derived ritual as a point of reference, as well as a controlling influence. Each play works to achieve the intended purpose of the ritual being used.

An Echo in the Bone begins and ends in the barn behind Crew's cottage nine nights after the killing of Charles - the Nine-nights is an African derived ritual ceremony to facilitate transition for the dead into the ancestral world. The play opens with Rachel as she gets ready to carry out the traditional wake for her dead husband. Soon enough, the audience is catapulted into the ritual proper with the entrance of Rattler, whose drumming precedes and precipitates the arrival of the dead in the room. Crew announces his arrival by possessing Dreamboat, one of those gathered for the ceremony. And once within the ritual matrix, the leaps and jumps in time and action begin, and it is accompanied by concomitant character transformations. Action moves between the present and the past so many times as the characters-actors are called upon to become so many personas from the past and present within so many dramatic moments which still are but one central action.

On the surface, some of the events appear unrelated to one another while the ritual is on, however, a closer look reveals an underlying principle of association that informs the overall meaning of the ritual. A similar principle underlies indigenous African performances. Gotrick's study of the Yoruba *Apidan* theatre ((1982: 40) and the analysis of *Enemma* masquerade festival of the Igbo (Okagbue, 1987, 2007) illustrate the central principle of traditional African theatre. This type of performance is best understood as a structure of totality in spite of the seeming un-relatedness of its constituent parts. Music provides an interpretative linkage to the various scenarios. This of course explains why music, and sometimes dance, in indigenous African theatre are not ornamental; these two elements are, in fact, structural necessities.

Most of the other African and African-Caribbean plays are arranged in much the same way. And central to all of them is the presence in each of a freedom of movement in time and space which reflects the African cosmology. For instance, within the ritual of the Nine-night ceremony, Scott is able to compress 'the actual and the supernatural, the past and the present, the living and the dead. They come together in a single consecrated space during a single night's watch' (Hill, 1985: 10). And in spite of the fact that the events are so far apart in time and dissimilar in character, they combine to explain Crew's killing of Charles. Applying the male pigeon courtship dance metaphor described earlier to the structure of the play, facilitates its understanding. The central action and context is the ritual wake organised by the living to enable them learn the hidden truths from the recently dead Crew. The drama constantly returns to this central point so the present can assess whatever information it has prised from the past, and also because in spite of the wanderings and meandering, the audience has to be reminded that it is at the wake.

The issue in *An Echo in the Bone* is the unanswered question of why and how Crew killed Charles. By taking the audience through this tour of the past, they are meant to arrive at the conclusion that Crew had killed because of centuries of injustice and other social injuries which he personally, and also as a representative of his race, has suffered at the hands of Charles, the person and representative of his own race. Through carefully cataloguing these events from the past, Scott is able to elevate two ordinary characters into symbols and the confrontation between them appropriately becomes one of races and classes. It is when approached from this perspective that *An Echo in the Bone* becomes the powerful play that it is meant to be. On the surface, the slave scenes of the remote past do not relate to the scenes of the immediate past, nor do they seem connected to the congregation at the wake, but they provide the weight of history which alone can explain the inequality, suffering and deprivation of the majority while Charles enjoyed unlimited luxury and abundance. Nothing in the play therefore is accidental, in spite of the seeming un-connectedness of the events.

Similarly, *A Dance of the Forests* roams in time and space. The play has a bipartite structure. Part One is a series of scenes which constantly alternate between the humans, the dead and the gods. The section is straightforward enough because, in spite of the ever-changing scenes and characters, the general hub of activity centres around the various participants as they make final preparations for the ritual dance of welcome which is the key event in the play. The dance is being organised by Aroni to welcome the restless dead and to 'chorus the future', to which Obaneji (Forest Head) is leading the unwilling but helpless humans as major participants. This section of the play works like a panoramic shot of different events with sufficient concentration on some so as to establish a connection between the key shots and isolated and peripheral ones. Here, the overall connection is suggested by a pervasive sense of hurry and frenetic movement towards the centre of the forest.

Part Two begins with the two gods, Murette and Eshuoro, confronting each other. Eshuoro is the missing link/factor in the divine power game being played out and his introduction at this point in the play is perfectly timed as he indeed provides the missing link. The scenes involving Murette are used to reveal the true designs of the warring deities, as well as that of Aroni. After the Murette-Eshuoro scene, the action proceeds to the summoning of the spirits for the ceremony, and for the second time in the play Soyinka utilises the indigenous masquerade (*Egungun*) motif - the first being the dead pair breaking surface at the beginning of the play. However, this time it is not only the dead who are summoned, but also nature forces and spirits who are asked to assume material forms for the communion between the realms. Through this, the action is firmly set within the liminal phase of the ritual and from then on, sequential time and space are completely abandoned making new experiences and states of being possible. It is significant that from this point on most of the characters are figures now under the liberating influence of the masks. Once within the liminal phase, Aroni takes the action into the past by calling up the decadent splendour of the court of Mata Kharibu of eight centuries ago. The scenes and narrative of the Mata Kharibu episode work in a similar manner to the slave scenes in *An Echo in the Bone* as both scenes help to establish the vital historical link between the characters in the present and their predecessors while present events are revealed to have had precedents in the past. With a dramatic jolt, Aroni brings the action back to the present for the ceremony of the dance of welcome for the dead, the chorus of the unborn and the living, and the final resolution of the conflict set up in the play. The action then moves to the edge of the forest where Demoke (one of the humans and a key character in the play) is discovered by his worried father who had been searching all night for him. *A Dance of the Forests* is almost Demoke's nightmare, just like Makak's in *A Dream on Monkey Mountain*.

Although not exactly like *An Echo in the Bone* with its disjointed and convoluted structure of action which moves widely in time and space, *A Dance of the Forests* too has an equally peculiar dramatic structure in which meaning only emerges with the final action or image. But like the former, it also is a journey in space and time designed to lead to knowledge of the past and of self. Both plays show that the past often holds the key to an understanding of the present, and the two provide glimpses of the future. The two also show the inter-relationship between the living and the dead, and that the living can learn a lot from the dead ancestors who can be summoned through ritual invocations. Both seem to have drawn inspiration from the masquerade tradition of African cultures in which the dead can be invited for a communion with the living - an invocation well captured by Soyinka in the Forest Crier scene in *A Dance of the Forests* as a prelude to the ritual dance of welcome. As in all masquerade appearances, the living initiate the rites because it is they who are in need of knowledge from the dead. The conflict in Soyinka's play however arises from the fact that the living who have invited the dead, out of guilt which they are not prepared to acknowledge, refuse to welcome their guests as is the custom, and so, as Aroni tells the audience in the opening testimony, he has taken the restless dead under his wing and the forest dwellers have consented to dance a welcome for them instead. In like manner, the appearance of Crew at the wake in his memory in *An Echo in the Bone* provides the knowledge which the living seek - the knowledge of who killed Charles and why. Basically therefore, the masquerade motif helps in an understanding of both plays.

The Road and *Dream on Monkey Mountain* also use masks as symbols, and actions in both plays take place within a ritual framework. The two are similar in many respects, and yet different in many others. For instance, each is structured as a rite of passage and involves a journey that starts from a pre-liminal phase of ignorance, through a liminal phase of stress and revelation, and ending in a post-liminal phase of new knowledge and heightened awareness. As in the previous two plays, the ritual-dream framework enables each playwright to explore a wide range of ideas as well as cope with many characters. Time, space and character are very flexible and versatile so as to cope with the physical and metaphysical realities which each play explores.

The setting for *The Road* more or less is around and within the liminal environment surrounding Professor's roadside shack. But even within this circumscribed space, the audience is still able to visit the church in Professor's younger days as a lay-reader; the sites of two ghastly road accidents; the drivers' festival in some unnamed place at which Murano is knocked down while performing as the masked dancer. All these events are differentiated in time and space, but as in *An Echo in the Bone*, the audience is able to follow the action as it slips effortlessly between the past and the present with unrelenting urgency and inevitability. Like the other plays, *The Road* is a theatre for the actor because it makes enormous demands on the actor's histrionic abilities - Samson, for instance, plays himself now and past, then he role-plays as the millionaire and later as Sergeant Burma. Salubi and Kotonou also manage between them a number of very challenging roles. The various situations in the play on the surface appear unconnected, but not too distanced and disparate as in *An Echo in the Bone*. But as in the former, *The Road* follows the pigeon-dance pattern as it makes forays into the past and to distant places, but returns always to the shack and the Aksident Store which is the central image and metaphor, as well as the anchor for the characters and the action.

The play starts in the present in the shack – it is early morning and those who have work to do leave for work and others idle about, waiting. This theme is introduced quite early and acts as a unifying idea because all the characters seem caught in limbo while they wait to move on to the next phase of their lives. Everyone is waiting for something or the other to happen - Professor is waiting for the Word to be revealed; Samson for Kotonou to return to the road as a driver; Salubi waits for Professor to forge a driving licence for him to get on the road; Kotonou is waiting to begin work as keeper of the Aksident Store; and the lay-abouts wait for any odd jobs and a chance to better their lives. Gradually from this first scene the action alternates in quick succession between the past and present until it gets to the end of Part One with Professor clutching his 'tower of words'. So far, the action heads everywhere but nowhere in particular. But at a deeper level, they in fact reflect one another while some act as narrative plants or hints for events that are to come in the future. The unconnected elements would all come together eventually in the final communion scene when the discarded mask comes to life and resumes its interrupted dance and Murano his interrupted *agemo* process.

Part Two begins with Professor admonishing Samson and Kotonou for neglecting his needs by not bringing any new revelation from a recent accident; and from talking about an accident the play transports the audience to the scene and it is the first serious warning to Kotonou that behind all the accidents and near-misses lies the unmistakable hand of Ogun, the vengeful god of the road and of drivers. Again, as in Part One, action alternates between past and present with measured consistency until the last scene that begins with the communion to the climactic moment when the possessed *egungun* emerges and dances leading to the play's resolution. This is when all the disparate elements of Part One find their complements as all action is impelled towards and concentrated in the symbolic figure of the masked Murano who dances himself into a 'lifeless heap of cloth and raffia'. This is the moment of revelation which Professor had been seeking and waiting for; it is also what had driven Kotonou off the road, the visual symbol of death and its resultant *agemo* which the mute Murano is.

Again, it is hard to find the connecting images, ideas or words in this medley of events. The task is slightly easier in *The Road* because it has a narrative structure and also because all the events revolve around the same key figures - Samson, Kotonou, Professor, Salubi, Say Tokyo Kid, most especially Murano and, of course, the ubiquitous road which unites them all. These characters are closely associated and in constant contact with each other, unlike in *An Echo in the Bone* in which character, time, space and events are so different and so far apart that any links between them are very well hidden. *A Dance of Forests* also illustrates Soyinka's sophisticated use of the cumulative association technique. In spite of the separation in time and space between the events, the characters are easily identifiable because he allows some character tendencies to survive and influence behaviour through time. For instance, Demoke, the carver, is the Poet in the court of Mata Kharibu and sends his apprentice, Oremole, to his death, thus repeating the crime of the court poet centuries ago who let his novice fall to death from a rooftop; Rola is the present day Madame Tortoise, the *femme fatale* queen who wantonly destroyed men and finally led a nation to war and destruction, and in her present incarnation she is a whore who gladly destroys men who come under her spell; Adenebi is the Court Historian who took a bribe to have the Warrior and his men sold into slavery, and now he takes another bribe to license the dangerous Incinerator; and Agboreko remains as in former life a soothsayer whose empty words are routinely ignored. This technique enables a past action or characteristic to inform a present one; it becomes clear that characters and motives link past crimes and present ones which has necessitated the ritual dance of welcome for the dead which the gods have arranged so that these perennial crimes may be expiated and the chain of errors finally broken.

Dream on Monkey Mountain stretches the frontiers of the dream medium quite significantly. Like the other plays, it has a circular structure, beginning and ending in the prison cell where Makak has been remanded overnight for disorderly conduct while drunk. Of the play's structure, Walcott writes:

> The play is a dream, one that exists as much in the given minds of its principal characters as in that of its writer, and as such, it is illogical, derivative, contradictory. Its source is metaphor and it is best treated as a physical poem with all the subconscious and deliberate borrowings of poetry. Its style should be spare, essential as the details of a dream (*Dream on Monkey Mountain*, p, 208).

The dream is thus a very suitable medium for an unhampered exploration and portrayal of the liminal nature of Makak's quest for the knowledge of self and race. With such detail from the author, the reader is prepped for the unexpected and the fantastic.

Dream on Monkey Mountain opens with Makak having been brought into the cell the evening before – a fact which the reader learns from the prologue. Once this has been established, the play catapults the audience into the past - eight years back to Monkey Mountain where Makak is found outside his desolate hut by his business partner, Moustique, delirious with malaria fever and full of his dreams about the white woman and a mission to lead the return to Africa. From this point, the action progressively moves further and further away from the cell 'towards Africa'. Like *The Road* and *A Dance of the Forests*, *Dream on*

Monkey Mountain is divided into two parts and Part One functions as a preamble to the actual journey at the centre of the play. All the major characters are introduced in Part One; also introduced are the ritual symbols, such as the mask, the spider and the moon, through which the events in the play can be comprehended. Part Two returns to the cell from where the prisoners (Makak, Souris and Tigre) escape and the action moves to the forest as Makak gets the others to join him on his dreamboat. Their journey deeper and deeper into the forest is similar to that in *A Dance of the Forests* in which Soyinka exploits the African perception of the forest as a zone of transition and of supernatural phenomena. Walcott also exploits this idea of the forest in *Ti-Jean and His Brothers*. As Makak and his two companions move deeper and deeper into the forest, they pull Corporal Lestrade and Basil along with them until finally they all meet in the heart of the forest where the ritual of identity retrieval takes place. Scene Three of this part is appropriately titled 'Apotheosis' where the forest is symbolically Africa. But the forest is also the soul of each character as they search for their cultural and racial identity which slavery and colonialism had undermined. Each character is meant to confront and come to terms with the submerged part of their personalities to rid themselves of their post-slavery and postcolonial alienation. Once inside the forest, action in the play becomes highly symbolic, culminating in the beheading of the White Goddess to herald the final freedom for Makak, the cultural pilgrim. The Epilogue returns the action to the cell where Moustique has come to secure Makak's release. This scene is used structurally to reveal that it had been a dream all along; all the action had been inside Makak's head. But it had been a momentous and vitally important journey which African-Caribbean characters make to engage with and understand the Africa within which they need in order to resolve their crisis of identity as peoples of African descent who have suffered centuries of exile and cultural denigration. Significantly though, the play demonstrates a unique African perception and structuring of experience as Makak's dream takes wings, flying to all corners of the earth, before returning to the sleeping head behind secure bars of his prison cell in his native Caribbean.

A Storytelling Theatre

Storytelling is a popular theatre form in African cultures; in fact, it is one of the most practised forms of theatre on the continent. Thus, another way African and African-Caribbean dramatists recuperate and reclaim their African cultural identities is through adopting storytelling dramatic style and structure. *Ti-Jean and His Brothers, Old Story Time, A Dance of the Forests* and *The Marriage of Anansewa* use elements of storytelling; and in fact, all four plays are structured as sessions of storytelling. All four contain suggestions of how to create the appropriate storytelling atmosphere, and besides, each play observes many of the narrative and structural conventions of African and African-Caribbean storytelling. However, within the formal structure of storytelling, individual playwrights have taken liberties where they feel that such liberties enhance the story being told. Of the four, *Old Story Time* and *The Marriage of Anansewa* are closest to storytelling theatre in style and structure. The two pretty much observe all the key conventions of the art - a standard opening formula which consists of a song, a welcome greeting for the audience and an introduction of the subject matter; there are occasional stoppages of the narrative to enable the narrator to comment, explain a few points, or like the delightful Pa Ben in *Old Story Time*, grease a dry and overworked throat. Sometimes, it is the audience who are given the chance to interrupt because the story is not being told 'properly' or some detail has been left out. And when the story is done, there is the final word from the narrator, usually a summing up or a statement of the moral or aetiological import of the tale, as in *The Marriage of Anansewa* and *Ti-Jean and his Brothers*.

Aroni (the Lame One) is the narrator in *A Dance of the Forests*, and he is also one of the characters. Although he is the prime mover, he is not as central to the action as Pa Ben is in *Old StoryTime*. Aroni's testimony is very illuminating and serves as narrator's opening address:

> I know who the Dead Ones are. They are the guests of the Human Community who are neighbours to us of the Forest. It is their Feast, the Gathering of the Tribes. . . . They asked us for ancestors, illustrious ancestors . . . . And I sent two spirits of the restless dead . . . . Their choice was no accident. In previous life they were linked with violence and blood with four of the living generation. . . . When the guests had broken the surface of earth, I sat and watched what the living would do. They drove them out. So I took them under my wing . . . and the Forests consented to dance for them (Soyinka, 1963: 1-2).

This introduction serves a number of purposes. The first is that it is a prelude; and within this tight opening speech, all the major characters are mentioned, the multiple conflicts established, the central action which is the 'dance of welcome for the dead', the judgement of the living and the chorusing of the future are all properly laid out. The speech also performs another key function, that of establishing the narrator's authority to tell the story - this right is born of Aroni's intimate knowledge of the story and acquaintance with the characters - he 'knows' everyone and everything that is going to happen in the story. Aroni's testimony is similar in style and function to the overture by Frog in *Ti-Jean and his Brothers*. According to Ben-Amos, the opening and the closing formula serve very important needs in folktales and storytelling sessions:

> They frame the expressions, setting the boundaries between formal and generic expressions and whatever type of verbal exchange precedes and follows them. Such phrases are not so much part of the narrative text as of the verbal interaction between the speaker and his listeners. They signal the nature of the tale and enable the listeners to prepare an attitude of belief, disbelief or humour toward a forthcoming narration (1977: 9).

Having achieved all these, Soyinka dispenses with the narrating voice and Aroni becomes just a minor character in *A Dance of the Forests*, but the action is still seen through him as the audience remain vaguely aware that what they are witnessing is what the unobtrusive Aroni is showing them and his voice from the testimony rings constantly in the ear throughout.

Once his testimony is done, the audience sees Aroni briefly with Murette in Part One, and not again until seven pages into Part Two when all preparations have been made, the final links completed and the 'Dance of Welcome' begins. Even then, he is on the side, not really involved in the action anymore. But like a conjurer, he summons the past into existence with an invisible wave of his magic wand. He actualises for his internal and external audiences the majestic court of Mata Kharibu. This is a key scene in the play because it provides both the structural and thus thematic link between the past and present and also between the living and the unborn. The scene also establishes a central concern of the play - the cosmic continuity characteristic of African thought and universe (the Yoruba model in this case). Through the structure of events and scenes in the play, the audience are able to experience the possibility of the co-existence of the past, the present and future, the dead, the living and the unborn, ancestors, men and gods - all existing in simultaneity in a single ritualised space and time. The past, the present and the future in the play are linked by a cosmic bond of mutual affectivity - a central element of African thought.

Structurally, the Mata Kharibu scene serves two very important purposes. First, it is a successful means of explaining the present in the light of the past. The human characters are made to become their previous personas and through this device the audience sees how each character reprises a past crime in their present incarnations. Demoke, Rola and Adenebi contribute to the cycle of crimes, the cycle which the ritual is designed to break. And through this scene Soyinka puts across a pessimistic vision of history which holds that present events have precedents in the past and antecedents in the future and that change can never come for as long as the present continues to brush the ugly memories of the past under the mat. The past, the play argues, has to be identified and acknowledged by the present, and atonement made for crimes, errors and sins before the future can become free of its effects. A similar view is also expressed in *Dream on Monkey Mountain* and *An Echo in the Bone*. Secondly, the Mata Kharibu scene brings together within the same dramatic envelope all the forces of the play's universe - evil, good, neutral, humans, spirits, the dead, and the unborn - which had been converging without actually meeting right from the beginning of the play. And once these links and the cosmic convergence are established, the meaning of the play becomes clear and the final resolution acceptable as a fitting finale to a grandiose though cumbersome drama.

Soyinka, like a good storyteller, does not forget to conclude his narrative in the appropriate manner. He remembers his closing formula, but instead of Aroni, he uses a group of narrators made up of Adenebi, Agoreko, Demoke, Old Man and Rola, who in a choric epilogue, tell the audience what the experience had been about and the purpose for which the ritual of the 'dance for the dead' had been initiated by Aroni. The divine and ancestral forces disappear or return to their original forms, and only the humans are left, at the very spot where they had been when the play began - somewhere at the edge of the forest. *A Dance of the Forests* therefore is a collective nightmare for this group of humans who have been skilfully manipulated by, on the one hand, the storyteller who makes them listeners and actors in his tale, and, on the other, by Aroni and Forest Head who force them into taking part in a ritual of expiation.

Similarly, Frog in Walcott's *Ti-Jean and His Brothers* gathers the audience together and takes them through heaven and hell before bringing them back to the starting point, leaving them with a parting aetiological and moral nugget to chew on while he goes on his way. The play is a moral tale which at the same time tries to offer a folksy explanation for a natural phenomenon - the presence of the lone man with a bundle of faggots and his little dog on the face of the moon. The play is obviously inspired by indigenous African–Caribbean storytelling. Of the play's narrative structure, Hill writes:

> In *Ti-Jean and his Brothers*, playwright Derek Walcott draws on St Lucian folklore for his story of a poor mother and her three sons who dwell on the edge of the forest. But this forest is magical. . . . Once again we are in the realm of fantasy where the actual and the miraculous collide and where man is thrown back on his own resourcefulness for self preservation (*Plays for Today*, p, 2).

It is not only its structure which has come from the folk tradition of storytelling; *Ti-Jean and his Brothers* also deals with a popular story type from Caribbean folklore. It is about the myth of the great or giant man who is defeated by the little man; this is a theme common in Africa and the Caribbean. The popularity of this theme in the Caribbean dates back to slave times when the poor helpless African slaves inspired and comforted themselves with the hope that they would always outwit and defeat their powerful masters - it is a myth of hope for the weak because it demonstrates that power is not all there is for survival and success. In this regard, one should note that *Ti-Jean and his Brothers* and *An Echo in the Bone* employ the standard conventions and matching archetypes of the folktale of the giant man who is usually unmasked in the end by the little man - Crew defeats Charles after years of oppression and cheating, despite the latter's immense power; while Ti-Jean outwits and defeats Papa Bois (Planter, Devil) where his two older brothers (raw power and excessive/vacuous intelligence) had failed. One thing which Walcott achieves in his skilful use of the conventions and archetypes from folk mythology is that he is able to deploy the archetypes for economy in his narrative. Because the story of Ti-Jean deals with easily recognisable archetypes, what each represents is obvious to the audience or reader immediately the archetype appears on stage or on the page. This is one primary advantage of myth appropriation in dramatic or literary structuring.

However, the ideas developed in the play are not wholly Caribbean - quite a few of them, including the central little man-great man confrontation, abound in much of the folk traditions of sub-Saharan Africa - the *Ananse* and *mbekwu* (tortoise) tales of the Akan and Igbo respectively are based on this. Of significance to Walcott's play is the theme of the White God who sends the black protagonist or little man to catch Death, a very dangerous and ultimately impossible task, very similar to the deviously impossible ones which the Plater/Devil sets for Ti-Jean and his brothers. As usual in such tales, the hero is lucky to meet some unusual creatures who help him to solve the problem in much the same way that the insects help Ti-Jean accomplish his tasks, to the annoyance of the Devil. Thus we see that the two Caribbean plays, *Ti-Jean and his Brothers* in particular, are based on a surviving African form which has helped to shape consciousness and expression in the Caribbean for peoples of African descent. The theme and form are therefore part of their African heritage and thus a statement of their African-Caribbean identity.

Ti-Jean and his Brothers combines the structure of the folktale with that of ritual as it is ultimately a rite of passage for the eponymous hero, Ti-Jean. In this respect, it shares with *Dream on Monkey Mountain* and *A Dance of the Forests*, the structure of the archetypal journey to the centre:

> the Centre, is pre-eminently the zone of the sacred, the zone of absolute reality, and the road leading to it is a difficult road. The road is arduous, fraught with perils, because it is in fact a rite of passage from the profane to the sacred. . . . Attaining the centre is equivalent to a consecration, an initiation (Eliade, 1965: 17-8).

The road to the centre is filled with danger, trials and obstacles; but the journey is one in which the hero, after much suffering but with assistance from unusual sources along the way, triumphs. Ti-Jean at the end of his tribulations and in spite of numerous traps on his path defeats Papa Bois and snatches life for the Bolom and for his dying mother.

For idea and structure for *Ti-Jean and his Brothers*, Walcott turned to the Akan *Ananse* folktale corpus which survives in African-Caribbean culture. In a sense, therefore, he is working from an indigenous base similar to because derived from the Akan *anansegoro* tradition from which Efua Sutherland derived George Kweku Ananse, the trickster hero and central character in *The Marriage of Anansewa*. According to Hill (1985: 2-3), Walcott 'unfolds his folktale with the formality of a practised craftsman' and shows that, 'like the traditional spinner of stories, he too can speak in many tongues using choral speech, singing and dancing to enhance his presentation' (2). Walcott acknowledges his debt to Africa when he says of the play that:

> What was there too, but too deep to be acknowledged, was the African art of the story-teller, a tradition which survived in my childhood through the figure of a magical, child enchanting aunt, and the memories of firefly-pricked rain forests at dusk . . . and those skin-

prickling chants whose words may change, but whose mode goes as far back and even past tribal memory (in Hill, 1985: 5).

All conventions of presentation are fully and effectively employed - the opening songs by the insects, the dances, choric chants, mime, all structurally contribute to enhance the performance as they do in the Ghanaian play. *The Marriage of Anansewa* begins with a song by the players, and intermittently there are chants (*mboguos*) which act as scene markers and commentaries on preceding or forthcoming actions.

Characteristically, it is evening when the insects meet - this is the time traditionally allowed in African and African-Caribbean cultures for storytelling, with moonlit nights often the best nights. This is also the time chosen by Pa Ben to gather his audience *in Old Story Time. Ti Jean and his Brothers* opens with the insects huddled together to shelter from the rain when Bird passes and is halted by Cricket:

> Cricket: Before you fly home, listen
> The cricket cracking a story
> A story about the moon.
> Frog: If you look in the moon,
> Though no moon is here tonight
> There is a man, no, a boy
> Bent by a weight of faggots . . . .
> That is Ti-Jean the hunter,
> He got the heap of sticks
> From the old man of the forest
> They calling Papa Bois
> Because he beat the devil
> God put him in that height
> To be the sun's right hand
> And light the evil dark
> But as the bird so ignorant
> I will start the tale truly
> (*Plays for Today*, p, 25-6).

This is a traditional formal opening which follows close on the heels of the choric chant and it performs a function structurally similar to Aroni's testimony in *A Dance of the Forests*. Through this initial formulaic exchange, rapport is established between the storyteller and his audience - both internal and external. Usually, the narrator follows this with a song to which his audience responds in chorus, as Pa Ben demonstrates in *Old Story Time* with his introductory banter and chants with his two audiences. Rhone's story makes the added effort of appropriating the already seated auditorium audience into Pa Ben's assembled listeners/guests. He steps out as it were and reaches beyond the stage to include the auditorium, an attempt which is not as overt or direct in Soyinka and Walcott. Aroni's address is to the audience, but unlike Pa Ben, he does not enlist their direct participation, and so Pa Ben's is much closer to African theatre and storytelling tradition by deliberately breaking the conventional Western barrier between stage and auditorium. Rhone's stage direction shows his desire to involve the whole house in the action on stage through reclaiming the communal nature of theatre:

> [*The stage and auditorium go to black. In the darkness we hear actors singing a quiet lyrical folk song. Very soon we see the glow of Pa Ben's lantern.*]
> Pa Ben: [*Over the song, sings*] Old Story Time. Old story Time . . . .
> Evening one and all. Everybody hearty? What happen, you people mouth join church or what? You don't have voice to answer me? Everybody hearty . . . . That's better . . . . Make yourselves comfortable on them nice chairs . . . .
> (*Old Story Time and Other Plays*, p, 8-9).

Like master storytellers, Frog and Pa Ben achieve an economic introduction of their stories and at the same time secure the audience's attention and participation. Also, both achieve what most traditional storytellers never fail to seek - a narrator must always stake their claim to the right to tell the tale. They have to convince the audience that they are the most qualified to tell the story. Frog claims that since Bird was 'so ignorant', he was the most qualified narrator. And Pa Ben, like the celebrated *griots* of West Africa, claims descent from a line of master storytellers - his father was the chief storyteller and so he is merely carrying on a family tradition. Story-teller in *The Marriage of Anansewa* tells his audience that he 'was present when all this happened' while Aroni begins *A Dance of the Forests* with: 'I know who the Dead Ones are. They are neighbours to us of the forests'. Pa Ben claims close acquaintance with the main characters, Len, Miss Aggy and Lois, as their neighbour and confidante.

Having introduced the characters and the story, Frog proceeds like Aroni to unobtrusively call up whatever scenes, places or persons he wishes so the story moves from scene to scene. In traditional African storytelling, once the story begins, the narrator can do one of three things. First, he or she can, like Pa Ben and Story-teller, stay with the action and participate all through, occasionally breaking off or stopping the action to make comments about what is happening, to respond to interjections or answer questions from the audience. Second, the narrator can step aside and relinquish their narrative voice and the audience neither hears their voice nor sees them again until perhaps at the end if they choose to reappear to make a final statement. Or third, they can relinquish their active narrative voice once the formal introduction is done and become just one of the minor characters, but the audience remains vaguely aware that they are narrating - in this capacity the narrator hardly comments on the action, and also does not come out in the end for a final statement. Soyinka and Walcott adopt the third option in *A Dance of the Forests* and *Ti-Jean and his Brothers* respectively. But unlike these two, Rhone makes Pa Ben personalise the story - he is both immersed in the action as well being able to step out and comment on it. This technique is quite effective and, with Pa Ben's hilariously comic antics, provides enchanting theatre. Story-teller in *The Marriage of Anansewa* provides comic counterpoints to the action in his relationship and interaction with the major characters - this is especially through his witty banter with those who seek information from him to help them out of their dilemma, such as Ananse himself and the postman. Story-teller offers no advice and would not be drawn to commit himself either way. Here he differs from Pa Ben and the insect narrators who gladly take sides.

Frog appears just three times as narrator throughout the tale. The first is when he begins the story. Again, half way through the action he makes a brief but significant appearance. The second appearance does two things - it reminds the audience of who the narrator is and, secondly, it marks a turning point in the story as from then onwards, the fortunes of Ti-Jean change and events tilt in his favour. The third and final time Frog appears is at the end when he sums up his tale and offers an aetiological statement.

Pa Ben in *Old Story Time* is the accomplished teller of tales. He is animator, actor, master-of-ceremony and singer, who busily arranges and directs the session. And he does so with consummate skill and delightful humour. As a master storyteller, he knows how to handle his audience as can been seen from the deft manner he helps them to immediately 'slap into the mood'. Besides, he controls the action effortlessly through appropriate pauses and suspense that are intrinsic to a good story. Pa Ben works in a very systematic way. First, he involves his audience by his formal greeting and by insisting on getting the right level of anticipatory and participatory responses from them. Having achieved this, he proceeds to introduce the story and by claiming intimacy with the characters and events, he establishes the authenticity of his narrative and also his right to tell it since it is also the story of his life:

> A did live in a certain big yard, next door to some of the people who the story concern, so you see A have first hand knowledge
> (*Old Story Time and Other Stories*, p, 10).

His humour is always bubbling on the surface and with it he enlivens his narrative, even when he talks of serious issues like racism and neurosis; this helps him win and keep his audience under his spell.

As soon as he creates the necessary atmosphere, the characters come to life and appear as they are called, as they do in *Ti-Jean and his Brothers* where the characters parade themselves and reveal their essential traits as Frog calls them. In *Old Story Time,* each actor - collectively they also constitute an inner audience - detaches himself or herself from the pool of players when their role or scene is to be played and then rejoins it after their performance. It is in this regard that the play resembles the *bori* and *An Echo in the Bone.* The technique is significant, however, because it allows both the actors and the audience to maintain a degree of artistic and emotional distance from the action on stage - this is a typical indigenous African performance sensibility in which the idea of playing is constantly fore-grounded and actors merely show the characters without claiming to be them. The technique makes both narrator and audience constantly aware that they are dealing with a fictional reality, no matter how close or similar that reality is to the lived one. This way it is possible, for instance, to see the actress playing Miss Aggy stand outside her and laugh at this neurotic woman desperately trying to escape from the prison of her skin colour. The same technique is employed in *The Marriage of Anansewa* where the pool of players is permanently before the audience and actors step out and back to perform their roles.

The narration in *Old Story Time* is more faithful to the folk tradition as it develops and maintains an atmosphere of storytelling more than any of the other plays. Of special significance is the playfulness and informality between the narrator and his immediate audience cum fellow actors. The latter are allowed liberties, such as, they could interrupt the story at any time they felt Pa Ben was not telling it right, or if they wanted him to clarify a point or, sometimes when their impatience got the better of them and they wanted him to quicken the action. They even interrupt to accuse him of being stingy with information. But of course, the old man sticks to his pace, refusing to be harried or hurried while feeling satisfied that he is in control of his material and his audience. All this goes to show that he is a master of his art who can even afford the luxury of breaking off his story to treat himself to a tot of rum to service his vocal apparatus, while his audience clamour and beg for him to continue.

Action in the play does not unfold as a linearly arranged sequence of events instead Pa Ben makes a lot of narrative detours and this manner of structuring places the play in the same associative mould as the other plays - the narratives, dreams and rituals. His story unfolds as a series of photographic shots achieved by an intricate panning and selection process. The play, for instance, begins with a shot of Miss Aggy and Pa Ben, one of Len and Pearl, another of Len and his mother, and then of Pa Ben and Miss Aggy again. These initial shots are a preamble - they establish whose story it is. The audience also learns from it of Pa Ben's centrality in the story - he is narrator, buffer between and confidante to the major characters. The story then makes a very long leap to many years later when there is a letter from Len who is studying in England. In between these shots, Pa Ben steps out three times to supply a linking commentary directed at the auditorium audience. As yet, the plot is near and in the past - the story so far is from Len's childhood to when he left home for school and then to England, the agony he caused his mother by not writing regularly and his shocking marriage to Lois instead of long-haired brown Margaret. But bits of the story are carefully left out for later and it is part of the technique of hinting but withholding full information until the right moment, with the result that the story is never completely told until the last bit has been told and heard. Sometimes, Pa Ben simply explains events that have happened or hints at those to come. But most often, they are used merely to narrate those bits of the story which are not to be enacted on the stage. There is a principle of selection at work here because it is Pa Ben alone who chooses what he considers vital enough to be shown and those that help the plot by being merely narrated.

By now the story takes the audience into the time of Len's return to Jamaica, and his mother's anguish at his 'unambitious' marriage. And from this point on, the leaps and hop-backs in the plot begin as the flashback scenes unreel in a carefully choreographed sequence, slightly deceptive, but overall, effective as a structural device. First, the audience sees George dupe Miss Aggy into investing her life's savings in his bogus housing scheme - at this point it is not clear who George is or what his relationships to Len, Lois and Margaret are. But what is significant from here on is that the dramatic technique becomes more intricate as Rhone creates so many levels of action which can be activated or frozen as needs arise, and of equal significance is the fact that most times the levels and actions are so seemingly unrelated that they could well be scenes from different plays with the only common thread or bond between them being the occasional appearance of one character in may be more than one of them. This is part of the narrative technique to enable the action travel far and wide for the moment until it is time to pull the various strands together. This technique is effective as the scene below in which Len is waiting to find out from his mother how she got involved with the dubious George (Mac) in the first place:

Len: How did Mac encourage you?
Mama: I was in the bank one day, the same bank A had a little savings in.
[Len *faces up stage and freezes.* Mama *removes her hat, goes into her bag and takes out a red one and puts it on.* George *enters*]
George: What a thing, eh?
Mama: What . . .
(p, 34).

And effortlessly the audience is in the bank some years back. Rhone uses this technique a number of times and its economy and ease of use helps the play to interconnect all the shifting times and all the scattered events that eventually give a clearer perspective on the play. This technique is similarly used in the prison scenes in *The Trial of Dedan Kimathi* when Kimathi goes back in time, back to the forest to put together for the audience the necessary information to help them understand events in the present.

However, this type of dramatic structure reflects the flexibility of indigenous African theatre in which the different realms, time schemes and events coexist with so much ease. The flexibility is such that one spot on the stage can become, without any physical change of scenery, a house now, a road, the forest, a playground, a bank, a stream, etc. Also, one actor can become five or more characters within a space of ten to fifteen minutes. This, of course, makes a lot of demand on the audience's willingness to accept what is being shown by suspending its disbelief. But this goes to prove the fact that actors and the audience, as well as the playwright, are conscious always of the theatricality of what is happening on stage. There is no attempt to pretend that the play is real, and because this is accepted by all participants, the dramatist is free to create and stretch the audience's imagination.

From the moment the flashbacks begin in *Old Story Time* the play becomes an endless series of shifts between the past and the present, and by the time the audience has travelled all that distance in time and space, all the hidden causes and effects, all the submerged motives and all the erstwhile loose nuts and bolts are tied up. Pa Ben takes his time in supplying his audience with information that will complete their knowledge - and his technique includes the 'use of interlocking images and details and also of transitional images' (Ben-Amos, 1977: 40-1) and hints which guide and link the action from one unrelated event to another. The total effect of this is that there is a unity of narrative and performance. The narrator merely drops bits of information which set up chains of association through the details, images and hints, and by the time action gets to the scene where an enraged Miss Aggy goes for George's jugular, all evidence has been presented to condemn the latter for all the evil things he did to her and members of her family.

Structures of Transition

The two East African plays, *The Trial of Dedan Kimathi* and *I'll Marry When I Want*, and the workshop plays from South Africa, such as *Woza Albert!* by Barney Simon, Percy Mtwa and Mbongeni Ngema and *Sizwe Bansi is Dead* by Athol Fugard, John Kani and Winston Ntshona, do not fall into either the ritual-dream or storytelling structures. However, they also use the cumulative associative mode of dramatic development. There are two ways of explaining this. The first is that underpinning all these plays is an essentially African non-linear narrative sensibility. Second is that by the nature of their history and development, African and African-Caribbean literary theatres are hybrid theatres, and like all hybrids, they are forms in transition still searching for their own voices and modes. This of course is also responsible for the high level of experimentation with dramatic forms, which characterise African and African-Caribbean dramaturgy. *The Trial of Dedan Kimathi*, *I'll Marry When I Want* and *Woza Albert!* will be discussed separately, not because they alone structurally reflect the creative tensions of hybridity and transition, but because they do not fit into the other two structures. However, they do combine features from these two as the section will show shortly.

Structurally, *The Trial of Dedan Kimathi* has the circular movement of action of the ritual plays. In some respect, it has the dream atmosphere of *Dream on Monkey Mountain*, but with a little less of the latter's convoluted drama. Its plot is non-linear; action unfolds, not in a series of causes and effects, but rather through a technique similar to the one used in *An Echo in the Bone*. Here the anchor image is the colonial court-room and the droning monotone of the judge repeatedly reading out the charges against Kimathi. This is the image which the play returns to from time to time, as the audience/reader returns to the barn in *An Echo in the Bone*, the prison cell in *Dream on Monkey Mountain*, and the roadside shack in *The Road*. The court-room provides a point of reference because it is central to the trial. The play is in three movements which in reality is a single movement, with the action breaking the barrier between formal and infinite time, so that past, present and future flow into one another. The scenes also flow into each other (wa Thiong'o and Mugo, 1976: 2). Like all the African and African-Caribbean plays a lot of use is made of flashbacks as a means of linking and explaining the non-linear structure. Again, in the play's plot there is a deliberate violation of normal time and space schemes to enable events and characters to coexist and inform one another, and to assume fuller significance only when all have been seen or heard.

The Trial of Dedan Kimathi is structured as series of trials, and each trial involves the central character, Dedan Kimathi, who is mainly the accused, but sometimes becomes judge and accuser, as in the trial of the traitors in the forest, or when he successfully makes Shaw Henderson and colonial law stand trial. Because the play is structured as a series of trials - there are six altogether which eventually lead up to the main trial of Dedan Kimathi by colonial law - the central image is the court-room to which the action returns since all events in the play lead to and end with the final trial and sentencing of Kimathi.

The play opens with a scene in the court-room as the presiding judge reads out the charge. This very brief scene is followed by the First Movement, consisting of a mimed scene of black African history that leads up to a final sequence of anti-colonial uprising, eventually transforming into real sung and danced action on the stage. The mime contains four sequences; these correspond to the four movements and also to the four internal trials of Kimathi in the play. The first sequence shows the betrayal of Africans by their chiefs, which leads to slavery. The same betrayal is going on in the present and has led to Kimathi's capture and impending trial. Sequence Two is about black African enslavement, which corresponds to colonisation brought about in part by further betrayal by Africans. The third sequence shows black overseers flogging the slaves in the same way that the third movement shows African traitors becoming watchmen and informants to white colonial masters. Sequence Four is the uprising which presages the final scene in the court after Kimathi's sentencing. The playwrights here skilfully build a dramatic structure that relies on cross-referencing and correspondences to put its meaning across. After the mimed scenes of past history, the action returns to the present, just a day or two before the trial as the police and their African collaborators round up the freedom fighters and other suspected villagers; then, there is a scene between Woman and Johnnie; between First Soldier and Second Soldier who discuss the capture of Kimathi and the commotion attending his impending trial; then enter Boy chasing Girl over money. The scene between Boy and Girl represents and gives validity to what Kimathi was fighting against - black people killing each other over crumbs from the coloniser's table. The pair then meet Woman who scolds him; then Boy and Woman meet alone and he is further drawn into the central action as a gun-carrier. All these encounters are on the street, just outside the court-room; the action then moves into the court-room where the charge is read out a second time. However, this time Kimathi makes his first appearance and proceeds to accuse colonial authority of illegality and highhandedness in its affairs in Kenya. This appearance helps to establish a conflict situation, and the next scene takes the action back onto the street where one encounters Fruit-seller, Boy and later, Girl. As yet, there is no discernable connection between these characters and the trial. In the major frame of the trial, Kimathi undergoes four internal temptations in his cell – reminiscent of the temptations of Christ – designed to make him betray the cause which he had espoused. Each temptation reveals something about Kimathi and about the struggle which he had come to personify. A fifth trial is organised by the freedom fighters against some of their ranks who had betrayed the cause. The purpose of the fifth trial, it appears, is to reveal Kimathi's basic humanness and the weakness that led to his capture. And it is after these trials that the final judgement is delivered.

Some of the action, especially the Kimathi and the Boy-Girl-Woman scenes, unfold in a manner that makes one feel as if they are watching two unrelated sequence of events. The only connecting thread is the frequent mention of Kimathi's name and his impending trial. And it is not until the storytelling scene when Woman begins to take Boy and Girl, and the audience, into the past that the jig-saw starts to fall into place – the identity of Woman is revealed, the costly mistake which Kimathi made which led to his capture, Woman's role and contribution to the freedom struggle, and the role she has chosen for Boy. All the frenetic activities of the past reveal themselves to be attempts to help Kimathi escape during his next appearance in the court-room. As in *A Dance of the*

Forests, a great deal of the action in *The Trial of Dedan Kimathi* is the preparation by all parties for the trial - each person, Woman, Girl, Boy, guards, Fruit-seller, Henderson, bankers, all are involved in the preparations for the big event. And in a characteristic cyclic manner, action begins in the court-room, travels all over the country, through the hills, valleys and forests, returning and ending where it began, in the court-room as judgement is delivered on Kimathi.

I'll Marry When I Want is unique in many respects. First, it is the result of a collaborative theatrical experiment by the Kamĩrĩĩthũ community on the one hand, and Ngũgĩ wa Thiong'o and Ngũgĩ wa Mĩriĩ on the other. And second, it makes use of a full complement of indigenous theatre and performance elements blended to create a loose but theatrically powerful dramatic structure. The play 'incorporates much song, dance and ritual from the people's shared tradition' (Cook and Okenimkpe, 1983: 168) and it also makes extensive use of mime and improvisation. By texture and composition, *I'll Marry When I Want* is a good example of a hybrid theatrical piece – what Balme (1999) refers to as 'syncretic theatre' – for it is both and yet it is beyond folk theatre and literary drama. It has been described as a play that borrows:

> from Mau Mau songs and celebration as well as from Christian church ceremony and hymns. The language flowers into proverbs and imagery. More than a quarter of the printed text involves singing and ceremonial forms (Cook and Okenimkpe, 1983: 168).

The play is a continuation of the experiment with content and form which was begun in *The Trial of Dedan Kimathi*. The play, according to Ngũgĩ wa Thiong'o and Ngũgĩ wa Mĩriĩ who recorded and transcribed it, originated as a draft outline which they had put together; this outline was later appropriated, modified and shaped by the Kamĩrĩĩthu community. The collective input is evident in the multi-layered theatrical modes which the play contains; this is matched by the abundance of rituals, songs and dances. *I'll Marry When I Want* is not intended as a play for reading since as a dramatic text it is not very strong; however, its strength is in performance when it comes to life because of the magnitude of its spectacle.

Like a folk theatre performance, it is not a 'well-made' play; in fact, it is more the creation of a free and uninhibited space for the crowd of dancers who fill the stage from time to time. The play effectively deploys a full range of indigenous theatre elements and techniques, especially mime, dance, choral singing, improvisation and swift transitions between the past and the present. These operate much in the same way rituals, dreams and the stories flashback to past scenes to enhance the action or embellish their narratives. For instance, if events in the present need clarification or amplification, scenes and characters from the past are brought up and in this way a present situation or character is given historical depth. Very often this technique is used to achieve contrast as when the scene of the traditional wedding ceremony contrasts and comments on the superficial and unnecessary Christian wedding which Kĩgũũnda and Wangeci were about to embark upon. There are other such contrasts as the play works by it a lot, with the central one being the contrast between Kĩgũũnda's and Kĩoi's homes, where the stark poverty of one stands accusingly against the overstuffed opulence of the other. Through this means, the theme of the play - which is that those who betrayed the struggle for independence are the very people who now enjoy the fruits - is subtly kept in focus throughout.

I'll Marry When I Want is in two parts and altogether they can be seen as making up an elaborate trap set by the Kĩoi family to ensnare Kĩgũũnda into surrendering his precious title deed and losing his daughter, Gathoni, in the process. The first part is like a slowly played out game of a hunter stalking his prey, with the section ending appropriately with Kĩoi, the angler throwing the bait and patiently feeding the line which the unsuspecting fish is already circling and nibbling at. Part Two is a well choreographed dance of the unwary fish as it debates whether or not to swallow the offered bait. Finally, Kĩgũũnda does, for the moment he agrees to the church wedding the audience knows that he and his family are utterly doomed. The play thus works well as an elaborately orchestrated hunting game, in which the hunter takes his time in the full knowledge that the victim had no chance of surviving. However, it is a game played through song and dance, ritual and mime; these elements are structurally vital since most of the time they are as much the vehicles of meaning as is the dialogue, which, one must point out, descends sometimes to the banality of revolutionary slogans and clichés.

The story in *Woza Albert!* unfolds as a structure of random images and snapshots of life for black people under apartheid. Like all the other plays already discussed, there is neither a single narrative nor are the characters developed in a conventional dramatic way; rather the two actors who devised the play with Barney Simon go through a series of characters, black and white, thereby providing a composite tapestry of life in South Africa during the apartheid era. The repressive and segregation policies of apartheid meant that mixed-race and mixed-cultural theatre was unlawful and because of that the workshop tradition emerged as an artistic response to a socio-political situation and in doing so created a thematically radical and subversive theatre style. By mixing the poor theatre techniques of Jerzy Grotowski (1968) and the flexible composite dramatic and narrative structure of indigenous African performance, the theatre makers created a theatre that was elusive and ultimately resistant to apartheid forces intent on silencing cultural and political opposition to the regime.

The play deals with the theme of what would happen if Morena (the Saviour) was to visit South Africa. Through this simple hypothetical question, the two performers take the audience through a breathtaking journey through South Africa - covering all races, classes, genders, ages and political persuasions. In the characters' reactions to this question, their expectations of what would or should happen were this visit to take place images of the different experiences of South African peoples are played out before the audience. The structure works as a panoramic sweep through the country, which covers everywhere and everybody - without any linearity but comprehensive and sometimes composite. Each scene is a mini play in its own right, hardly having any identifiable link with those immediately preceding or coming after it; the only link is the two actors who play all the characters. It is only when all scenes - some very short and made up of only a few lines - have been played out that the audience get a sense of the scope of the peoples and places covered within such a short period.

Chapter 7

INDIGENISATION, DOMESTICATION AND POSTCOLONIAL SUBJECTIVITY

Folk Elements in African and African-Caribbean Theatre

The uniqueness of African and African-Caribbean theatres derives from the fact that both incorporate a lot of folk theatre and performance elements. Having looked at plays from both regions, it is evident that an indigenous African or African-derived cosmological system provides the perspective and spatial envelope for action and characters. This cosmological system, shared by black peoples around the world, has over time generated its own folk forms for exploring and expressing the unique universe of African peoples. In exploring their worlds, African and African-Caribbean dramatists often search for forms that best accommodate the expansive and constantly shifting universe of Africans and peoples of African descent in the Caribbean; and by a curious consensus, they all tend to settle for the versatile and expansive forms of the indigenous performance repertoire. Of the various forms, which the African and African-Caribbean cosmological system has engendered, the dramatists favour mainly two – storytelling with its captivating theatricality and ritual theatre with its composite and symbolic mode of presentation. These two forms translate into two dramatic structures under which a majority of the plays from Africa and the Caribbean can be categorised; and these are the ritual-dream structure and narrative or storytelling theatre. The two, in turn, combine in varying degrees in plays depending on each playwright's material, theme and purpose. This means that the two structures are merely heuristic models for analysis; there are other models in which elements of both and others are combined. However, apart from combining these structures, the plays have other things in common; an underlying unifying characteristic being the freedom that playwrights exhibit in their dramatic plots. Significantly, they all shun linear plots in which action progresses strictly based on a principle of causality, in which events follow each other in an uninterrupted stream of inevitability. Aristotle's theory in *The Poetics* of a beginning, middle and an end does not operate in this context. Rather, in these plays action can begin anywhere and develop in any direction and in whatever order the playwright chooses. This, however, is not to say that African and African-Caribbean plays lack order or that they are very loosely structured. On the contrary, an inherent principle of organisation holds the plays together and this principle of cumulative association, this book argues, is a product of the African cosmological system from which these plays are conceived. Besides, the deliberate rejection of Aristotelian principles of drama is part of the process of liberating African and African-Caribbean theatre from an essentially Western dramatic mode of structuration.

African peoples (this includes all peoples of African descent) have a uniquely African mode of perceiving the world and this is based on what can best be described as an associative sensibility – a sensibility that refuses to be bound by beginnings or endings, or a compartmentalisation of human experience. Another major premise of this mode of perception is that nothing is perceived as complete or finished until seen and understood in relation to other things. Thus, one can only comprehend the full meaning of an event or phenomenon when one has seen all the possible and potential sides of that event or phenomenon. The Igbo people express this idea perfectly in the proverb of the dancing masquerade, which they believe can never be fully appreciated when viewed from only one spot. For the Igbo, the world is like a masquerade dancing and the spectator would need to change positions in order to get a better and more comprehensive view of the spectacle. Applied to the theatre, this means that the full significance and meaning of a play can never be known until the performance is over or the text is finished. With this notion of totality in mind, African and African-Caribbean dramatists construct plays guided by the principle of cumulative association or a process of accretion of ideas and images in which full comprehension only comes when the last image or idea has been received or perceived. This structural device owes, consciously or unconsciously, a debt to African folk theatre practices in which performances hardly have linear narrative plots or structures, but instead are often made up of a series of skits that may or may not have the same ideas or characters, and in which any of the skits can come in anywhere or at anytime in the performance. What determines the impact and meaning of a performance is the association which the collected skits call forth in the minds of the spectators. This means, in effect, that a performance must be conceived as a total or composite event. And one sees this as the principle on which so many of the African and African-Caribbean plays can be understood; and this is irrespective of whether they are structured as rituals, dreams, storytelling or improvisations. To achieve this unique sense of totality, the plays rely a lot on elements of the folk performance traditions, which easily lend themselves to manipulation by dramatists. These elements are: music, dance, mime, improvisation, multi-local action, heightened theatricality, all blended harmoniously to achieve a high degree of involvement of and/or participation by actors and spectators.

The concept of 'total theatre' applies to African and African-Caribbean theatre and is crucial for the realisation of the two structures, which this book explores. Total theatre is a term closely associated with indigenous African performance practices and implies a coming together of various art forms in a synthesis in which each is as vital as the other. Applied to contemporary African and African-Caribbean plays, total theatre would therefore mean an attempt to balance the emphasis between elements of theatre, like music, dance, mime, the plastic arts and dialogue, in a blend that is unique and fresh. In the main, African and African-Caribbean playwrights do not see theatre as just an art of speech as is the case in many Western European and North American theatre practices. This, however, is not to suggest that only Africans or Caribbean peoples of African descent believe in a theatre that is not built around dialogue; in fact, Japanese, Chinese, Indian and other Asian performance and theatre traditions are hardly dialogic. The fact, however, is that among Africans and peoples of African descent in the Caribbean, theatre is essentially an action and dialogue can be part of this but not its soul as it sometimes is in Western theatre traditions. Indigenous theatre and performance in Africa most times is not a vocal activity; rather, it relies more often on other expressive mediums like music, dance, mime, sometimes trance and possession, and the plastic arts. It is theatre, which communicates mainly through images, in which what is seen is more important than what is heard, and that is why it uses a lot of symbols.

Dance and Music

Dance and music are key structural elements in African and African-Caribbean plays – in fact, only very few plays from Africa or the Caribbean are without these two artistic and expressive mediums. When they are used, they are not just cosmetic since they contribute greatly to the texturing and structuring of the plays, as well as being very dependable codes of meaning in themselves. In fact, some plays, such as *A Dance of the Forests*, *An Echo in the Bone* and *Singuè Mura* are incomplete without dance and music. In *A Dance of the Forests*, for instance, the central event is, 'the dance of welcome for the dead', and around this there are others such as 'the dance of the Half-Child' and 'the dance of the Unwilling Sacrifice'. Together, these are structurally arranged events that become ciphers through which meaning is relayed in the play. The title of the play itself suggests the key role which dance plays as the central action, the dance of welcome for the returning dead to which all other actions in the play are directed. The drama itself is a dance and the series of minor dances are but preparations for the main one in the centre of the forest when the Half-Child is tossed around in a game between Eshuoro and his accomplices. It is obvious that at critical moments in most of Soyinka's plays, dance and music become the repositories and transmitters of meaning, more than what the characters say. This happens in the climactic central scene in *A Dance of the Forests* and shows that in the African world, music and dance are languages of action as some moments are utterly beyond the expressive capacities of words, and at such moments human beings go back to primordial sounds, echoes and movements which only music and the dancing body can capture, interpret and express.

The central conflict in *A Dance of the Forests* arises from the fact that, as the Dirge Man says, the living are not prepared to 'leave the dead some room to dance'. Soyinka carefully arranges the dances as the action moves gradually towards the centre of the forest where an explosion of dances by various characters occurs, each dance designed as an action conclusive by itself but acquires deeper significance only when seen in relation to the others. The 'dance of the Half-Child', for instance, looks unconnected to, say, 'the dance of the Unwilling Sacrifice', but it is because Demoke instinctively interrupts the dance of the child that Eshuoro is finally able to claim him. Demoke's dance as the unwilling sacrifice also brings to a climax the primal conflict between Ogun (Demoke's protector god) and Eshuoro (the god he has wronged by first chopping off his sacred tree and then killing the god's acolyte). Once these dances begin, little else is said as they sequentially constitute the 'welcome for the dead', the trial of the living, and the 'chorusing of the future and the unborn'. And it is only when they are done that judgment is pronounced and action resolved.

Dance is structurally central to *An Echo in the Bone*; it is used in a very sophisticated manner, almost in the same way that it is used in *The Road* and *I'll Marry When I Want*. In Scott's play, dance and music combine as a springboard into possession for Dreamboat, Rachel and Sonson. The possession scenes are very crucial to the development of the action in *An Echo in the Bone* because without them it would be difficult for the drama to move from the present into the past, a transition and knowledge without which the historical perspective necessary for an understanding of the present events would be lost. Also, apart from helping the action slip in and out of the past, possession is important because through it elements of the supernatural are inserted into the world of the play. The same is true of *The Road* where through possession, the spirit of Sergeant Burma is brought back by Samson to reveal the past and thereby giving a historical dimension to the theme of violent death on the road, as well as establishing Ogun's place and role in all this as the god of war, metal, the road and of the drivers who make a living on it.

The two plays are suffused with the aura of supernatural forces, the unseen but strongly felt presences in the plays. The hand of Ogun is felt throughout the happenings in *The Road*, but he is not fully felt until the moment in the final scene when the discarded mask comes to life again in its final dance of possession and dissolution. Equally, the frenzied jerks and bodily contortions of Dreamboat in *An Echo in the Bone* bring to the notice of the other characters, as well as the audience, the powerful presence of the dead who have arrived for the wake. Apart from its function as an aid to possession, dance is a necessary part of the rituals in both plays which have brought the characters together, and so it creates the required atmosphere, as well as propels the actions in the desired direction.

In *I'll Marry When I Want*, dance is similarly used to lead the action back into the past. The flashback scenes in particular are used to explain the long suffering of the poor in Kenya, as well as the foreign rape of their culture and resources. These ideas are contained in and expressed through the courtship and marriage dances between Gĩcaamba and Njooki. The Kĩgũũndas, who are in danger of losing touch with their culture by flirting with a foreign and apparently corrosive and domineering culture, watch the dances intended as a warning against the cultural and economic suicide which they were about to commit. But it's too late, however, because they are in the end beguiled by the new culture. Of significance though is how the dances are used to reinforce the dangers of cultural imperialism or economic exploitation; the songs of the Mau Mau freedom fighters, the ritual dances of the *Ngurario* wedding ceremony, and the *Mũcũng'wa* dance are expressive enough in themselves to articulate these conditions. Their richness in cultural symbolism and rootedness contrast sharply with the emptiness and artificiality of the church wedding Kĩgũũnda and Wangeci are trying to exchange them with.

But can it be claimed that dance and song function in contemporary African and African-Caribbean plays in the same way that they do in the folk theatres? The answer is yes and no. Yes, because in the indigenous theatre in which action and skits appear to be self-contained and unconnected, music and dance are used as linking devices as is illustrated by the Yoruba *Apidan* which Kacke Gotrick (1982) has studied and the *Enemma* performance (Okagbue, 1987, 2007) previously mentioned in this study. These elements make the indigenous theatre shows the unified performances which they turn out to be. And to a large extent, the dances in African and African-Caribbean theatre do the same. But then no, because dance and music do not just link the skits in the indigenous theatre, they, in fact, are the action and the drama. As a matter of fact, the skits cannot exist without the music and the dance.

In this respect then, it is mainly the West African plays such as *A Dance of the Forests, Death and the King's Horseman* (Soyinka), *Hopes of the Living Dead* (Rotimi), *Singuè Mura* and *La Puissance de Um* (Liking), *La Termitière* (*The Ant-hill*) and *La Guerre des Femmes* (*The War of the Women*) (both by Bernard Zadi Zaourou), and *I'll Marry When I Want* (to some degree) which use the two elements effectively and very much like in the folk theatre style. In Soyinka, in particular, at crucial moments the spoken word becomes inadequate as a vehicle for action, and at such moments action passes into dance and music which are the primal languages and echoes of the human soul under stress. Of the African-Caribbean playwrights, only Walcott approaches this level of complexity in his use of music and dance; this is evident in *Dream on Monkey Mountain*, especially in the opening dance scene between the mysterious figure of death and the gossamer figure of the silent dancer as both circle the symbolic disc of the moon and the sun. Unfortunately, Walcott does not extend this expressive dance language or sustain it as Soyinka does or as in *I'll Marry When I Want*. For other Caribbean dramatists of African descent, music and dance (the latter in particular) are useful but can be left out sometimes without impairment or impoverishment of the dramatic action. For Africans, dramatic action would be drab without music and dance, and this is one of those instances in which Africans at home and peoples of African descent in the diaspora differ in their expressive sensibilities. One suspects that this must be the result of the acculturation which has taken place in the Caribbean between the African cultures of the African slaves and the West European cultures of their masters.

Music does not always go with dance in the African-Caribbean plays, but on its own can stand and perform functions which are usually performed by dialogue. Walcott, for instance, uses music in a special way in his theatrical folktale, *Ti-Jean and his Brothers*, as a means of characterisation and for introducing the principal characters. Just as happens with *Bori* spirits, each character has a personal signature tune. The soft sad music of the flute is for the poor unfortunate mother who sits by and watches her children go off to do battle with the greedy Devil. The Devil and his entourage of obscenities are appropriately announced by or dance in to a 'crash of cymbals', shrieks and 'claps of thunder'. And when the first two sons, Gros-Jean and Mi-Jean, set out, they are accompanied across the stage by 'martial music, comic quatro' punctuated by a 'roll of drums'. The comic quatro points, of course, to their lack of intelligence, and also gives them a ludicrous appearance. A weird hard to define sound announces the emergence of the Bolom (suitable for his neither-nor character), but this soon changes to a crash of cymbals once the Bolom becomes the Devil's messenger of doom. There is therefore a conscious use of music in the play; a kind of soundscape in which no piece of sound or music is wasted as each is designed to contribute something to the play's overall meaning. Walcott arranges the music in such a way that it creates a pattern reflecting the progress and significance of the action, and when the individual pieces of music are grouped in opposition, they also reflect the play's binary opposition of good versus evil, honest innocence against devilish cunning. In a way therefore, music tells its own story in *Ti-Jean and his Brothers*, in much the same way that dance does in *A Dance of the Forests*.

In her plays, especially *Singuè Mura* and *La Puissance de Um*, Liking creates a soundscape which provides a textual backdrop and envelope in, and through which her characters navigate their ritual passage into knowledge of themselves and their societies. The soundscape also provides structure to the movements which is the dramatist's characteristic way of demarcating her scenes. The music often provides the overlaying ambiance for the ritual experience and purgation which her theatre performances are intended to achieve. The *kiyi mbock* which informs her theatre sensibility are female initiation rites from the Bassa culture of the Cameroon (her native country) and these rites are designed to transform young girls into women and mothers. Her plays are meant to emulate or acquire this transformative capacity. In a similar manner, Zaourou's use of the *didiga* (the hunter narratives) of the Bete people in Togo with its music means that in his drama, music is not cosmetic but is used as a structuring, expressive and interpretative device without which the drama would be flat. This is the case in *La Termitière* and *Les Guerre des Femmes*, two of Zaourou's best known plays. Zaourou explains the uniqueness of this indigenous form and his adaptation of it in his search for a uniquely African contemporary dramatic/theatrical form. Of the first play he writes:

> **La Guerre des Femmes** est un <<**Didiga**>>, c'est-à-dire un theater à vocation initiatique.... Comme nos contes et come nos mythes qui lui ont fourni l'essentiel de sa matière et des formes, comme nos grands rituals, elle est un mode de questionnment aussi bien pour l'acteur qui l'interprète que pour le public qui la decouvre...
> (*La Guerre des Femmes suivie de La Termitière*, p, 7).

> [*The War of the Women* is a Didiga, that is to say, an initiatory vocational theatre.... Like our stories and our myths which provided the bulk of its subject matter, its forms and major rituals, it is a way of questioning, both for the actor who plays and for the public to learn more... (my translation)].

Didiga is a specialised art form of the hunters and is a combination of the mythical, mystical, epic, mysterious, poetic, profane and sacred initiation music. Zaourou then describes how he adapts thess in his plays:

> A la base de cet art, un instrument de musique qui est un instrument parleur: dôdô, connu en français sous le nom d'arc musical.... Dans cette œuvre commes dans *la Termitière*, c'est l'arc musical qui assure la progression dramatique du récit et coordonne les différentes actions des personages centraux ou des scenes de foule.

> [At the base of this art is a musical instrument, a loud speaker: dôdô, known in French as the musical arc.... In this work, as in *La Termitière*, is the musical arc (dôdô) that ensures the progression of the narrative drama and coordinates the actions of the central characters or crowd scenes].
> (124-133)

Thus, music is a central element of African theatre, including the hybridised literary theatre of western educated African playwrights. One can argue that this insistence on and use of music as a structuring device and envelope for dramatic action is part of their postcolonial quest for an African identity that is neither enslaved by nor ashamed of its colonial experience.

A good storyteller relies a lot on music as it is an integral element of the art of indigenous African storytelling and its Caribbean offshoot. Pa Ben in *Old Story Time* does not forget to sing lustily in between his narration, nor does he forget to get his on-stage audience involved in the singing. The same applies to Storyteller and his pool of players in *The Marriage of Anansewa* in which the songs and the *mboguos* which they introduce are structural components of the story of George Kweku Ananse and the intricate web of deception which he spins around his daughter and the four chiefs. The songs in the plays, apart from complementing certain aspects of the stories, perform useful structural functions. In *Old Story Time*, they are used effectively a few times to entertain the audience while the actors change the set. In other words, the songs help to maintain the mood and tempo generated by the action in the story, while also acting as instructional work songs for the actors turned stagehands. Pa Ben leads the songs and through them directs his team on what to do, on where to place what and so on. The songs in *The Marriage of Anansewa* perform similar functions, as well as acting as linking agents between ideas and scenes. The other songs in *Old Story Time* perform a formulaic function which songs perform in indigenous storytelling theatre. A customary 'once upon a time. . .' song begins Pa Ben's narrative session and it is chanted in chorus by everybody. Its purpose is to announce the start of the storytelling session. In between, other songs feature as needed and directed by Pa Ben – the change of scene songs, songs to cheer Miss Aggy from her gloom, another song is used to characterise George as the 'sly mongoose' whose crime is widely known, and finally there is the ritual chant to free Miss Aggy's soul from the possible wrath of the angry spirits she had let loose. Again, as in *The Marriage of Anansewa*, *Singuè Mura* and *La Termitière*, the songs are not ornamental, rather they are part of the structuring and they contribute as much as the other elements of dialogue, dance, mime etc. to the total meaning of the play.

Although music is also used thematically in the East African plays, they hardly achieve the blended brilliance which they do in Soyinka or the other West African playwrights. Rotimi, for instance, achieves a magnificent integration in *Hopes of the Living Dead* in which the songs capture in detail the constantly shifting moods of despair, hope and joyous fulfilment of the characters. Songs feature prominently and work well in *I'll Marry When I Want* and *The Trial of Dedan Kimathi*, except that sometimes the music does not properly blend with the dramatic action and its purpose at such moments becomes a little too obvious and contrived for effect. The songs do not grow organically from the action as, say, the songs of hope of Harcourt Whyte and his fellow lepers as they contemplate and struggle for their utopian dream of a place of their own. In *I'll Marry When I Want*, in particular, there appears to be a conscious attempt to use music because it would be effective and not because it is the right idiom to use at that moment, and this, as has been pointed out earlier, is Soyinka's forte in *The Road, Death and the King's Horseman* and *A Dance of the Forests*. In these plays, his artistic sensibility is finely tuned to recognise and exploit such moments. Strictly speaking, the problem with the songs in *The Trial of Dedan Kimathi* and *I'll Marry When I Want* is that most of the pungent attacks on colonialism and neo-colonialism and the messages of unity and solidarity to the Kenyan peoples are contained in them and so inevitably the deliberateness takes the place of the spontaneity which characterises songs in the folk theatre. Thus, the conclusion is that the music in the Kenyan plays, although powerful in performance, draws attention to itself.

In Soyinka, as in Rotimi, Liking, Zaourou and a host of new generation West African dramatists (Osofisan and Sowande for example) there is a delicate blend of dance, music, mime and dialogue in the creation of an exciting dramatic structure. The elements are used as in indigenous African performance traditions. But it is also because they are combined in ways that are not purely folksy that Soyinka's dramas possess freshness and beauty for Nigerians and non-Nigerians alike. His plays have a strange familiarity which makes them compelling theatre, whether or not one understands the sometimes unfathomable metaphysical concerns explored in them. Soyinka's choreographic sense is such that in his theatre the dances are hardly separate because they are made to feed on the music, and both, as in moments in *A Dance of the Forests, The Road* and *Death and the King's Horseman*, become the only discernible activity going on in the play. For him, certain emotions, states of mind and ideas are beyond words; these have to be chanted or intoned or danced. It is a typical African expressive sensibility at work at such moments, and the moments are often the most powerful and intense times in his plays. The final scene in *The Road*, for instance, is a good example of such a moment of dramatic intensity – the scene when the interrupted dance of the killed *egungun* is resumed, right until the point when the frightened Say Tokyo Kid stabs Professor, is the most intense scene in the play. Once the dance begins, there are no words, only the dance and the music, and yet the meaning of the play is contained and revealed in this heightened moment. Another such scene is the series of dances in the forest during the welcome for the dead which eventually culminate in the vigorous dance of the Half-Child and then on to the dance of the Unwilling Sacrifice in *A Dance of the Forests*. It is to Soyinka's credit that he creates these moments of intense dramatic activity and feeling in his plays, and it is usually at moments like these that the notion of 'total theatre' becomes fully demonstrated. It is a concept which seems to have disappeared from the theatre sensibilities of the Caribbean playwrights, despite the hesitant groping towards it by Walcott and Scott. It is part of that sense of a partially lost origin which peoples of African descent in the diaspora have to faithfully recover, or else, their attempts would only amount to vague imitations of models from a distant African 'homeland' or as Walcott puts it, trying to invoke with the names of 'exotic gods' who do not answer.

In summary, African and African-Caribbean playwrights express a common world view born of sharing a unique metaphysical understanding and philosophy of the universe. Theirs is an expansive universe which allows a contiguous interrelationship between the past, present and future; between the dead, the living and the unborn; and finally between the world of the gods, humans and ancestors. In between these worlds is a chthonic realm, the gulf of transition. Crossing from one world to another often requires a rite of passage across this gulf and this explains the importance of rituals in African life because they provide humans with the tool and means of breaching the gulf of transition, of diminishing its danger and negotiating with the very powerful forces which guard the paths through it.

For theatre to encode and transmit such a world, it has to search for forms that are flexible enough to accommodate such an immense and constantly changing universe with its contradictions. In searching for forms to use, African and African-Caribbean dramatists, perhaps, because of a shared though tenuous ancestry and expressive sensibility, settle for two basic forms derived from the indigenous folk traditions of Africa – the storytelling theatre and ritual-dream theatre. These two forms in various combinations generate structures that can at times admit of the fantastic and the impossible, the real and unreal. With these structures, the improbable tales are not so improbable anymore and when successfully used, the structures seem well suited to the content which they express. And in most cases, to understand and appreciate the latter, one needs to unpack the former to reveal patterns each dramatist has created, and it is through a structural analysis of this kind that one is able to unearth the meanings of the plays.

Chapter 8

LANGUAGE AND IDENTITY IN AFRICAN AND AFRICAN-CARIBBEAN THEATRE

The Master's Language: Anglophone and Francophone

My first introduction to African-Caribbean theatre was in 1982 when I read *Dream on Monkey Mountain*. What struck me most about the play was its language, but also striking was the underlying but undeniable African presence which bounced back at me from every page as I heard, in my mind's ear, the characters speak. Africa was the source; it was also the imagined landscape in the distant horizon on the other side of the Atlantic calling to and resonating in her children from across the centuries. I was particularly struck by the strange and yet familiar rhythm and resonance of the language of *Dream on Monkey Mountain*, a dialect which seemed to be an exotic but a lexically and semantically enriched version of the pidgin English of my Nigerian society. It was as if Makak and his companions spoke of their racial anguish and longing for Africa in a language which I understood ver well because this strange language excited in me an echo of recognition and identification. Thus was born my curiosity and what has turned out to be an abiding interest in African-Caribbean cultures and theatre. And having explored the cultural, thematic and stylistic similarities between African theatre and its African-Caribbean counterpart, I feel it is fitting to devote sometime and space to an exploration of that language bond which first attracted me. Besides, it is my view that language is an important element in the theatre and therefore needs a special treatment. It is also crucial to do this because language is very central to the discourse and politics of identity within situations of enslavement, colonialism and post-colonialism which African and African-Caribbean peoples have experienced over the past four hundred years and which is the focus of this study. The book will trace the source of this language similarity and identification between Africa and its Caribbean diaspora.

The first contact between African languages (mainly West African) took place around the 15th Century, and it happened in the context of trade. Africans and Europeans needed a language to facilitate trade between them, and the contact language which emerged in response to this need was a form of pidgin based on borrowings from African and

European languages. This was a language which had evolved out of a mutual need, a contact language that was not native to any of the groups who used it. The Africans had and still have their specific ethnic mother-tongues and so had the Europeans. However, slavery, and later colonialism, altered all that by tilting the balance in the contact in favour of European languages so as to reflect the master-slave and the coloniser-colonised relationships between Europeans and Africans in the two eras. Whereas during the trade contact, Africans had made the choice to use a contact language in dealing with Europeans while retaining their ethnic languages, the situation was entirely different for the unfortunate African slaves in the Caribbean. They had no choice but to master or acquire a bit of the language of the master since that was the best way of surviving and rising to a tolerable social level in the slave and colonial social structure of the New World. The process through which European languages such as English, French, Portuguese, Dutch and Spanish became the compulsory languages of contact between Africans and Europeans was a carefully orchestrated one which began during slavery and continued into the colonial period.

One of the strategies used to achieve the dominance of European languages during trans-Atlantic slavery was, as long as it was economically possible, to keep people from the same area or ethnic group apart because it was considered dangerous to have those who shared a language staying together. So, part of the process of breaking in the new slaves was to make sure that each new arrival was deprived of the use of his or her native tongue, and the result was that over time, an atrophying process set in because a language is only able to survive and grow through use. And of course, in the absence of other people to speak his or her language with, the slave had to use the only available medium of communication with fellow slaves, and the master's language was handy, and soon was handled and 'mangled' into shape to facilitate communication. However, significantly with the loss of their language began for the slaves also the process that led to the loss of identity which was a central feature of the slave experience in the Caribbean and North America. Language is a tool for self-definition and this being the case, the slave, and subsequently their descendants, were forced into defining themselves in the languages of their masters and thus being reduced to a perpetual state of alienation.

The Africans brought to the New World could lie down at night and reflect on life in their own languages (Roberts, 1988: 122), but in the day they would have had to go out and confront reality in the master's languages; and the reality of the slave society had decreed that only those who were better at acquiring the rudiments of the master's language had any chance of a tolerable life. It is hardly surprising that the desire to be able to communicate in the dominant European languages of the places of their enslavement was strong on the part of the African slaves. And through them, their children had inherited, not an African language of their ancestors, not a pure European language of the oppressors, but a hybrid language and hence the 'dialect' (English) or 'patois' (French), which is a further creolisation of the pidgins which their parents had developed, either in Africa, on the slave ships or when they arrived in the New World. To a large extent, the prediction of one of the slaves on the ship in *An Echo in the Bone* that: 'If we stay here longer, we'll learn to speak the same tongue. All the tribe. Of Dahomey' (in *Plays for Today*, p, 89), eventually comes true. Forms of dialect and patois have since become the uniform and undisputed mother tongues throughout the Caribbean.

Colonisation achieved a similar result by imposing a language (the coloniser's) on the colonised, but it never succeeded in wiping out the indigenous languages of African peoples. However, it managed to elevate the West European languages of the colonisers into the national languages of the colonies. Thus, the Berlin Conference of 1884 was a glotto-political act which divided Africa into the different languages of the colonising European powers. The result of this act has since become part of the 'burden' or 'boon' inherited by most African nations at independence – that is to say that although there was political independence in the fifties, sixties, seventies, eighties and nineties, there is still today a language bondage reflected in the lingering divisions and accompanying allegiances of Anglophone, Francophone and Lusophone Africa and the Caribbean.

The reason for the successful imposition or rather the easy acceptance of Western languages by colonised African peoples has been attributed to the existence of numerous languages within most of the arbitrarily created geographical and national boundaries in the continent. Thus, one of the great ironies of the African colonial experience was that languages of oppression and subjugation such as English, French and Portuguese, came to be accepted as neutral languages which could unite the various ethnic groups and peoples of each colony and between ethnic groups across boundaries under the same colonial authority such as Great Britain and France. A country like Nigeria, with nearly four hundred ethnic languages has Igbo, Yoruba and Hausa as the dominant languages, but everyone recognises that it would be politically explosive and naïve to suggest any of the three as a national language without invoking the lurking phobia of ethnic domination which has remained the bane of Nigerian politics. And yet, English is seen as neutral and has remained, in spite of the fact that it is the language of colonisation and bondage; in spite also of the fact that the domination of a people's language by that of the colonising power was crucial in the domination of the mental universe of the colonised (see Ngũgĩ wa Thiong'o, 1986:16). One other outcome of the language situation was the creation and continued polarisation of African and Caribbean peoples between Anglophone, Francophone and Lusophone – with the result that these language zones still control and or dictate intellectual, educational and cultural traffic and affiliations between African states in particular. In West Africa, for instance, the Francophone countries associate more with each other and with France, the Anglophone with themselves and with the United Kingdom, while those of the Lusophone look toward each other and to Portugal. However, this book is not concerned so much with the cultural implications of the historical accident that was colonialism as it is with exploring what the former slaves and colonised have been able to make of the linguistic boon that was part of the slave and colonial experiences and heritage of Africans and African-Caribbean peoples.

Evidence suggest that a majority of the slaves who crossed the Atlantic to the New World came principally from the Gulf of Guinea and the stretch between the Bights of Benin and Biafra; the slaves also came from two main linguistic families of the West African coast – notably, the Kwa and Mande language groups (see Roberts, 1988: 112-3). This book will reveal the linguistic implications of this later on when it examines the consequent creolisations which occurred between these languages on the one hand, and English, French, Portuguese and Spanish respectively on the other. It will also look at the comparative duplication and spread of syncretism on both sides of the Atlantic.

Through slavery, peoples of African descent in the Caribbean inherited European languages, first through their inter-language variants which were pidgins and creoles, and through a further process of creolisation, the present dialects and patois which have become the first languages of Caribbean peoples. Interestingly, this is the language of much of Caribbean theatre while Caribbean Standard English and French (CSE and CSF) remain the official languages of education, politics, and international exchange. And in Africa, the Africans inherited English, French and Portuguese pidgins, but these have remained inter-languages because of the existence and continued use of indigenous African languages, while African Standard English and French (ASE and ASF) are the main languages of instruction, politics and international exchange. The pidgins, however, are also powerful languages for inter-ethnic exchange among the uneducated populations within and sometimes beyond national boundaries. Thus, not only do black peoples in the Caribbean diaspora and those in Africa share some cultural similarities as a result of African survivals in the New World, they also share a common heritage of imposed alien tongues.

In acquiring these alien tongues on both sides of the Atlantic, however, it has been obvious that one of

the major limitations on achievement in second language learning is that the learners seldom achieve native speaker competence in the target language, especially in its phonology. In the learner's language the native language surfaces sporadically and unpredictably, sometimes in situations of stress (Roberts, 1988: 121).

This has been responsible for the gradual evolution of a form of African and African-Caribbean English or French through a process of phonological and syntactical domestication of English and French by African and the Caribbean peoples of African descent. The effect of this act of domestication is also evident in the 'Black' English of African-Americans. This explains the unmistakable similarity between the 'dialect' and 'patois' of African-Caribbean plays and the pidgins in Africa, these being languages written as spoken and which are therefore very refreshing and dramatically realistic and effective as markers of African and African-Caribbean identities.

Mastering the Master: Hybridity and Identity

Just as the slaves had to be broken in by their masters when they arrived in the New World, the Africans attempted right from the first contact to break in the European languages in order to make them conform and more malleable to their African palates. This process occurred out of choice on the African continent but was a necessity for the slaves in the New World. The process is described by a righteously enraged character in Ishmael Reed's novel, *Mumbo Jumbo*, who sees nothing, but sacrilege and profanity in what the slaves were doing to his precious English language:

Son, these niggers writing. Profaning our sacred words. Taking them from us and beating them in the anvil of Boogie-Woogie, putting their black hands on them so that they shine like burnished amulets. Taking our words, son, these filthy niggers and using them like they were their god-given pussy (quoted in Gates, 1984: 1).

This, however, is part of the story of domestication, a process that is becoming more deliberate and sophisticated as Chinua Achebe points out while defending his attempt to tame and use English as his language of choice in his novels:

> The price a world language must be prepared to pay is submission to many different kinds of use. The African writer should aim to use English in a way that brings out his message best without altering the language to the extent that its value as a medium of international exchange will be lost. He should aim at fashioning out an English which is at once universal and able to carry his peculiar experience.... But it will have to be a new English, still in full communion with its ancestral home but altered to suit its new African surroundings (1975: 61-2).

The result of this alteration is the educated African Englishes and varieties of French one finds in African novels, poems and plays. But does this too account for the West African Pidgins (WAP), *français de Mousa* or *français de Treichville* (the street French of Abidjan in the Ivory Coast), *nouchi* (a French slang spoken by gangs in Abidjan), *kamtok* in Cameroon, the Caribbean Dialect (CD), Caribbean Patois (CP) and their relationship to the original English or French which the Africans had come into contact with?

One feels that in the formation of the pidgins, dialect and patois, the alteration went far beyond the subtle experiments which Achebe and others like Soyinka, John Pepper Clark-Bekederemo, Césaire, Ndao, Dadie, Ama Ata Aidoo, Zaourou, Thierno Ba, Rotimi, Gabriel Okara and Efua Sutherland carry out in their works. The formation of the pidgins, patois and dialect involved a far more radical alteration in the lexical, phonological and syntactical structures of the European languages. Pidgin, patois, varieties of French and African Englishes can be better understood in the light of this observation by Cook:

> ... there are English-speaking Africans... who are 'taking the white man's language, dislocating his syntax, recharging his words with new strengths and sometimes with new meanings before hauling them back in his teeth, while upsetting his self-righteous complacency and clichés ... (quoted by Gilliam in Harrison and Trabasso, 1976: 100).

Collectively, these efforts are attempts to domesticate European languages, to temper their phraseologies so that they become attuned to the African ear and mouth, and more able to carry the full weight of the black and African experience. Significantly though, these were also political acts that enabled the colonised and enslaved to take hold of one of the major instruments of oppression, master it through disfigurement and then turn it against the oppressor who becomes estranged from the new language. To master the language was a way of getting the knowledge of the culture of the oppressor, thereby upsetting the desire for knowledge and power over the other, which Edward Said (1978) argues was one of the major assumptions on which the imperial project was based. The pidgins, creoles, dialects were not intended as bastardisations of the masters' languages, rather they were meant to be new languages which sometimes succeeded in excluding and alienating the master.

Attention will now turn to these 'blackened' Englishes and varieties of French in African and African-Caribbean plays in order to find out which features of African languages went into the process of domestication and also to see if it is African linguistic features which explain the remarkable likeness between African pidgins and Caribbean dialect and patois, and between varieties of African Standard English or French and Caribbean Standard English and French.

Levels of Domestication

Domestication has produced various levels and types of language usage in Africa and the Caribbean. There are three levels of domestication and all three are fairly well represented in the plays. The first level is the inter-language level that produced the English and French pidgins found throughout Africa, from the Cameroon to the Gambia and Senegal, and from the Congo to Zimbabwe and South Africa. One finds the pidgin, for instance, in plays such as Soyinka's *The Road*, *Death and the King's Horseman*, *The Trials of Brother Jero*, Rotimi's *Ovonramwen Nogbaisi*, *Hopes of the Living Dead*, and *If...* Many other writers use ranges of pidgin in their plays but the study will concentrate on the plays mentioned above. It is surprising though that it is mostly Nigerian and Cameroonian playwrights who represent pidgin (*kamtok*, Cameroon pidgin which has both French and English versions) speaking characters, while Ghanaian playwrights such as Aidoo and Sutherland, Kenyan and South African dramatists do not create any pidgin-speaking characters (the latter though have some *Tsotsiaal* speaking characters – *tsotsiaal* is a towship slang derived from Bantu languages and English and Afrikaans). It is even more surprising in Ghanaian plays given that the Ghanaian society that a play like *The Marriage of Anansewa* depicts is as multi-ethnic as the Lagos of *The Trials of Brother Jero* or the Port Harcourt of *Hopes of the Living Dead*. This is not intended as a criticism of the playwrights since it is possible that the characters speak indigenous African languages which the playwrights then translate into standard Ghanaian English. Pidgins though are a part of any modern urban African society and their inclusion, in my view, gives a realistic and representative feel to plays in which they are used.

Broadly speaking, pidgin may be characterised as a language that is nobody's native language. It often arises in contact situations where speakers of mutually unintelligible languages come together as social subordinates to a socially dominant group who speak yet another language (see Traugott In Harrison and Trabasso, 1976: 59), as the slaves were in the plantations of the Caribbean and North America. Generally, pidgins and patois do not display complex sentence structures or extensive vocabulary; rather they show an ingenious employment of limited structures to express complex relations. They often have 'a vocabulary that is related to one or more of the languages of the dominant or superstrate group and a grammar more closely related to one or more socially subordinate or substrate languages'(60). It is this aspect of pidgin that is of interest to this book, which is particularly keen to trace the African contribution to the grammar of both pidgins and dialects as this is part of the African heritage of black peoples on the two sides of the Atlantic.

From what has been said above about the evolution of pidgins, it would therefore imply that the lexicon was borrowed from the superstrate languages, in this case English and French, while the grammatical structures and phonology came from the various West African languages of the Niger-Congo family. The Kwa sub-family which provided most of the slaves is made up of the following languages: Akan, Bassa, Baule, Bete, Edo, Efik, Ewe, Fanti, Fon, Ga, Igbo, Ijaw, Twi and Yoruba, among others. Despite their apparent mutual unintelligibility, these languages share similar phonological and syntactic structures. It was thus easy for syntactically and phonologically similar pidgins to emerge from the contact between the speakers of these West African languages and those who spoke English or French. It would not be easy, for instance, to identify the correct ethnic origin of say a character like Chume in *The Trials of Brother Jero*, Samson in *The Road* or Betty in *If …* by the kind of pidgin they speak since they could be Yoruba, Igbo, Edo, or even Akan, Fanti or Ewe.

The second level of domestication, the kind found in Caribbean plays, is domestication that has progressed into a post-pidgin continuum. This is a second stage domestication of the pidgin which may have originated on the West African coasts, on the slave ships, or as in most cases, a pidgin developed in the Caribbean by the slaves who had not acquired any pidgin before becoming enslaved. A good example of this is the group of slaves in *An Echo in the Bone* who obviously are speaking their indigenous West African languages which Scott translates into an Africanised English, as this speech from one of them shows:

> But a chief's son learns easily how to make the best of things. I will tell you. Once the house is empty, what happens to it is of no importance. I saw your woman. When they loosed the chain, she fell on her face onto the ground, and they dragged her with her mouth open through the shit we lie in, and took her away. Do not weep for her, my brother. She tasted nothing (90).

This speech is quite distinct from the prevalent dialect of the ritual scenes in the barn, and it is also different from the Standard 'British' English of the two shipmates as they discuss their investments and hopes. It is possible that Scott tries to show through the occasional gestures of incomprehension that his slave characters are, in fact, speaking in their own mother tongues, even though some of the languages may be intelligible to other people. One of the slaves actually speaks what must be the beginnings of a pidgin when she says – 'he worse than me' (the kind of 'bad English' spoken by Joseph, the Pilkings' houseboy in *Death and the King's Horseman*) – and it is obvious the others do not understand her. However, between the characters there is the desire to communicate with one another, so as to be able to comfort one another. The speech quoted previously shows characteristics of an African language speech, especially when rendered into English – a tendency for metaphorical phraseology, short sentences which attempt to balance one another, and the attempt to yoke clauses which gives the long sentences a looped and slightly lilting structure and cadence.

As already pointed out, very many slaves who spoke a variety of African languages were transported to the Caribbean. Very few of them had much contact with Europeans, especially the field slaves, and so the most pressing problem for them was how to communicate with one another, rather than with their masters and their families. This explains why the pidgins they evolved owe a lot more to African languages than to the European languages. The result is that this pidgin or patois was similar to the one which had evolved in West Africa because it too was 'a simplified form of communication, its vocabulary was small, very few grammatical rules, lost inflectional endings and speakers relied heavily on gestures' to provide meaning (Edwards, 1986: 40).

However, if the situation which gave rise to a pidgin remained stable, important developments usually take place in subsequent generations as the pidgin gradually develops into a *creole*. The latter, in time, becomes a language of its own as 'whereas pidginization is marked by simplification, the hallmark of creolization is elaboration' (40). This difference between pidgin and *creole* is very evident in African and Caribbean plays. Whereas the pidgin speakers in the African plays appear to the audience or reader as persons struggling to communicate using a limited vocabulary, as Chume, for instance, appears compared to his verbally assured chatterbox of a wife, Amope, in Soyinka's *The Trials of Brother Jero* or Sergeant Amusa and Joseph in comparison to the lyrically philosophical Iyaloja or the pithy and poetic Elesin in *Death and the King's Horseman*, the creole (dialect and patois) speakers in the African-Caribbean plays are quite articulate and comfortable in their world. In fact, they are more fully developed than the Standard English or French speakers, who often appear as caricatures of real people – such as Jean in *Meeting*; this again is where the African characters differ from the Caribbean ones as the opposite is the case. The one dimensional and stiff Basil, who represents the character of Death in *Dream on Monkey Mountain*, speaks a formal kind of English and thus appears out of place in the world of the play, and so is Corporal Lestrade when he is being officious. Len in *Old Story Time*, on the other hand, is saved from this by his frequent code-switching, as through this the audience/reader is able to see that beneath the veneer of Europeanness resides a comfortable hybrid postcolonial African-Caribbean person.

A pidgin, by nature, allows for only limited communication, whereas a creole, with a greatly expanded lexicon and grammatical structure, is capable of fulfilling all the speaker's linguistic and expressive needs. Creole (dialect or patois) is the native language of the Caribbean, with national varieties as will become evident when we look at plays, such as Matura's *Meetings, Dream on Monkey Mountain, Ti-Jean and His Brothers, An Echo in the Bone, Old Story Time* and *Redemption Song*, with their Trinidadian dialect, St Lucian patois, Jamaican and Montserrat dialects respectively. At another linguistic remove, however, is Walcott's *O*

Babylon!, a play about a Rastafarian community fighting against the oppression and exclusion of Babylon. The language of the latter play is generously spiced with 'rasta talk' or what has been referred to as the 'emperor's "Iyaric"' (Pollard in Örlach and Holm, 1986: 159); it is the emperor's iyaric because Rastafarians believe in the godhead of Ethiopean Emperor Haile Selassie and their predilection for the phono-semantic properties and possibilities of the letter 'I'. On the whole though, Rastafarian language is a dialectal innovation in the primarily English lexicon and the West African derived grammar of the Jamaican creole which the Rastafarians found inadequate in articulating and expressing 'the religious, social, cultural and philosophical positions' which they wish to reflect in opposition to Babylon (Pollard, 1986: 157).

There is no doubt that both West African pidgin and Caribbean dialect – the latter with all its variants – owe their grammatical and phonological structures to indigenous languages of West Africa. This, one supposes, must have been responsible for the similarity and strange echo of recognition which I felt when I first read *Dream on Monkey Mountain* which is written in dialect, the same echo which the Guyanese linguist, Van Sertima, had had on reading Gullah folktales for the first time (Sertima in Harrison and Trabasso, 1976: 123).

Third level domestication produced the new standard Englishes which have become part of colonial and slave histories and legacies. These varieties of English are also the result of English having become an international language and for which it pays the price of use and 'abuse' in so many different ways, in different parts of the world. The same is true of the French language which is second only to the English language in international currency. French has also undergone different disfigurements and modifications to suit different contexts and users. This has therefore given rise to varieties of English and French, of which the African Standard English and French (ASE and ASF) and the Caribbean Standard English and French (CSE and CSF) respectively are just examples. However, within these broad categories, there are national varieties, such as the Nigerian Standard English (NSE), Ivorian Standard French (ISF), Kenyan Standard English (KSE), South African Standard English (SASE), Ghanaian Standard English (GSE), Senegalese Standard French (SSF), Martinican Standard French (MSF), Jamaican Standard English (JSE), St Lucian Standard English (SLSE), Barbadian Standard English (BSE) and Trinidadian Standard English (TSE). Cameroon has Standard English (CSE) and French (CASF).

However, these national varieties share a homogeneity in the morpho-syntactic and phonological structures of the native languages which influence all the Englishes and French spoken along the West African coasts and other parts of Africa, with the result that it is possible that the same elements which form the core of the first language interference occur in the way characters like Elesin in *Death and the King's Horseman* and Anowa in *Anowa*, Brother Jero in *The Trials of Brother Jero* and Ananse in *The Marriage of Anansewa*, or Banji in *If...*, Kimathi and Woman in *The Trial of Dedan Kimathi*, Singué Mura in *Singué Mura*, Hilun or Ngond Libii in *Le Puissance d'Um*, Dona Beatrice in *Béatrice du Congo* or King Albouri or Prince Laobe Penda in *L'Exil d'Albouri* phonologically and syntactically render English or French. As Bohamba points out with regard to English in Africa:

> These Englishes share certain properties that can be identified as Africanisms, in that they reflect structural characteristics of African languages. Specifically, these properties can be discovered at all linguistic levels – phonological, morphological, semantic and syntactic (in Kachru, 1982: 78).

The same can be said of French in Africa because the same first language influence also creates similar Africanisms in the French spoken in Africa whose peculiarities include lexical modifications such as the presence of words which do not exist in Standard French; words given meanings different from their standard French ones or the tendency among educated African French speaker to go for hypercorrect speech which makes the characters sound conservative and old fashioned. Combined, these domesticating acts give a distinct flavour to the French of sub-Sahara Africa (see Emmanuel Kwoffie, 1976); thus, there is a distinctly Ivorian (mainly Abidjan) French, apart from the *nouchi* or *Francais de Mousa*, which are forms of pidgin French. In Nigeria, Dapo Adelugba (1978: 216) coined the term *Yorubanenglish* to refer to this flavouring.

Except in the question of personal style, there is not much difference between the English used in Aidoo's *Anowa* and that used by Soyinka in *The Trials of Brother Jero* or Rotimi in *If...*, or between Sutherland in *The Marriage of Anansewa* and Rotimi or Soyinka in *Hopes of the Living Dead* and *A Dance of the Forests* respectively. The only difference may be a matter of style; while most of Soyinka is in verse, the others seem to prefer straight everyday prose. But there is something definitely African in all the characters' speeches, and this Africanness, this book argues, results from a deliberate colouring of the sentences with Yoruba and Fanti speech features, such as the timely and apt use of proverbs, the peculiar African imagery which dances through the lines, and other key structural and rhetorical features of African discourse and language use. And it is in this respect that Caribbean Standard Englishes differ from the West African Standard Englishes. The reason for this is not far to seek.

For where indigenous African languages provide the influence on the rendering of the educated West African English which Aidoo, Soyinka, Rotimi and Sutherland give their characters, the Caribbean educated English of Scott, Rhone, Matura, Walcott and White are two removes from the original African languages which had influenced the pidgin and subsequent dialect/patois which now provide the first language interference for the educated Caribbean person of African descent writing or speaking English. It is not surprising therefore that one is able to identify West African language features in the speech of a Caribbean character, such as when Miss B in *Redemption Song* uses a proverb to drive her point home to Verity. However, Miss B's speech lacks the customary colour and vibrancy of African proverbs, it is a rather watered down version though still powerfully meaningful and apt in the context in which it is used. But sometimes these features and influences are so difficult to identify, even though the echo of similarity is unmistakable. A similar difference exists between the French of Césaire in *Une tempête*, *Une Saison au Congo*, *La Tragédie du Roi Christophe*, Ina Césaire's *Mémoires d' isles: Maman N et Maman F* (*Island Memories*), Marise Condé's plays and the bulk of Francophone African plays in which the direct influence of African languages colour and flavour the French differently from the creole influenced French of the African-Caribbean dramatists.

Most of the major African writers, at one point or another, have commented on the deliberate effort to Africanise English and French in their works. Rotimi, for instance, sees domestication as essentially involving a tempering of the foreignness of the English language through deliberate but skilful restructuring and manipulation of phraseology that owes a lot to his native Yoruba speech patterns. As Adelugba sums up:

> Rotimi is creating a new language which is neither exclusively English nor Yoruba but a mixture of both. At the middle of an English sentence Rotimi can introduce a Yoruba exclamation, greeting, or speech tag, as occasion dictates (1978: 214).

This is an experiment which began with his first major play, *The Gods are not to Blame*, and went on throughout his writing, culminating in his bold use of as many as fifteen Nigerian languages side by side with his own authorial African transliterated English, that of his English speaking characters and the pidgin speeches in *Hopes of the Living Dead*.

Wole Soyinka, without question, is a master in the creation of an English that is colourfully African, but 'still in full communion with its ancestral home' (Achebe, 1975: 61-2) in England. Awoonor summarises Soyinka's achievement in fashioning an English that is Yoruba in its imagery, syntax and flavour:

> I read Soyinka and have a feeling that he is not exactly writing English – he's got a hybrid of Yoruba strength which is married to English which he uses very well. . . (in Duerden and Pieterse, 1972: 34).

It is correct to affirm that in the works of Soyinka there is a deliberate and sustained effort to give a distinctly Yoruba colouration to English and this is achieved, either through choice of expression, of insults like the string of them which issue forth from Amokpe's mouth in *The Trials of Brother Jero*, from Oba Danlola in *Kongi's Harvest*, and from Murette in *A Dance of the Forests*; but more ambitiously he successfully renders in English some traditional Yoruba poetic diction and rhythm of speech, the type one finds in *Death and the King's Horseman*, and the traditional saws of Oba Danlola. This is the strongest feature of Soyinka's dramaturgy in *Death and the King's Horseman*, his linguistic masterpiece, and in which Elesin Oba and his praise-singer hypnotise the audience with their exquisite verbal display modelled on traditional Yoruba *oriki* chants (praise poetry). Of equal lyrical beauty are the Danlola lines in *Kongi's Harvest* as he laments the world being swept away by Kongi's new autocratic dispensation. But in the ritual scenes in *A Dance of the Forests*, Soyinka's poetry actually reaches sublime heights in metaphorical and image-laden lines such as:

> Red is the pit of the sun's entrails, and I
> who light the crannies of the bole
> Would speak, but shadows veil the eye
> That pierces with the thorn. I know the stole
> That warms the shoulders of the Moon
> But this is not its shadow. And I trace
> No course that leaves a cloud. The sun cries Noon
> Whose hand is it that covers up his face! (*A Dance of the Forests*, p, 76)

What lines of poetry can surpass these or the hauntingly soporific reminders of a noble life from Praise-singer to a somnabulant Elesin Oba, whose dancing feet are already touching those of the dead as he treads his passage across the gulf of transition in *Death and the King's Horseman*? In these lines, Soyinka successfully enriches his idiom and imagery by drawing heavily from his traditional Yoruba sources and the product is the kind of English which must have prompted Penelope Gilliatt to say of a production of *The Road* at the Commonwealth Arts Festival, that Soyinka,

> has done for our napping language what brigand dramatists from Ireland have done for centuries; looted it awake, rifled its pockets and scattered the loot into the middle of next week. (in *The Observer*, London 1965 reproduced on the covers of both *A Dance of the Forests, Kongi's Harvest* and *The Road*)

The Nigerian writers are not alone in this effort to Africanise English and French languages, for the same process of hybridisation is at work in the plays of Aidoo and Sutherland from Ghana, Ngũgĩ wa Thiong'o, Micere Mugo, Ngũgĩ wa Mĩriĩ from Kenya, and Francophone dramatists, such as Cheik Ndao, Bernard Dadie, Werewere Liking, Zadi Zaourou, Zenoufou Zinsou, Birago Diop, Thierno Ba and Jean Pliya, and also in the workshop plays of Fugard, Kani, Ntshona, Mtwa, Simon, Ngema which display influences of indigenous African languages and township slang. These playwrights people their plays with characters whose language registers are coloured by speech patterns borrowed from the numerous languages of Ghana, Kenya, South Africa, Senegal, the Ivory Coast and Benin respectively.

This, however, is more evident in some dramatists than in others. For instance, it is easier to notice experimentation in Aidoo than it is in Sutherland, although the latter's *The Marriage of Anansewa* remains a fine example of a play cast in the indigenous mould, both in form and content. In the play, the most prominent speeches which show a closeness to indigenous Ghanaian languages are Ananse 'sugary' letters to the four chiefs to entice them to send him money and gifts to 'oil the wheel of custom', and also his laments when his scheme goes awry and he is compelled to stage a fake funeral for the 'dead' Anansewa. Aidoo's two plays, *Anowa* and *The Dilemma of a Ghost*, especially the former, show a rendering into English of speeches from the vernacular while retaining as much of the native flavour as possible without obscuring the meanings and feelings intended. Thus, Aidoo is able to create an English which can be traced to her native Fanti linguistic heritage, but which because Fanti shares with other languages of the Kwa language sub-family the same syntactical and phonological structures can easily be identified as belonging to the West African region. Ato, a central character in *The Dilemma of a Ghost*, could well be any educated West African speaking to either his American-born wife or to his uneducated relatives. And the characters in *Anowa* are definitely Fanti speakers who know no English, so whatever English they speak is a product of the translation, transliteration and transmutation by Aidoo herself. The same can be said of the 'French' speech of King Albouri and the entire court in Ndao's *L'Exil d'Albouri* – the speeches are coloured by the dramatist's native tongue in the same way that Iyaloja's or Elesin's English belongs to Soyinka their creator as he translates/transliterates their Yoruba into English. So also is Woman in *The Trial of Dedan Kimathi*, who must be a Kikuyu speaker, and, in fact, speaks occasionally without being translated by the dramatists. Invariably, it is the playwright's competence that accounts for the effectiveness or otherwise of the translation, because it is at the level of the playwright that the first language interference occurs and is subsequently transferred to the characters.

Studies show that in the acquisition and use of a second language, there is always an unconscious interference from the speaker's first language. In all cases, the speakers of a second language bring from their mother tongues internalised linguistic systems of enormous complexity which ultimately play a significant role in the way they handle the new language. This happened with Africans who inherited European languages as 'national' languages. So, playwrights who wish to translate the African vernacular of their characters into English or French exhibit a first language interference and this raises a question of whether they can convincingly create non-African characters since these too are products and subject to the same first language interference. Even when playwirghts are not translating native African language speakers, the languages of their non-native characters can never in all cases be free of the African flavour – that, in effect, their non-Africans end up speaking as Africans speak. Good examples of this are Jane and Simon Pilkings in *Death and the King's Horseman*, Henderson, Scottish farmer and Indian in *The Trial of Dedan Kimathi*, the Europeans in *Béatrice du Congo*.

In the case of Jane and Simon Pilkings in *Death and the King's Horseman*, for example, although they are not Yoruba speakers, neither are they, strictly speaking, English-English speakers. Even Simon, the most British and English of the characters adopts a very African use of proverb and circumlocution in Scene Five during his heart-to-heart talk with Elesin in prison:

I have lived among you long enough to learn a few sayings or two. One came to mind tonight when I stepped into the market and saw what was going on. You were surrounded by those who egged you on with songs and praises. I thought, are these not the same people who say: the elder grimly approaches heaven and you ask him to bear your greetings yonder, do you really think he makes the journey willingly? (*Death and the King's Horseman*: 206-7)

Simon is not so insensitive and impervious after all that the flavour and spirit of his African environment leave him untouched; in fact, he is a good example of the contamination that underpins postcolonial notions of hybridity. However, Soyinka is still able to maintain a remarkable difference between his African and non-African speakers because the Simon-Jane scenes are nowhere near or similar in emotional intensity and verbal virtuosity to the Iyaloja-Elesin or Elesin-Praise-Singer scenes; it doe not even come close to the Olunde-Jane scene, the latter coming midway between the African scenes and the non-African ones. However, Simon's speech above sounds African nonetheless and this is simply because it is written by an African who exhibits an unconscious avoidance of consonant clusters which is often a distinguishing characteristic of nativised African English. Thus, because he avoids the clusters Simon sounds more African than English or European, despite Soyinka's attempts to the contrary. Even the French of the Europeans in Dadie's play syntactically sound like their African counterparts because the dramatist's French can only be an African French.

For Caribbean peoples of African descent, on the other hand, their first language interference comes from dialect or patois, their mother tongues. For the original slaves, however, the process of second language acquisition would have been similar to that on the West African homeland, in which case, they would have evolved pidgins similar in both phonological and syntactical structures to those which developed in West Africa, and later a variety of Standard English or Standard French which share syntactic structures and phonological elements with the Standard French or English of educated Africans. This latter point is more likely and to an extent is supported by the peculiar similarities in the use of English between, for instance, in *An Echo in the Bone* in Dennis Scott's translation of the dialogue of his West African vernacular speaking slaves and Aidoo in *Anowa,* and also the seeming likeness between Samson's pidgin in Soyinka's *The Road* and Bramble's creole in White's *Redemption Song*. In both plays certain words such as 'di', 'de', 'wey' and other features like the missing copulas, the absence of possessive and plural markers, as well as the presence of peculiar forms of verb inflections are characteristic features; all deriving from structures and phonology of indigenous West African languages. These similarities occur because, as Roberts highlights:

> Interlanguage transfer or heavy dependence on native language implies that in the case of the Africans, whether on the West coast of Africa, or in the early days of slavery in the Caribbean, or those late arrivals in the Caribbean, their language, as they attempted to learn English, was dominated by features of West African languages (1988: 117).

Similarly, because of the interlanguage transfer educated Caribbean peoples of African descent when speaking English or French experience interference from the creolised dialect or patois, their native or first language. There is a lot of evidence from the plays to support this. Len in *Old Story Time*, for instance, who throughout the play tries to stick to speaking educated Standard English, often makes the occasional slip into dialect whenever he is intensely worked up, especially during arguments with his mother. In *Dream on Monkey Mountain*, Corporal Lestrade and his assistants in the mock court scene have patois intrusions into their speeches which they obviously intend to be in formal Standard English to reflect the legal roles they are playing. Even white characters, such as Master Charles in *An Echo in the Bone* and George in *Old Story Time* do not escape these linguistic slips as both freely code-switch between creole and standard. Three reasons can be suggested for the creole interference.

For Len, it is a psychological response to intense pressure and anger. People, in general, tend to fall back on their native tongues when angry, when lacking in confidence, or when they have their backs to the wall. For Lestrade, Tigre and Souris, the first language interference occurs when they suddenly forget that they are playing the role of judges in a court of law. Their role as judges of course requires them to speak formal Standard English, however, their limited competence makes it difficult for them to sustain such a demanding performance and they occasionally get carried away. Walcott, in fact, draws much comedy out of this because the audience is made aware that the three characters are not competent in the language and as soon as the impostors begin to enjoy themselves in the roles, the dialect surfaces as it is the language natural to them, one which they are most comfortable in. And for George and Master Charles, however, one can argue that it is interference and deliberate code-switching; but both are still psychological responses to situations in which the characters find themselves. In situations in which

George and Master Charles revert to dialect, both men are desperate to win the confidence of the listener and such an attitude bears out Edward's (1986) observation that the use of dialect or patois in the Caribbean was widespread (serving almost as a national language), even among educated speakers of Caribbean English or French, and that,

> ... like the local languages, and to some extent the pidgins and Krio in Africa, it signifies for its speakers a feeling of belonging, of shared local beliefs and images (Edwards, 1986: 19).

Creole - dialect and patois - in the Caribbean, as native (first) languages, are markers of identity and people use it to show they belong. However, speaking dialect or patois as George and Charles do also cynically reflects a tendency which characterised slave and colonial speech relationships; between slave and master and between colonised and coloniser. It can be argued that these two white characters choose to, as it were, come down to the level of their black and socially inferior interlocutors so as to enable the latter who it is assumed have not mastered or cannot cope with the complexities of Standard English because they do not speak it. This response too is psychological and is explained well by Fanon:

> A white man addressing a Negro behaves exactly like an adult with a child and starts smirking, whispering, patronizing, cozening.... Talking to Negroes in this way gets down to their level, it puts them at ease, it is an effort to make them understand us, it reassures them (1967: 31-2).

And listening to George talk to Miss Aggy at the bank or Charles trying to come down to Rachel's level is symptomatic of this attitude which is a carry-over from slavery. Charles still sees himself as the master who must get whatever he desires from his slaves, and George knows he can talk his black into doing whatever he wants her to do. Both, however, still play on the idea of associating with their black compatriots/interlocutors as a means of getting what they want from them.

The intrusion of creolisms into the speech of educated African-Caribbean peoples may also, according to Edwards, be a product of a post-creole continuum where because of the continuing contact between Creole and English or French, a process of decreolisation is already taking place (1986: 40). The result of this is that there is a linking of the broadest variety of the Creole with the local standard variety of English or French. This, one supposes, explains the mixed speeches of characters such as Lestrade in *Dream on Monkey Mountain*, Legion in *Redemption Song*, and all the other educated characters in *Old Story Time* who experience first language intrusions and interference.

Having looked at the shared origin and development of pidgins, creoles (dialect and patois) and varieties of Standard English and French in West Africa and the Caribbean, it is clear that these languages evolved out of situations of contact between West African languages and European languages. It also was evident that in the formation of these varieties, the mode of combination had been to base a greater proportion of the lexicon on English or French while the phonology and syntactic structures came from the West African languages. The lexical items which were extracted from the European languages provided the European speakers an ease of entry into the pidgin or creole, while the altered grammatical structure and phonology made the foreign languages easy to speak and understand for the West Africans. It is thus clear that domestication began from the earliest contact and not just the efforts of literary artists of recent years

But does the fact that pidgin, dialect and patois, and African Standard English and French and Caribbean Standard English and French at their base all have features of English or French and African languages point to similarities, say, between dialect or patois and the various pidgins in Africa, or between African Standard and Caribbean Standard? I feel it does, but more especially between pidgin and dialect as my own experience on first reading dialect in *Dream on Monkey Mountain* shows or patois as Van Sertima's experience indicates:

> I for one, coming from the coastlands of Guyana in South America, have never met a Gullah Negro from South Carolina or the Georgia Coast. A vast ocean lies between us which we have hardly crossed, my Gullah brother and I, since the days of the middle passage. Yet when I read Gullah in the folktales... something turns on in me like a second ear, something reechoes the words and structures of that dialect within me like a submerged speaker and tongue. What you may ask is that something? What is really moving and playing, like a drummer in shadow, behind me? (1976: 123).

Being fluent in pidgin myself and also having a West African language as my first language, I had been struck by the very strong similarity in the phonology and syntax of the languages which I spoke in Nigeria and the patois of the St Lucian characters in *Dream on Monkey Mountain* and the dialect of the other characters in the many other Caribbean plays that I subsequently read. When I heard Pa Ben in *Old Story Time* begin his story with the words: 'Evening one and all.

Everybody hearty? What happen? You people mouth join church or what.... Make yourselves comfortable on them nice chairs'(8), I could almost take him for a Nigerian from another ethnic group telling me a story in pidgin because he does not speak my native tongue. I could read and understand these characters as if they spoke one of my two languages. So, what then are the elements that unite me to the Caribbean characters, to the *français Mousa* and *kamtok* speakers in Abidjan and Yaounde respectively, and all of us to our Gullah brothers and sisters of South Carolina and Georgia?

The first feature which struck me about pidgin and dialect was the phonological similarity reflected in the pronunciation of certain consonant and vowel sounds, and which in turn affects the way these words or the sounds representing them are written. Two key sounds – the ð and θ English sounds, as in 'the' and 'thief' respectively - will help to illustrate the point being made here. West African languages, in general, do not have these two sounds in their phonetic schemes and so, in their place, West African speakers of English, even the very highly educated ones, tend to go for the closest substitute sounds available in their languages, these being the **d** and **t** sounds respectively. One can only conclude that it is this kind of substitution which must have occurred in the formation of pidgin and dialect subsequently. It is not surprising therefore to come across lines like these in a Caribbean play:

Mooma, don't cry
Your son in **de** jail a'ready
I pass by **de** police station
Nobody to sign **de** bail bond (*Dream*: 213);

or Lestrade admonishing Souris with '**Dat**, you mange-ridden felon, is **de** King of Africa'. And Tigre tells his cellmate who complains that his hand had been broken by the angry corporal – 'Well, you can't **t'hief** again' – which obviously signals a difficulty in dealing with the θ sound in the word 'thief'. Walcott separates the 't' and 'h' by an apostrophe to indicate that just the first sound is heard or the two must be made distinct, and as his character is supposed to speak in a formal register and so he goes for the 'hypercorrect' pronunciation. These lines display some of the characterising features of dialect and pidgin, and it is present in Betty, the most consistent pidgin speaker in Rotimi's *If...*, who constantly makes a similar substitution in lines such as: **Di ting** way una take belle talk, way una **tink** say I no hear... (5). In Betty's speech, there is use of both the **d** and θ in one sentence. Betty also uses the word 'una' (to mean 'you' plural) which could have come from the Igbo word *unu* (meaning you plural), and one comes across 'una' a few times and a few more African sounding words in the Caribbean dialect speech of some of the characters.

However, it seems linguistically at least, that these characters can swap places between plays. But because the other phonological peculiarities of pidgin and dialect can be appreciated fully only in the spoken form, and also because the playwrights, even the linguistically accomplished ones like Soyinka and Walcott, show levels of inconsistency in their respective rendering and use of pidgin or patois, it is difficult to analyse these features in detail. With Walcott, however, there is occasionally a conscious effort to represent the dialect sounds on paper as one would imagine them being uttered by his characters or as real Caribbean peoples would speak them. He does this remarkably well in *O'Babylon!* with words like **bwoy, gyal, cyan't, lickle** for 'boy', 'girl', 'can't' and 'little' respectively. Soyinka writes more or less an educated pidgin which in any case is acceptable since there is not as yet a standard orthography of Nigerian or any of the other West African pidgins such as *francais Mousa* or *kamtok*. One doubts if there is yet a standard orthography of Caribbean dialects or patois.

One feels, though, that the playwrights, both the West Africans and the Caribbean ones, should make more effort to write the sounds, and with some consistency, because in the theatre the spoken is more important than the written and the task of the playwrights is made easier because they have the actor to help them realise their lines of dialogue on stage. One suspects that it is a realisation of this which must have prompted Roberts to write that:

> ... the playwright in a certain sense has a less difficult task (than the fiction writer) from the point of view of language because actors have liberties in converting the text to speech. The West Indian playwright then does not necessarily have to be fastidious in his orthographic representation, except to the extent that he is aware that plays are also treated as books to be read (1988: 146-7).

The same freedom applies to the West African playwrights who write pidgin. Soyinka's is definitely different from Rotimi's, both in the spelling of some common words and also in grammar. Even Rotimi's pidgin changes from one play to another, sometimes the pidgin degenerates into an unnecessary exoticism as one moves from the really good pidgin used in *If...* and *Hopes of the Living Dead* to the almost unintelligible one in

Ovonramwen Nogbaisi. And even then, the pidgin used in *If...* differs grammatically and phonologically from that used in *Hopes of the Living Dead*. This is not meant as a criticism of Rotimi as there is a recognition here that it is only from attempts such as these that a much needed standardised orthography for Nigerian pidgin will emerge, and perhaps some day one can have Samson from *The Road* speaking the same language as Betty or Adigha in *If...* or Sergeant Amusa in *Death and King's Horseman*.

Because of the lack of any orthography for pidgin and dialect (patois), the focus of the study will be on the syntactic features of pidgin and dialect which show similarity, uniformity and consistency. The aim is to find out what debt both languages owe to the grammatical structures of the West African languages they were formed from. Sertima's observation on the nature of Black speech in North America is very relevant here. He points out that:

> ... since it is true that the main vocabulary of American blacks is non-African, the crucial African element to watch is not vocabulary at all, but a grammatical base, a syntactical structure. It is the African structure underlying the top layer Anglo-Saxon words which accounts for the peculiar combinations, patterns, and transformations in the speech of peoples as far apart as the Guyanese of South America, the Gambians of West Africa, and the Gullahs of Georgia (1976: 127).

This study agrees completely with this observation because it is this underlying African base which is responsible for the echo of recognition mentioned previously.

The distinguishing features of African pidgins and Caribbean creoles derived from West African languages can be summed up as follows:

- usually short verb-centred sentences which rely more on finite verbs
- there usually is a noticeable absence of possessive as well as plural markers
- tense usually is never marked by any change in the inflection of the verb
- use of predicative adjectives to function as the verb and predicate of sentences
- a peculiar form of serial verb construction is a feature of the syntax of pidgin and dialect where there is the occurrence of two or more verbs in a clause or sentence without intervening conjunctions
- an absence of copula

- occasional use of the double superlative.

There are many others, including the avoidance of consonant clusters in English pidgins, creoles, as well as in English standards pointed out earlier, but those listed above are the key features which anyone familiar with West African languages cannot fail to identify, and it is these that account for the similarity between the various languages derived from the mixing of African with European languages in slave and colonial contexts on either side of the Atlantic. As already highlighted, dialect and patois are, in fact, the result of the creolisations of what must have been African inspired French and English pidgins, and so are merely elaborations of their grammatical and lexical structures.

But even if one were able to use the features above to explain or establish the close resemblance between pidgin, dialect and patois, it is not so easy to establish a similar closeness between African Standard English and French and Caribbean Standard English and French. It won't be out of place, however, to argue that since dialect and patois are syntactically derived from West African language based pidgins, that the Standard English or French production of Caribbean peoples of African descent with the inevitable interlanguage interference and transfers from dialect or patois should bear a resemblance to the Standard English or French of West Africans. The plays, however, do not support this argument since both the educated English and French speakers and the native language speakers from both regions appear quite different from each other in their speech patterns. This may best be explained as being the result of a process of attenuation brought about by time and distance. This means, in effect, that the residual West African languages' features which get transferred through dialect or patois into Standard English or French speech generally lack the purity, force and freshness which writers like Soyinka or Aidoo or Dadie or Ndao or Liking, who are still close to and rooted in Yoruba, Fanti, Baule, Wolof or Bassa, can transfer from these first languages into the English or French that their native and educated African speaking characters use. Thus, Walcott's powerful praise-chant to Makak in *Dream on Monkey Mountain* (reminds one of Ananse's praise oration to the chiefs in *The Marriage of Anansewa*), with its African style phrasing and intended mode of delivery, cannot match Ananse in full verbal flight as he pays 'homage' to the chiefs:

> These are the conquests of Makak
> King of Limpopo, eye of Zambezi, blazing spear…
> Who has bundled the tribes like broken sticks…

Who has scattered his enemies like grain in the wind…
Drinkers of milk from the Mountains of the Moon.
Who has held captivity captive,
Who has brindled the wind,
Who has fathered the brood of the crocodile.
Whose eyes is the sun,
Whose plate is the moon at its full,
Whose sword is the moon in its crescent
(*Dream on Monkey Mountain*, p, 308-9).

What is missing in Lestrade's speech is the absence of the supporting philosophical system which informs Ananse's speech and eulogy; a similar speech system underpins the pithy and earthy Yorubanness of Soyinka's dialogue in lines such as these from *Death and the King's Horseman*:

Who would deny your reputation, snake-on-the-loose in dark passages of the market! Bed-bug who wages war on the mat and receives the thanks of the vanquished! When caught with his bride's own sister he protested – but I was only prostrating myself to her as becomes a grateful in-law. Hunter who carries his powder-horn on the hips and fires crouching or standing… (158).

But having said that, the fact that these, including Walcott's, belong to a recognisable tradition of African praise-singing testifies to the African cultural influence on both African and African-Caribbean writers. The only distinction, however, being that the proverbs, the gnomic sayings, the riddles and verve that are peculiarly African and present in Soyinka, Dadie, Ndao, Rotimi, Sutherland, Aidoo and Liking, are missing from the works of their Caribbean counterparts, and where there are suggestions of them they seem to have shed the colourful pithiness of the African proverbs and other speech features. This arguably is the price paid for the time and space which have intervened between Africa and her diasporas. Besides, the African dramatists do not have the post-creole continuum effect that narrowed the distance between dialect or patois speakers like Miss Aggy, Pa Ben, Makak, Bramble and the Standard English or French speakers like Len, Lois, Mrs Power, George, Master Charles, Toussaint l'Overture, Christophé, Dessailine (the last three from Césaire's *La Roi du Christophé*). On the other hand, the distance between Elesin and Iyaloja (*Death and the King's Horseman*), Ananse (*The Marriage of Anasewa*), Albouri (*L'Exil d'Albouri*), Dona Béatrice (*Béatrice du Congo*) or Ngond Libii (*Le Puissance de Um*) and Simon Pilkings (*Death and the King's*

Horseman), Superintendent (*Hopes of the Living Dead*) is remarkable and there is hardly any cross-over or bridge between their registers; moreover, the usual ease with which code-switching or code-mixing occur among the Caribbean characters is absent in the African characters, who as a rule stick to one register, with the exception of the linguistically dexterous Samson in *The Road* who moves effortlessly between pidgin and a native language.

Language and Characterisation

Theatre principally relies on language for its effectiveness, and language plays a significant role in African and African-Caribbean theatres because of their postcoloniality. In general, African and African-Caribbean playwrights use language in many ways to localise character and setting; however, they also use language registers as markers of identity. African dramatists through domestication create levels of language usage which they manipulate to achieve two major theatrical objectives – to contextualise their plays and as a means of distinguishing between categories of characters. The same principle also guides Caribbean playwrights in their use of language; it is significant that African-Caribbean plays are mostly in dialect or patois. The importance of language in Caribbean literature as a whole is well captured by Roberts:

> West Indian literature, reflecting as it does the life of the West Indian classes, colonialism and racial injustice, has language in primary focus. Language is both the artistic medium and part of the subject matter. The writer therefore has to manage language in such a way as to show distinctions between generations, racial groups, social groups, religious groups, the educated, the uneducated and the pretentious parvenus (1988: 143).

Although not applicable to African theatre completely, some aspects of Roberts' statement are evident in African theatre. Language in African and African-Caribbean theatres is a powerful instrument for character differentiation, especially since in the theatre language as spoken is far more important than language as written. African-Caribbean playwrights show an awareness of this in how they distribute language registers to correspond to characters' social types and levels.

Trevor Rhone's use of language in *Old Story Time* has already been mentioned. In the play he creates two groups of characters who represent, rather loosely, two distinct Caribbean social classes – an upper class which includes Len, Lois, George and Margaret who speak Jamaican Standard, and a lower class which includes Miss Aggy, Pa Ben and Pearl, who speak dialect (creole). Thus in the play class identity is also marked as a linguistic identity. But for dramatic effect and also in order to achieve a psychological deepening of character, the playwright makes Len and George slip in and out of dialect at appropriate moments. Through this clever use of language mixing and code-switching, Rhone is able to reflect in a realistic manner the complex web of social relationships which characterise Jamaican society – the language and code of behaviour between individuals and between social groups and races. The same principle underpins Walcott's deployment of language registers in *Dream on Monkey Mountain,* a play in which all the characters speak patois, except for the vacillating and officious Lestrade who in his capacity as the city's police corporal has to maintain a 'formal' language register in keeping with his authority. His language has to be different, even though his African sensibility nudges him to speak patois, the language of the majority in his mainly homogeneous St Lucian society. Walcott, however, draws much comedy out of the fact that Lestrade cannot keep up a sustained flow of Standard English speech, since he is not a highly educated public official - a classic pretentious parvenu – desperately trying to rise above his normal language competence because he feels he needs to use a formal register in order to successfully impress his authority on his prison wards.

In Lestrade's speeches, especially the longer ones, there is constant first language interference as the syntactical and phonological structures of dialect play havoc with his lofty aim of maintaining formal speech; this forms part of his characterisation as a bumbling officious police corporal. The tension between the two languages represents the crisis of identity that Lestrade is experiencing as a mixed-race person who is not sure of which of his ancestral identities to adopt. His preference, it is obvious, is for his white European ancestry whose language he clings to, but his African identity refuses to let him be by successfully tripping him up at crucial moments and making him look like a fool before the prisoners, Tigre and Souris. Thus, one can see that Walcott uses Lestrade to explore the crisis of identity which is a major feature of Caribbean life and society. One also gets the impression from the play that Walcott implies that the crisis of identity which Caribbean peoples suffer is also a crisis of language. The Caribbean person, like Lestrade in his speeches in the early part of the forest scenes, tries to speak all languages – patois, French, English, Swahili, Urdu, Igbo, Papiamento – but speaks none well. The

Caribbean person is therefore a mulatto of language as well, which is the central crisis that almost drives Lestrade insane. But he is not alone. In these scenes, Lestrade's struggles reflect an internal dilemma which comes out in his language which fluctuates desperately between patois and standard. But, like Makak, Lestrade finds himself and a language only when he accepts that he is of African-Caribbean descent too:

> Was that my voice? My voice. O God, I have become what I mocked. I always was, I always was. Makak! Makak! Forgive me old father (*Dream on Monkey Mountain*,p, 300).

At this point in the play, his voice becomes one with those of the others and there is no more code-switching or mixing between patois and Standard English. Other Caribbean dramatists explore pretty much the same theme, although not in the same complex symbolic way that Walcott does in *Dream on Monkey Mountain*.

Of all the Caribbean playwrights, Dennis Scott in *An Echo in the Bone* comes closest to the language experiments of his African counterparts in the way he translates the speeches of the slaves into English, and in his attempt to create a separate register for the white slave traders, as well as the dialect of the slave descendants who are gathered in the barn for the wake. His experiment works well dramatically as it helps to set these groups of characters apart. But above all, the value of the experiment is that it helps the playwright to economically delineate the large scope and canvas of the world of the play. Scott's dramatic action and structure require in performance a recycling of characters and actors and it is only through this kind of language manipulation to achieve differentiation that he is able to carry the audience with him through the numerous transitions that take place in the play: from the present to the past, from the slave ship off the coast of West Africa to a barn in Jamaica where the ritual wake is taking place. It is a bold experiment designed to task the elocutionary resourcefulness of actors – some of them are actually required to travel back and forth between the three language ranges, from an African language in English to dialect, and from dialect to Standard English.

What Scott does in the play in terms of translation and creation of levels of language is comparable to what Soyinka does in *Death and the King's Horseman* and Rotimi in *Ovonramwen Nogbaisi*. In the Nigerian plays, there are African language speakers, pidgin speakers, West African Standard English speakers and speakers of English-English. This is also similar to the registers used by Ndao in *L'Exil d'Albouri* to reflect the broad spectrum of characters, from Albouri, Samba, Prince Laobé Penda, the queen, the king's sister and mother and other native speakers who speak Wolof to the governor's envoy who speaks French-French. The same can be said of Dadie in *Béatrice du Congo*, a play which has an equally wide array of characters demanding different registers. In Soyinka, these distinctions are clearly marked because the usually pithy, proverb-suffused and lyrically hypnotic lines of Elesin, Praise-singer and Iyaloja contrast sharply with the matter-of-fact, economical and direct and almost clinical register of the Pilkings, Aide-de-Camp and Resident. In between these two are placed the Yoruba educated English of Olunde, the uneducated 'bad' English of Joseph and the 'foreigner's' pidgin of Sergeant Amusa. There is no doubt that the Elesin group and the Simon group speak two different languages, just as there is no doubt that the group represented by Dona Béatrice, the Mani Congo and Le Nganga and the other group represented by Henri, Lopez, Lapoudre and Bonnechère also speak two different languages. Both Béatrice and the king spice their sentences with proverbs and other pithy sayings such as this exchange between the king and Dona Béatrice:

Le Roi:	… Le bouc même parfumé sentira toujours le bouc. La terre appartient à Dieu; le chrétien étant fils de Dieu, il est partout chez lui et peut donc en tout lieu déposer sa fortune
Dona Béatrice:	Non! Ne me bousculez pas. Il est temps qu'on vous crache la vérité en face.
Le Roi:	Enfin, savez-vous que vous parlez à votre roi, roi de par la grace de Dieu?
Dona Béatrice:	Roi de par la grace des Bitandais… Vous cracher la vérité en face… Il y a les chrétiens qui vivent couchés sur les lois, festoyent sur le lois, et les autres, tous les autres qui attendant la resurrection couchés sous la dale des lois… de vos lois… Ah! S'il fallait tout vous dire… (*Béatrice du Congo*, page 89)

[King:	The goat will always have the scent of a goat. The earth belongs to God; the Christian is the son of God, he is at home everywhere …
Dona Béatrice:	No! Do not push me aside. It's time one spat the truth to your face.
King:	Finally, do you know that you are speaking to your king, king by the grace of God?
Dona Béatrice:	King by the grace of the Bitandis…. To spit the opposite truth to your face… There are the Christians who live

> sleeping on the laws, been feasting on the laws, and the
> others, all the others who wait for the resurrection
> sleeping under the paving stone of the laws... of your
> laws... Ah! If that was everything necessary to say to
> you...

(my translation)]

On the other hand, the register of the Europeans is direct as they avoid the typical African embellishments, although Dadie tries to write in French embellishments for them instead. But like Soyinka, he too can not escape his first language interference in this exercise. Of the African-Caribbean plays, *An Echo in the Bone* is the most African inspired, both in its form and in its handling of language because it alone contains native African characters in the persons of the slaves on the slave ships and the play is structured like an African possession ritual ceremony and wake-keeping . Scott successfully creates different registers for all these groups of characters.

Another notable experiment in language is Walcott's bold and largely successful attempt to capture the language of Jamaican Rastafarians in *O Babylon!*. There are three language groups in the play – the African-Caribbean characters who are not Rastafarians speak plain dialect, the agents of Babylon speak Jamaican Standard English, and the Rastafarians themselves use *Rasta* talk, also known as the emperor's *Iyaric*. Walcott successfully centralises the conflict in the play in the opposition and tension between the language of Babylon and the *Iyaric* of the Rastafari. Dialect, as spoken by Rude Bwoy and Dolores Hope, stands in-between these two contesting modes of expression and being and in a way suggests that those characters who speak dialect are caught in a no-man's land. As characters, in relation to the central conflict in the play, they remain nebulous and hard to pin down to any specific idea or theme; they remain ambivalent personages throughout the play, never developing beyond who they were when they first appear.

Rasta language lexically, phonologically and occasionally syntactically, marks a deviation from, as well as a radical innovation in Jamaican Creole and Walcott acknowledges that it is a unique language which, to be understood, requires total conversion into and submission to the spiritual thought, linguistic philosophy and the practicalities of Rastafarianism. The emperor's Iyaric is a language for initiates and its sole purpose is to defy, mystify and exclude intruders from Babylon. As well as the physical symbol of the dreadlocks, Rasta language is one major marker of identity for Rastafarians. Of the group and its language, Walcott writes:

> The Rastafari have invented a grammar and a syntax which immune them from the seductions of Babylon, an oral poetry which requires translation into the language of the oppressor. To translate is to betray. My theatre language is, in effect, an adaptation and, for clarity's sake, filtered (*O Babylon!*, p, 156).

The Rastafarians retain the flavour and core rhythm of Jamaican dialect speech, but at the same time they stretch the individual words and concepts to give them new and startling meanings. The letter 'I' bears most of the brunt of this treatment as it is twisted and turned to achieve highly unimaginable but refreshing semantical combinations. Thus, one comes across a statement like 'I-and- I shall hide him' which means 'we shall hide him' in *O Babylon!*. They use other words in very strange and unexpected ways, such as 'me write a-next song' or 'with four next-rasta-man', where 'next' can mean either 'another' or 'other'. Of course, the absence of a plural marker is evident in 'four next-rasta-man' where the word 'man' retains its singular while its plural meaning is established by the word 'four' and the context – the absence of a plural marker is definitely borrowed from dialect and from African languages.

Another feature of the language is that the Rastafarians borrow extensively from the Bible, but having done that, they proceed to creatively twist and subvert the biblical materials by pressing them into newer and often diametrically opposed contexts and meanings that are in keeping only with Rastafarian philosophy and intention. Dolly, who stubbornly refuses to accept Rasta doctrine and language, disparages them thus:

> Dem nah want work, so dem call work 'Babylon'
> Dem twist up de Bible to dem convenience
> like was jackass-rope. Ganja illegal,
> but fe dem, dear, is Genesis: 'The Tree of Life,
> for the healing of nations' (*O' Babylon!*, p, 195).

On the whole, Rastafarianism is a revolt against Babylon whose language of operation is Standard English; the Iyaric is therefore a part of the rejection of Babylonian oppression by substituting its language with one of revolt and freedom. Iyaric seeks to exclude all who do not belong, but especially agents of Babylon, through its complex philosophy and intricate syntax, and it works because in the play, the Babylonians do not succeed in penetrating and destroying the hopes and bond of Zion, represented by the Rasta community. In creating a Rasta play, Walcott acknowledges and pays tribute to a reality which is part of his Jamaican society. The language is now part of the heritage of the Caribbean and elements of it have begun to pass into mainstream use. But in writing about the Rastafarians, Walcott's attitude to the language of the group shows an awareness and sympathy for the group identity which the Rastafarian movement is; their longing for Africa and their adoption of Emperor Haile Selassie of Ethiopia as their living God is central to their project of seeking a collective and ennobled identity that would counter the collective sense of loss which being descendants of a horrible slave experience means for a lot of Caribbean peoples of African descent. To speak a language, as Fanon (1967a) and Ngũgĩ wa Thiong'o (1986: 16) point out, is to declare a world, culture and world view, and so to create their own language is literarily to create their own world, their own culture and their own world view, which distinguishes them from other worlds, cultures and world views. It is a remaking of themselves, free of previous negative representations.

Of the Caribbean plays studied in this book, Matura's *Meetings* is significantly the only one which does not try to differentiate between characters, social classes and educational backgrounds through language. The three physically present characters in the play – Hugh, Jean and Elsa – all speak a form of Trinidadian dialect characterised by its peculiar twang and spelling, as well as other uniquely distinguishing features which one supposes owe their presence and origins to the highly polyglot history of Trinidad itself. Trinidad has the most cultural, as well as linguistic mix of all the Caribbean islands because of the manner of its settlement and eventual composition. Trinidad's linguistic history has been described thus:

> There are men from all quarters of the globe, and with a little exaggeration, it may be said that in Trinidad, all the languages of the earth are spoken (Gamble, 1985: 182).

The Trinidadian dialect, however, is not all that different from other creoles found in the Caribbean or the ones in the play texts. This is because the grammatical roots are the same, coming as they do from the influence of the dominant African populations. So, in a way, Matura has written a monolingual play in the manner of Soyinka's *A Dance of the Forests*, Liking's *Singué Mura* and *La Puissance de Um*, Aidoo's *Anowa* and Sutherland's *The Marriage of Anansewa*. The difference, however, is that unlike them Matura does not translate his characters from the native dialect into a form of Caribbean (Trinidadian) English. All three characters speak alike, however, within the shared frame of their dialect, Matura introduces subtle distinctions which suggest age, education and thus class, as the speeches of Hugh and Jean demonstrate. Their affectation and occasional rendering of educated English into dialect misses the natural freshness, spontaneity and folksiness of Elsa's. With subtle manipulation of the dialect, *Meetings* manages to achieve character identification which places individual characters close or far away from the central theme depending on the register of dialect they speak. Elsa, who represents the play's ideal of remaining true to an African-Caribbean cultural roots, speaks an earthy and unadulterated dialect, while Jean's speech is full of Americanisms, indicating her strong desire not to be associated with Trinidadian folk culture and practices. By giving his characters a basic dialect speech, the playwright successfully creates the realistic atmosphere which he seeks to impose on the action of a play whose home setting requires an air of informality and intimacy. Besides, Matura through this uniformity of dialect speech makes the point that his characters belong to the same cultural and national context, sharing the same cultural, racial and national identities in spite of their differing status and class orientations and positions.

Domestication in African theatre is a bit more complicated than it is in African-Caribbean theatre because the African playwrights have the added task of translating characters speaking African languages into an English or French that would be distinctly African in flavour and phraseology, and at the same time, to write other varieties of English and French to reflect other speakers. Soyinka, Aidoo, Sutherland, Ndao and Liking avoid this problem in their monolingual plays in which they simply look for the most appropriate African idiom in English or French to best carry the weight of the thoughts and actions of their African characters. They succeed because listening to characters such as Anowa, her mother, Badua, the two indubitable bags of ancient wisdom, The Mouths-that-Eat-Pepper-and-Salt, in *Anowa*, or Aroni, Forest Head and Agoreko in *A Dance of the Forests*, or the Hilun and Ngond Libii in *La Puissance de Um* or Singuè Mura or any of the characters in *Singué Mura*, one is immediately struck by the distinct African texture and timbre of their 'English' and 'French'. The characters localise themselves, as it were, through the way they speak. In them, one hardly finds the mixed register of Olunde in *Death and the King's Horseman* who betrays his education and therefore the influence of his contact with and sustained exposure to the

English language and culture. None of the characters from the monolingual plays mentioned above suggest in their speech any contact with English or French. So, whatever English or French they speak is surely that of the playwright who translates them from Fanti or Bassa or Yoruba respectively. And it is to the credit of the three dramatists that they successfully retain elements and colours of the West African languages in the new English or French they write so that it becomes quite easy to place these characters within their West African settings. This, the Caribbean playwrights achieve through their predominant use of dialect, a language which, according to Walcott, must go beyond mere mimicry of Africa or Europe because it too has become home grown and has all the attributes of a native language (a postslavery and postcolonial hybrid language). It is, as he says, a

> ... dialect which has the force of a revelation as it invented names for things, one which [has] finally settled on its own mode of inflection, and which [has] begun to create an oral culture of chants, jokes, folk-songs and fables (Walcott, 'What the Twilight Says', 1972: 17).

It is significant that about ninety-percent of African-Caribbean plays are written in either dialect or patois which is the dramatists' way of creating and claiming their unique identity, given the history and hybrid nature of their Caribbean societies.

In the other African plays, however, because there are differences in the languages which characters speak, the playwrights have had to create different registers as a means of reflecting the multi-lingual world of their plays. This, one must hasten to point out, brings with it a problem of believability for the audience. How, for instance, one wonders, do Elesin and Simon Pilkings in *Death and the King's Horseman* communicate with each other in the prison scene – there are numerous instances of this linguistic gaps in African plays. And this does not just occur when African and European characters meet as above, but also when African characters who speak mutually unintelligible African languages meet – Amusa in *Death and the King's Horseman* comes to mind. Elesin speaks Yoruba throughout, there is no doubt about that, and Pilkings is definitely English through and through. There is no indication that either of them understands the other's language and there is no interpreter between them, but the audience is expected to accept that they manage to understand what the other is saying and the action of the play remains unimpaired. This is not a very big point, but it does highlight a major incongruity in African writings in European languages. Caribbean writers avoid this problem by creating in their plays a majority of characters who have a common origin and so a common tongue. The African writers could have indicated the gap through various means, including the characters showing the struggle to understand the other, as Scott does in *An Echo in the Bone* with one of the slaves on the ship.

The observations made above should, however, not detract from the successful experiments by West African playwrights to fashion a useful theatrical African English and French idioms to reflect the African reality which their plays deal with. Their ability to create within plays categories of English and French registers should be seen as an achievement to be commended. Some of the playwrights show an awareness of the incongruity of the language situation and each dramatist in their own way tries to find a way round the problem. Rotimi provides a good example of such an effort in his two plays, *If...* and *Hopes of the Living Dead*. Banham (1989) highlights Rotimi's skilful use of multiple-simultaneous translation and interpretation in *If...* in his analysis of the scene between Banji, Mama Rosa and Fisherman. Three languages are used simultaneously in this scene – Banji speaks Standard English, Fisherman speaks and understands only Kalabari, and Mama Rosa speaks pidgin and Kalabari. It is assumed that Banji understands pidgin and so Mama Rosa becomes the language intermediary in this linguistically interesting scene between lawyer and client:

Mama Rosa:	[*Introducing Fisherman*] Dis na my broder wey I go bail now-now for Police Station sah. Dem catch am for fishing - port say eno pay tax.... I beg, make you help me.
Banji:	What really happened?
Mama Rosa:	[*To Fisherman, in Kalabari language*] Mioku, duko o pirii. Ye goyegoye duko pirii. [Meaning: Now tell him everything]
Fisherman:	Duko o pirii, yeri njibabo.
Mama Rosa:	He say him be fisherman...
Fisherman:	Yei! Au igbigi nyana-aa
Mama Rosa:	Him no get money, o!
Banji:	Tell him not to worry. I shall do my best...
Mama Rosa:	Tank you, sah. [departing with Fisherman] Yee wa so. Du mee wa sote kaladikite boo. Boo, biomgbo lokomama

(*If...* , p, 25-8).

The whole scene is a fine piece of experimentation with language and the nature of communication which offers immense scope for dramatic possibilities on stage. The same can be said of Rotimi's other linguistic experiment, *Hopes of the Living Dead*, in which he deploys up to fifteen languages on stage at the same time in single scenes. In this instance, communication and movement of action are achieved through simultaneous translation between the inmates of the leper wards. Rotimi makes a sizeable number of the characters bilingual like Mama Rosa in the previous play, and some like Nweke and CC in *Hopes of the Living Dead* are trilingual, but Hannah beats them all as she speaks five languages; and to these multi-lingual characters fall the responsibility of translating respectively for their monolingual companions. This way the momentum of the action is maintained through the 'each one tell one' refrain which echoes as a sustaining chorus of unity throughout the play.

On the whole, African and African-Caribbean playwrights use language in a variety of ways as an index of character in their plays. For Africans, it is even more so because of the high value placed on an individual's ability to use and manipulate words. Words are held to be sacred and they can be used to make or unmake the world, to bless and to damn, and thus an ability to use words is important in African contexts. In African societies a person's intrinsic worth is also measured by the person's mastery of use of words, an ability to manipulate language as occasions demand. There is the saying that you can assess a person by what and how they speak. Moreover, it requires linguistic competence, maturity and intelligence to understand when language is used in that special way which is a mark of African rhetoric; for when proverbs are used only the wise understand and the not-so-wise merely become confused. African and Caribbean playwrights show themselves to be competent in the manipulation of language of language to create special effects, in the same way that indigenous *griots*, oral poets and praise-singers of West Africa and the *Izibongo* poets of Southern Africa have been masters and mistresses of the word for ages.

African playwrights, in particular, employ the full range of traditional African oratorical repertory, from the pithy proverbs to brain-teasing riddles, from the gnomic and cryptic sayings to the highly developed figurative language and the skilful technique of indirection in speech. There are in the plays those who speak well and there are also those who do not; there are owners of words like Elesin, Iyaloja and Praise-singer in *Death and the King's Horseman*, Danlola in *Kongi's Harvest* and Kweku Ananse in *The Marriage of Anansewa*, Dona Béatrice and the Mani Congo in *Béatrice du Congo*, the major characters in *Singué Mura* and *La Puissance de Um* whose language 'is couched in sayings and proverbs or in esoteric jargon whose meaning can be grasped … only by initiates or those who are conversant with the rituals in which these speeches are made' (Jeanne Dingome *et al*, 1996: 18). But there are also those like Agboreko in *A Dance of the Forests* and Professor in *The Road* for whom words are not as sacred and sometimes just meaningless babble. Samson's complexity and verve as a character in *The Road* arises from his linguistic dexterity which he deploys to great effect against his enemies in much the same way that Danlola uses his word skill to cut his opponents down, including the almighty Kongi himself whose words are as meaningless as his mechanistic vision of progress.

For Caribbean dramatists, language is used as an index to external characteristics such as class, race, education and other forms of social categorisation. There are, in this respect, two main types of language to be found throughout Caribbean societies – creoles (dialect for the Anglophone or patois for the Francophone) and Standard English or French. There is of course Iyaric, the almost cultic language of the Rastafarians. Those who speak standard all the time belong to the top five percent of the population and this group is made up mainly of white people – incidentally, there are very few of them in the plays - and a few black people like Len and his wife who qualify through education. Len's language marks him out as being 'hoity-toity', a social climber who has managed to rise above the confines of his racial origins. We have already mentioned Lestrade and his struggle to keep up a steady flow of Satandard English speech, a struggle which he constantly loses because of his underlying incompetence in English. Apart from using this charade to expose Lestrade as a pretentious parvenu, Walcott also uses it as a means of probing the contradiction and psychic tension inherent in Lestrade's mixed-race personality. As a mulatto, Lestrade struggles throughout *Dream on Monkey Mountain* to deny or stifle the African part of his identity. He must not speak the same language as the other black characters, but this deep African base in his personality refuses to be subdued and manifests itself in the ease and frequency with which dialect creeps into his speech to remind him of this haunting black eclipse threatening his aspirations to be seen as a white only person. Because of this struggle, Lestrade is neither-nor, neither black, nor white, and so his speech, accordingly, is neither standard nor dialect. His companions all speak patois. And it is significant that it is only in the forest when he finally comes to terms with his descent from the black 'ugly' Makak that Lestrade abandons his bumblings with/in Standard English to speak like Makak and the rest of the 'tribe'. He finds a language and himself only when he finds and accepts his ancestry and his race. One finds, therefore, that with the Caribbean plays, reflecting as they do the Caribbean society, to speak a language is to declare a class, a social group, education, and in most cases, it is also to pronounce a racial origin. Hugh, Jean and Elsa speak Trinidadian dialect, and despite the subtle difference in register, especially in Jean's speech, this is used by Matura to indicate an unequivocal acceptance by the three of their collective Trinidadian national identity.

In the African plays, language use is a little more complex because it is of a slightly different nature. In both, language is a means of characterisation, but in the African texts it is more about the internals of character and not with social status as in the Caribbean plays. In the former, what is important is not the language a character speaks, but how that character speaks it because in the final analysis, it is how a person employs his or her words that determine their effectiveness as communicators and subsequently how they are regarded. Words are sacred, delicate and very powerful in their ability to invoke reality into being. They are like eggs in their delicateness and they break once they are dropped. Thus there are 'owners of words' like Elesin and his Praise-singer in *Death and King's Horseman* or Hilun in *La Puissance de Um* who sweep the audience along the floodtide of their images and metaphors, confront the listening ear, intelligence and imagination with the delicate aptness of their proverbs and oratory. Such characters are the real owners and guardians of the word, and not Agboreko who allows his 'horses of speech' to gallop out of control. Agboreko spouts strings of proverbs which are as vacuous and pedantic as his ineffectual spiritual ministrations to his society. By making him such a windbag, Soyinka makes the audience realise the futile hope and desperation of a society that relies on a medium like Agboreko to divine and mediate between it and its angry gods. Through this, Soyinka achieves a subtle but very effective piece of characterisation.

All in all, language is a vital element in the plays of African and African-Caribbean playwrights. For the latter, the choice of what language to use is part of the subject matter, especially as most of the plays are concerned, as most Caribbean literature is, with the search for individual or collective identities. For Caribbean peoples of African descent, dialect is an integral part of their Caribbean identity in the same way that Bassa, Baule, Igbo, Yoruba, Fanti, Akan, Gikuyu, Wolof and Luo are part of the identities of different African peoples; to speak any language is to represent the world whose soul, voice and values are embodied in that language. It is thus to the credit of the Caribbean playwrights that about ninety percent of them write in dialect and that

Culture and Identity in African and Caribbean Theatre

when they create Standard English speaking characters, they do so merely for dramatic reasons – either for a realistic portrayal of a bi-glot Caribbean society, or as foils against which to offset their dialect speaking characters. So, making their characters speak dialect is in fact an act of affirmation of their Caribbeanness on the part of the playwrights as it is on the part of the characters themselves. But the African playwrights, on the other hand, are still labouring under the burden of the foreign languages which they inherited as part of their colonial histories. Unlike the Anglophone and Francophone Caribbean diaspora which has either dialect or patois respectively as a uniform language as it were, most current African nation-states are still made up of different ethnic languages which, though sharing basic similarities in their diversity, are largely mutually unintelligible. However, because of the strong presence and predominant use of the indigenous African languages, the pidgins that evolved out of the contact situation between these languages and European languages have not gone through a process of further creolisation which would have enriched and expanded their lexicon as in the Caribbean. Therefore, they remain what they have always been, contact languages, which are not native to any of the groups who speak them. This perhaps is the reason why pidgin speaking characters in African plays often appear ambiguous and sometimes underdeveloped, and at best as comic characters. These characters are often one-dimensional, even at their most captivating liveliness. Samson seems to be an exception, and this is perhaps because of the bi-lingualism implied in the way he is characterised. Many African playwrights therefore are constrained to conceive and then translate their thoughts and characters into English or French in order to avoid becoming ethnic or provincial writers. However, they all in their individual ways try to write English or French that would be 'native' to Africa and sometimes to their individual nation-states or ethnic groups, and in doing so, give a stamp of Africanness to their characters and their situations.

On a final note, one can say with some justification that the cultural similarity which this study has established between African and Caribbean plays also extends to the languages in which these plays are written; at least, they all share a heritage of European and African languages in one form or another. In the first place, the slaves who crossed the Atlantic carried within and with them elements of Africa which they put to use once they arrived in the New World and one of these was their specific African languages. Although in most cases they could not or were not allowed to use these languages, but like their brothers and sisters on the African continent, they had to call upon some of the internalised linguistic features of their native tongues when they came into contact with and were required to communicate in the European languages of their enslavers. The result of this first level of interlanguage situation was a pidgin, similar in many respects to the pidgins which evolved along the coastal regions of their former African homelands. Subsequently, the dialect which came out of the creolisation of the pidgin by the children of the slaves retained key features of the pidgin, especially its grammatical and phonological structures which had been borrowed from the African languages. This means that the dialect or patois as spoken in the Caribbean today are, to a degree, products of Africa and this explains the ease with which an African reader, especially one from West Africa like me, could enter into the linguistic field of a Caribbean play like *Dream on Monkey Mountain*. Pidgin and dialect/patois are similar because of their shared root of elements of African and European languages. Besides, Africa was and has remained the spiritual-cum-cultural homeland for all peoples of African descent, and for her children in the diaspora Africa's influence lies deep like Walcott's 'black Atlantis buried in a deep sea of sand' (quoted in Lyn, 1980: 50). Scratch any of her children and one will discover Africa at the centre of their being, always there and waiting to be discovered and acknowledged for a complete and settled identity to emerge to counter centuries of denigration and degradation. Africa will, therefore, always excite an echo of recognition in her children, irrespective of where they are located on the face of the earth.

Chapter 9

CONCLUSION

Africa and her Children

Dream on Monkey Mountain introduced me to African-Caribbean theatre, but it also did more than just that; it opened my eyes to the similarities between the worlds of this theatre and that of my African (Nigerian) society. It enkindled in me a desire to explore the totality of the African-Caribbean experience, and then to compare this with mine since the dialogue of the characters of the African-Caribbean plays resembled, almost, those of the common folks around me on the streets of my Nigerian home, as well those of the ordinary characters in much of African drama that I had studied. The interest and search for the common source inevitably led to two momentous events in black and African history: trans-Atlantic slavery and African colonisation by Europe. These were two epochs of shame, trauma and humiliation for African peoples in the continent and all peoples of African descent in the diaspora.

Slavery and colonisation had impacted upon and continue to colour African and African-Caribbean experience in world history. To begin with, trans-Atlantic slavery had created the first known African diaspora in recorded history in the Caribbean and the Americas; the cultural umbilical cord which ties all dispersed African children to the African homeland arose from this. This cord is responsible for the unique bond which unites all 'African' peoples throughout the world, for Africa was and remains a physical (for some) but a spiritual home for all peoples of African descent. One is then not surprised at the strong yearning for Africa in almost all the African-Caribbean characters; from Makak in *Dream on Monkey Mountain* who is compelled to make a symbolic return to a pre-slavery African homeland in order to deal with his crisis of identity and feeling of inferiority, to the group of African-Caribbean characters in *An Echo in the Bone* who equally visit Africa in their minds in order to understand and to come to terms with the present in their Jamaican home; from Hugh in *Meetings* who has to go back to his African-Caribbean folk traditions in order to overcome his feelings of alienation, Len in *Old Story Time* who makes a passing return to Africa in his student days, to the Rastafarians in *O Babylon!* who long for an African paradise home which they hope would put an end to their exile and bondage in Babylon. What all these varieties of attachment to Africa point to is the fact that in spite of centuries of separation, dehumanisation, degradation and cultural emasculation, Africa refused to die in the souls of her dispersed children. And it is this Africa of the mind which is responsible for the similarities between African and African-Caribbean cultures, plays and playwrights; it is the reason for that echo of recognition excited in me when I first read Walcott. The dialect which Makak and his companions spoke had strongly reminded me of the pidgin of my Nigerian and West African home. All this had been brought about by slavery, that traumatically momentous and transformative contact between African and European cultures four centuries ago.

One of the things that has emerged from this study is the fact that the enslavers and colonisers, in order to justify their actions and to mask the economic motive behind them, sought theories and myths to make the actions seem right or divinely ordained. What the theories amount to is this, that because African peoples as presented by Europeans are naturally inferior to Europeans, the latter therefore had the incontrovertible right to dominate and exploit them, while the former were expected to see this relationship as being for their own good. Also, because African peoples were described, again by Europeans, as primitive, savage and barbarous, they ought to be thankful that Europeans had undertaken the selfless task of coming to bring them out of their darkness into light and civilisation. In these racist theories and myths, black peoples are assigned so many psychological and physiological defects that their only hope of salvation was in their becoming like white people, if not in body, at least in mind through the adoption of white cultural values. Some of the mythic images which dominated trans-Atlantic and colonial cartography did have some effect for it was not possible for the African peoples so tagged to escape behind a wall of indifference. The negative images succeeded in creating in some the sense of inferiority intended; this process was helped, on the one hand, by the fact that within the slave societies of the Caribbean and North and South America and colonial contexts in Africa and the Caribbean, the slave owners and colonisers controlled most instruments of representation; and reinforced, on the other, by the glaring inequalities between black people and white people in both slave and colonial societies. The two societies had ensured that the lowest white person was better than the average black person, and in some cases, even better than the best black. The slave societies of the New World did not even recognise the humanity of the African slave and so there was no question of comparing a black to a white, since one was a person and the other a thing, someone else's property who featured in the economic and social structure only as an element of production.

Both slavery and colonialism were inherently racist. Both needed social structures based on relations of inequality and privilege; structures in which people of black colour, as a collective, found themselves utterly disadvantaged. As slaves, they had functioned in the social system merely as factors of production; they were presumed to have no minds and so were treated as objects to be used and abused by those who controlled, manipulated and hugely benefited from the system. And as the colonised, they fared no better than their slave brothers and sisters, except perhaps in the degree of dehumanisation and cultural emasculation needed to keep the racially unequal social structure in place. The slave was not a person, so he or she was not paid for their labour; the colonised was an inferior person, and so received inferior pay. Neither the slave nor the colonised had any say in the mechanics of their respective societies. The enslavers and colonisers, for their part, had to justify the atrocities which had been committed on the enslaved and colonised peoples by creating myths of African inferiority versus European superiority; the animalism and savagery of black people against the humanity and civilisation of white people. And the poor slave and colonised, assaulted on all sides and at all times by these negative images of themselves, were not left unaffected, especially since the social system and the reality arising from it were on hand to reinforce these sub-human images of themselves. There is no doubt that slave and colonial experiences brought about psychic devastation which left in their wake men and women who began to doubt even their basic sense of being human; like Makak who sees himself as 'ugly as sin' and only fit to live alone away from other humans on Monkey Mountain, or Miss Aggy who is so full of self and race-hate that she would have nothing to do with black people and flies into an extreme rage with her son for marrying one. These are typical of the characters one finds in Caribbean plays, and it is their alienation and how to combat it which engages the imagination of African-Caribbean playwrights such as Walcott, Rhone, Scott and Matura. The playwrights explore the facet and frontiers of the alienated African-Caribbean psyches and through their dramas they attempt to find answers or put forward solutions.

In Africa, the colonial social structure attempted to destroy as much of African culture as it could, and besides, it insisted on perceiving and treating the colonised natives as factors and products of 'European' history; that is that Africa had no history until its encounter with Europe through trade, slavery and colonialism. All this was done in order to create a de-cultured, inferior and thus pliable colonised population; in effect, to create men and women who suffer from various stages and forms of 'colonial mentality'. A lot of Black and African literatures and theatres are thus attempts by African writers and writers of African descent in the diaspora to give voice back to the slaves and the colonised who for so long had been denied a voice and humanity in slave and colonial writings, and in this respect the plays studied here belong firmly in the domain of postcolonial theatre – a theatre that wears two faces, with one face it writes to the slave and the colonised, and with the other face writes back to the enslaver and the coloniser. Above all, this book argues, it is a theatre that transforms the slave and the colonised into subjects of their own histories and narratives as opposed to the objects they were in the master narratives and historiography of imperial Europe; it is a theatre which gives them a space and location from which to speak their subjectivity.

As post-slavery and postcolonial texts, African and African-Caribbean plays specifically try to counter racist theories, ideologies and myths which had been used to justify slavery and colonialism. The plays adopt postcolonial strategies of cultural affirmation, counter-narrativity, counter-discourse, domestication, retrieval and recuperation of history. Thus, the plays are either reconstructing and representing the distorted facts of African and African-Caribbean histories; Rotimi does this in a lot of his history plays, but especially in *Ovonramwen Nogbaisi*, as do Ngũgĩ wa Thiong'o and Mĩcere Mugo in *The Trial of Dedan Kimathi*. The two plays engage with colonial contact and conquest and they recuperate the portraits of two African leaders in their confrontation with colonial invaders. A significant number of Francophone African plays deal with African history and the colonial encounter, with the following texts being good examples: *L'Exil d'Albouri, Béatrice du Congo*, Thierno Ba's *Lat-Dior: Le chemin de l'honneur*. Quite a reasonable number, such as *Le Mort de Chaka, Les Amazoulous*, are devoted to the heroism of Chaka, the 19th Century Zulu king, whose legendary encounters with European colonising powers has become part of a collective African folklore. Another Zulu leader, Cetsewayo, is celebrated in *Cetsewayo* by Herbert Dhlomo. Césaire's *Une saison au Congo* (*A Season in the Congo*, 1973) not only looks at a colonial encounter in Africa, but actually follows this history to the decolonisation moment with the Congo gaining independence from Belgium and the catastrophic events that followed in its wake including the brutal murder of Patrice Lumumba, the first democratically elected prime minister of the new country. Quite a few African-Caribbean plays explore Caribbean history, the most notable ones being Césaire's *La Tragédie du Roi Christophé* (1970), Walcott's *Henri Christophé, Drums and Colours* and *Haitian Earth,* Glissant's *Monsieur Toussaint* and C. L. R. James' *The Black Jacobins (Toussaint l'Overture).* These six plays explore the 19th century revolution by black slaves which led to the independence from France of the island of San Domingo which became the Republic of Haiti. Ivorian dramatist, Dadie also celebrates this glorious moment in African-Caribbean history in *Iles de tempête* (1971). A great many Caribbean plays choose instead to create characters who undertake soul journeys as a means of getting to the bottom of their psychic alienation as Makak and his companions do in *Dream on Monkey Mountain*, Hugh in *Meetings* and the characters in *An Echo in the Bone*. But others, like Soyinka in *Death and the King's Horseman*, do not bother with creating counter-myths, but rather concentrate on creating an African world which observes its own internal social rhythms and systems as dictated by its own metaphysics, in spite of the intrusive and meddling presence of the coloniser. But, in general, all the plays try to create characters who do not answer to the racial stereotypes of black and African peoples created by and still lodged in the collective unconscious of Europe having been circulated widely for centuries in and by slave and colonial literature and narratives.

Theme therefore has been found to be a unifying factor between African and African-Caribbean theatres because, apart from exploring the psychic states of its African and African-Caribbean characters, the plays are also critiques of the structures of inequality in social relations, which exist in both Africa and the Caribbean. The overriding argument in the plays seems to be that the underdeveloped state of African and Caribbean societies, and thus the disadvantaged position of African and black peoples in world socio-economic relations, stem from the unjust social structures which slavery and colonialism had needed and had set-up in order to function and which, sadly, have remained in place, in spite of emancipation and decolonisation. African-Caribbean plays, such as *An Echo in the Bone* and *Ti-Jean and his Brothers*, show that nothing has changed for the majority who incidentally are descendants of African slaves and who are still consigned to the periphery of things like their slave ancestors of many centuries ago, while lone white characters like Charles and the Planter own and control large estates which they can hardly use fully. It is simple; the rich (a minority population) in Caribbean society are white, while the poor (the majority) are black. And in the African plays, because the social structure which supported colonialism had been left untouched by the emergent native bourgeoisie and political elite, a handful of Africans have stepped directly into the shoes and hammocks vacated by the European colonial masters. What this means is that, in effect, life has hardly changed for the numerous peasants who fought to secure independence and win African lands stolen or expropriated by white settlers. This is the theme of *I'll Marry When I Want*. It was so that a situation such as this became abolished or does not arise in the future that the Mau Mau war discussed in *The Trial of Dedan Kimathi* was fought. The play looks at the conduct of the liberation struggle by the peasants under their leader, Dedan Kimathi, his capture and trial; *I'll Marry When I Want* highlights the bitter irony and tragedy of neo-colonial exploitation in a post-Mau Mau postcolonial Kenya. It is a Kenya in which the dreams of *uhuru* have become aborted and betrayed and in which black tenants are forced into squatters on the immense holdings and estates of black bourgeois landlords like Kīoi. The irony, the play points out, is greater because it is the very people who had been against the freedom struggle and became home guards in support of the colonial administration who have become the ultimate beneficiaries of independence.

On the whole, both African and African-Caribbean plays show that relations of inequality exist, but where the latter show inequality as arising from race, the former show it as being dependent on economics and therefore on class and other forms of social categorisation. This difference in perception can be attributed to the experience of slavery and the concomitant existence of a multi-racial society in the Caribbean, whereas the Africa in the plays is mainly racially homogenous and its social structure was affected only by colonisation. This difference in how inequality is perceived, of course, has implications for character orientation and dramatic action in the plays. Because they perceive their social positions mainly in racial terms, African-Caribbean characters, carrying as they do centuries of psychological conditioning, tend not to be as aggressive or strong-willed as the African characters who do not feel racially inferior to other Africans who happen to be on a higher social scale. Thus, where the Africans are proud, angry, assertive and cynical sometimes, like the nobles in *Death and the King's Horseman*, *The Trial of Dedan Kimathi*, *Kongi's Harvest*, *L'Exil d'Albouri*, *Une saison au Congo*, *Béatrice du Congo*, *Ovonramwen Nogbaisi*, the farmers in revolt in Osofisan and Sowande, the scheming Ananse in Sutherland, the Caribbean characters tend generally to be lacking in self-pride and almost self-effacing like Makak and Miss Aggy. The latter do not, like the African characters, plot and bide their time hoping to either climb up the social ladder or topple those at the top. Even the lepers in *Hopes of the Living Dead* and the layabouts in *The Road* have their eyes set on getting to the top, whereas the Caribbean characters merely seek ways to get by or just to slightly improve their lot, like Lestrade, Miss Aggy and Makak who desire to become white or less black. This the study found is a major difference between African-Caribbean and African plays; the former are essentially conservative in inspiration and temper, while the latter appear mildly radical and sometimes combative in comparison; and while the latter question the status quo, the former hardly ever do. What the plays from Africa and the Caribbean have in common, however, is a deep commitment to a cultural politics designed to be in the service of their respective peoples and societies.

Because the process of conquering the minds of black people both in Africa and in the diaspora had been achieved by means of all manner of racist literature and through the legitimisation by church doctrines, African and Caribbean writers therefore employ the same instrument of literature and theatre to help the affected minds to unlearn and to critically evaluate the European cultural values which they have been fed. The writers try to help the enslaved black minds to break out of the prison of European and colonial indoctrination and culture in which they have been placed all these years. For the African playwrights and some Africa-Caribbean writers such as Scott, the process of re-education has to be communal as we find in *Ovonramwen Nogbaisi*, *The Trial of Dedan Kimathi*, *L'Exil d'Albouri*, *Béatrice du Congo*, *An Echo in the Bone* etc. This is apparently because, unlike their Caribbean counterparts, black people in Africa had not been physically uprooted, they never really took leave of their culture and geographical location in a physical sense as is evident in *Death and the King's Horseman* or in the plays of Werewere Liking and Zadi Zaourou – the latter make extensive use of their native *kiyi-mbock* and *didiga* performance traditions respectively. What Africans suffered rather was a denial and inferiorisation of their cultures and their humanity, as well as a distortion of their histories. What they needed therefore was to have these histories and cultures re-presented or reclaimed so that they can begin to take pride in them again. For the Caribbean dramatists, the search is mostly individual because the main problem for African-Caribbean peoples is one of crisis of identity arising from the higher degree of deculturation which they as a group have gone through over many centuries; thus, the quest for identity seems to dominate Caribbean consciousness more than it does the African, and this explains why a majority of the characters in the plays are often individuals experiencing one form of psychic crisis or another. A lot of the Caribbean plays studied are often structured as journeys into the self which the characters make to acquire an understanding of who they are, and through that to an understanding of the society. The plays are like psycho-dramas that unfold at two levels and where the cure is both for the characters in the plays and the audience members who become vicarious participants. What the characters go through in the plays are similar to the problems and dilemmas members of the audience experience in their daily lives. The slave experience had been traumatic for African-Caribbean peoples who are the descendants of the unfortunate African slaves and thus their memories of history and race are rather unpleasant. To fashion a new meaningful life and a new image of themselves as individuals and as a people in the land to which they have been violently relocated and which they must now reluctantly accept as home, the children of slaves have to understand their history, their origins, the middle passage which remains the dominant image in the collective unconscious of Caribbean peoples of African descent. Thus a play like *Dream on Monkey Mountain*, as Slade Hopkinson rightly argues, is:

> . . . in part, about West Indian man's rejection of his home, and therefore of himself. It is about the psychology of mental and cultural emigration . . . the psychology of the 'red' official who, in the play, is a mental and cultural emigrant to a Europe of the mind; the psychology of the black bush recluse who is, in the play, a mental and cultural emigrant to an Africa of the mind . . . . Makak, crazed by loneliness, futility and longing for psychological status and self-respect, makes a dream escape from the prison of his island and condition and emigrates to a dream Africa (1977: 79).

It is this urge to escape from their present harsh condition, to find an anchor and a new meaning in their lives which drives African-Caribbean characters in their dreams or moments of trance or possession to reach back to slavery and to an Africa before slavery, an Africa only dimly remembered. The plays suggest that these unpleasant memories and histories have to be retrieved, repossessed and understood for Caribbean peoples of African descent to move forward in their present home as is the case in *Dream on Monkey Mountain* where Makak 'within the dimensions of reality re-emigrates to an island where he has been freed from his prison' of complexes (79), and Lestrade, the mixed-race police corporal, finds personal peace after accepting his African and European ancestry. A physical return to Africa, the central idea of the Rastafarian movement, is an unrealisable daydream, a mere escape from facing reality. Africa, therefore, in the play, while remaining in their dreams, must be acknowledged as a root which goes deep and which can provide them with an anchor. But ultimately the Caribbean is a home which they must accept because it alone is the reality they have. And it is a home fed from elements of many former homes, including Africa, the Caribbean and Europe.

Whatever approach to the quest for identity adopted, the dramatists are all involved in the one endeavour of helping alienated blacks or those who have strayed to see the signposts that would lead them back to the centre, the soul of race and the cultures of their ancestors. The plays show that black people have nothing to be ashamed of, nothing to feel inferior about with regard to their histories and cultures, or in themselves, as human beings and members of a race. The plays echo in different ways Kimathi's assertion that:

> Here in the forest armed in body
> Mind and soul
> We must kill the lie
> That the black people never invented anything
> Lay for ever to rest that inferiority
> Complex
> Implanted in our minds by centuries
> of oppression
> (*The Trial of Dedan Kimathi*, p, 68).

The plays therefore are calls for action, whether physical or mental, which would eventually lead to the liberation of the enslaved minds. The dramatists do not recommend that black people should begin to prove or ask for equality with white people because that in itself, they believe, is a temptation as well as a trap. Rather, they advocate that African and African-Caribbean peoples should prove and celebrate their difference from European peoples, for ultimately it is the differences between blacks and whites which would command attention without pleading for respect. And by preaching the difference, the characters would by the same stroke announce their acceptance of the fact and unchangeability of their blackness. The plays are thus attempts to teach black people to be proud to be black – African and African-Caribbean.

The book also reveals that, in general, African and African-Caribbean playwrights share and express a common world view, born of a single African derived metaphysical and philosophical understanding of the universe. Theirs is an expansive universe which allows a contiguous interrelationship between the past, present and future; between the dead, the living and the unborn; and finally between the worlds of the gods, of humans and of the ancestors. In between these worlds is a chthonic realm which is the zone of transition. Crossing from one world to another often requires a rite of passage to negotiate a path through this gulf that divides the worlds and this explains the importance of rituals in African life because they provide humans with the tool and means of breaching the gulf of transition, of diminishing its danger and making peace with the very powerful forces which guard the paths through the gulf.

For theatre to encode and transmit such a world, the book argues, it has to search for forms that are flexible enough to accommodate such an immense and constantly changing universe with its contradictions. In searching for forms to use, African and African-Caribbean dramatists, perhaps, because of a shared though tenuous ancestry, settle for two basic forms derived from the indigenous folk traditions of Africa – the storytelling theatre and ritual-dream theatre. These two forms in various combinations generate structures that can at times admit of the fantastic and the impossible, the real and unreal. With these structures, the improbable tales are not so improbable anymore and when successfully used, the structures seem well suited to the content which they express. And in most cases, to understand and appreciate the latter, one needs to unpack the former in order to reveal patterns each dramatist has created, and it is through a structural analysis of this kind that one is able to unearth the meaning of the plays. These forms are also chosen because traditionally in Africa they are forms used to functionally enable the human society to explore its world, interrogate itself, affirm its values, educate its young, and finally commune, communicate and negotiate with other worlds. However, the study argues that no matter how unwieldy the dramatic structures which emerge from adopting the two performance forms appear to be, that an essentially African mode of perception which avoids linearity needs to be used to understand what is happening in the plays; thus the book proposes a cumulative associative approach in which meaning can be gained or constructed only when all has been seen or heard.

What this study also found is that the similarities between African and African-Caribbean plays extend to the language - the first thing that struck me on reading Walcott. The various pidgins and varieties of Standard English and Standard French spoken by the characters in the plays also reflect the deep influences of original African languages which have interacted in numerous ways and periods with European languages prior to slavery, during slavery and then during the colonial period. In the formation of the pidgins, whether in Africa, on the slave ships or in the Caribbean, the two main African language families of the slaves, the Kwa and Ga, had provided the grammatical and phonological structures while the European languages supplied the lexicon and hence the closeness of the pidgin of characters in Rotimi's *Hopes of the Living Dead*, *If . . .*, Soyinka's *The Road*, *Death and the King's Horseman* and the patois of characters in *Dream on Monkey Mountain*, Scott's *An Echo in the Bone*, Rhone's *Old Story Time* and White's *Redemption Song*. Equally, the standard French spoken by the characters in Césaire's *Une saison au Congo* and *La Tragédie du Roi Christophé* are similar although these characters' identities are African and African-Caribbean respectively. Similarly, the Standard French of characters in Liking's *Singué Mura* and *La Puissance de Um* and those in Dadie's *Béatrice du Congo* resemble in many respects that spoken by Césaire's and Glissant's characters. The conclusion which this book has arrived at is that these similarities in a way reflect that peculiar echo of recognition, the same strangeness and familiarity which Walcott's characters excited in me when I first heard them speak their anguish. The reason for the echo is because of the underlying presence of the African languages in the phonology and grammar of the pidgins, creoles (dialect and patois), the varieties of Standard English and French of African and African-Caribbean peoples.

Beside sharing this similarity in language, African and African-Caribbean plays use language as a means of characterisation. The language a character speaks is used as an index of their personality and sometimes of their self-worth, reflecting an essentially African sensibility which places a lot of value on people's ability to manipulate words to achieve the effects they desire. Serious characters such as Iyaloja, Praise-Singer, Ananse, Singué Mura, the Hilun, Ngond Libii, Makak, Rachel, Crew, Dona Béatrice, King Albouri, speak well and are effective; others like Agboreko and Professor are windbags whose words are empty or Amusa who struggles to make himself understood as the language he speaks is not his. Others, like Lestrade, reflect in their language their crisis of identity - as a mixed-race character who is not completely comfortable with his dual heritage he struggles to suppress one language and use the other, but the language (patois) being repressed refuses to go away and Lestrade's identity is resolved in the end and he is able to speak both languages, switching from one to the other with ease and out of choice.

The dramatists also use language, generally, as a statement of identity. The fact that almost ninety percent of African-Caribbean plays are written in dialect or patois, within the postcolonial scheme of things, is a major affirmation of their African-Caribbean identities given that these creoles have been despised as the language of the common people, a language that is not fit for literature, learning and for the office. Also the African writers through domestication of the European languages of the coloniser make these languages their own, able as Achebe (1975: 61-2) points out, to carry the full weight of their African experience.

A Black (African) Theatre Aesthetic?

Having looked at the spectrum of African and African-Caribbean theatre and performance and given the great similarities in perception and creative expression which exist between African and African-Caribbean playwrights, is it possible to talk of an essentially Black (African) theatre aesthetic? Basically speaking, a unique African cosmological system is central to the universe of African peoples and peoples of African descent in the diaspora. This cosmological system influences all aspects of life and all manner of cultural expression of African peoples, whether in Africa or in the diaspora. All black people tend to perceive life and the world in much the same way since they see the universe as a total structure of lived experience. They also tend to reflect this totality in their various structures and modes of cultural expression, such as architecture, plastic arts, theatre and literature. However, the greatest area of similarity between African and Caribbean plays is the area of dramatic structure and form, and especially in the way in which the dramatists tend to employ the former as an index to meaning.

African and black literatures and theatres reflect the African universe of contraries and harmonies, an African metaphysics that accepts the coexistence of different planes of existence. It is a universe made up of different floating orbs that constantly interpenetrate the ever-rotating orbits of one another. These orbs represent the different planes of existence and imply different spatial and temporal relationships. The unique fluidity of the African world and its complex metaphysics which form the generative and sustaining fount of much African, African-Caribbean and black literatures and theatres demand unique structures that have the flexibility to cope with the expansive and constantly changing African universe of harmony and opposition. This, the book has argued, is responsible for the peculiar structures of African and Caribbean plays - African-American plays also display this complexity in structure – and that these structures demand a different set of aesthetic rubrics for their appreciation and explication. It also explains why it is totally unfruitful to approach African or Caribbean plays using Western European critical frames of reference because these plays are very often well outside and actually do resist the Western European predilection for a linear structuring of dramatic action and narrative. African and African-Caribbean plays very often reflect the African mode of perception, which can best be described as 'cyclic' because it tends to see in any event the beginnings and ends of a unit of action. That is to say, that time past is contained and co-existent with time present and both are to be found in the orb of time to come. Indigenous African theatre reflects this worldview very well in its composite structure of dramatic action; and contemporary black African and Caribbean theatres have inherited this structuring principle. Playwrights modify it extensively to come up with different kinds of dramatic structure, such as the dream-ritual structure which Walcott uses in *Dream on Monkey Mountain*, Scott in *An Echo in the Bone*, and Soyinka in *The Road*, *Death and the King's Horseman* and *A Dance of the Forests*. Another favourite of the dramatists is the storytelling form, as used in Rhone's *Old Story Time* and Sutherland's *The Marriage of Anansewa*. Some writers actually combine the various models in single plays. The result of all this is that there is a healthy explosion of experimentation with dramatic form which has become a hallmark of African and African-Caribbean theatres. As a result of the constant experiment with form, African and African-Caribbean theatres and performances are hybrid forms; they are forms of transition which in their embrace of transition reflect the recognition within African and African-Caribbean thought that life, worlds and cultures are constantly in the making and thus all forms and identities deriving from them are always in transition. The linear form of narrative is a fixed form whereas the cumulative associative approach acknowledges and is based on the instability of form, on change and the celebration of impermanence and growth. These are essentially African.

BIBLIOGRAPHY

Primary Texts

Aidoo, Ama Ata (1987), *The Dilemma of a Ghost and Anowa*, Essex: Longman African Classic

Ba, Thierno (1987), *Lat-Dior: Le chemin de l'honneur*, Dakar: Les Nouvelles Editions Africaines

Césaire, Aimé (1963), *La Tragédie du Roi Christophé*, Paris: Présence Africaine

Césaire, Aimé (1969), *Une tempête*, Paris: Editions du Seuil

Dadié, Bernard B (1970), *Béatrice du Congo*, Paris, Dakar: Presence Africaine

Liking, Werewere (1996), *African Ritual Theatre: The Power of Um and A New Earth*, transl/ed Jeanne Dingome et al, San Francisco – London - Bethesda: International Studies Publications

Liking, Werewere (1979), *La Puissance de Um*, Abidjan: CEDA

Liking, Werewere (1996), *African Ritual Theatre: 'The Power of Um and 'A New Earth'*, transl. and edited by Jeanne N. Dingome *et al*, San Francisco, London, Bethesda: International Scholars Publications

Liking, Werewere (2001), 'Singué Mura' in *Theatre Forum*, Issue 19, Summer/Fall

Mais, Roger (1945), 'Edward William Gordon' in Errol Hill ed. *A Time and a Season: Eight Caribbean Plays*, Trinidad: Extra-Mural Studies Unit, UWI, 1976(revised 1996)

Matura, Mustapha (1982), *Play Mas, Independence and Meetings*, London: Methuen

Ndao, Cheik Aliou (1985), *L'Exil d'Albouri, Le Fils de Almamy, La case del'homme*, Dakar-Abidjan-Lomé: Les Nouvelle Editions Africaines

Ngũgĩ wa Thiong'o and Micere Githae Mugo (1976), *The Trial of Dedan Kimathi*, London: Heinemann Educational Books

Ngũgĩ wa Thiong'o and Ngũgĩ wa Mĩriĩ (1982), *I'll Marry When I Want*, London: Heinemann

Osofisan, Femi (1982), *Morountodun and Other Plays*, Ikeja: Longman Drumbeat

Osofisan, Femi (1977), *The Chattering and the Song*, Ibadan: Ibadan University Press

Rhone, Trevor (1981), *Old Story Time and Other Plays*, Essex: Longman Drumbeat

Rotimi, Ola (1974), *Ovonramwen Nogbaisi*, Benin & Ibadan: Ethiope Publishing Corporation and Oxford University Press

Rotimi, Ola (1983), *If: The Tragedy of the Ruled*, Ibadan: Heinemann Educational Books

Rotimi, Ola (1987), *Hopes of the Living Dead,* Ibadan, Nigeria: Spectrum Books Limited

Scott, Dennis (1985), 'An Echo in the Bone' in Errol Hill (ed.) *Plays for Today*, London: Longman Caribbean Writers

Sowande, Bode (1979), *Farewell to Babylon and Other Plays*, London: Longman Drumbeat

Sowande, Bode (1986), *Flamingo and Other Plays*, London: Longman Drumbeat

Soyinka, Wole (1963), *A Dance of the Forests*, Oxford: Oxford University Press

Soyinka, Wole (1965), *The Road*, Nairobi and Oxford: Oxford University Press

Soyinka, Wole (1967), *Kongi's Harvest*, Oxford: Oxford University Press

Soyinka, Wole (1975), *Death and the King's Horseman*, London: Methuen

Sutherland, Efua T (1987), *The Marriage of Anansewa and Edufa*, Essex: Longman African Classic

Walcott, Derek (1972), *Dream on Monkey Mountain and Other Plays*, London: Jonathan Cape

Walcott, Derek (1980), *Remembrance and Pantomime*, New York: Farrar, Straus and Giroux

Walcott, Derek (1979), *The Joke of Serville and O Babylon!,* London: Jonathan Cape

Walcott, Derek (1985), Ti-Jean and His Brother' in *Plays for Today*

White, Edgar (1985), *Redemption Song and Other Plays*, London: Marion Boyars Ltd

Zaourou, Bottey Zadi (2001), *La Guerre des Femmes suivi de La Termitière*, Abidjan: Nouvelles Éditions Ivoiriennes

Secondary Sources

Achebe, Chinua (1985), 'The African Writer and the English Language' in *Morning Yet on Creation Day*, London: Heinemann

Achebe, Chinua (1988), *Hopes and Impediments*, London: Heinemann

Adelugba, Dapọ (1978), 'Wale Ogunyẹmi, 'Zulu Sọfọla & Ọla Rotimi: Three Dramatists in Search of a Language' in *Theatre in Africa*, eds. Oyin Ogunba and Abiola Irele, Ibadan: Ibadan University Press.

Aldrich, Virgil (1963), *Philosophy of Art*, New Jersey: Prentice Hall Inc.

Alexander, Samuel (1933), *Beauty and Other Forms of Value*, London: Macmillan and Co

Amuta, Chidi (1986), *Towards a Sociology of African Literature*, Oguta: Zim Pan Press African Publishers

Anozie, Sunday (1981), *Structural Model and African Poetics*, London: Routledge and Kegan Paul Ltd

Balme, Christopher (1999), *Decolonising the Stage: Theatrical Syncretism and Postcolonial Drama*, Oxford: Clarendon Press

Barthes, Roland (1974), *Mythologies*, London: Cape

Bathold, Bonnie J (1981), *Black Time*, New Haven: Yale University Press

Baugh, Edward (1978), *Derek Walcott, Memory as Vision; Another Life*, London: Longman Group Ltd

Ben-Amos, Dan (1977), 'Folklore in African Society' in Bernth Lindfors (ed) *Forms of Folklore in Africa*, Austin: University of Texas Press

Bhabha, Homi (1994), *The Location of Culture*, London, New York: Routledge

Bhabha, Homi (1997), Keynote Lecture, Trinity Week, Dublin: Trinity College

Boal, Augusto (1979), *Theatre of the Oppressed*, London: Pluto Press

Boas, George (1967), *Wingless Pegasus*, Baltimore: The John Hopkins Press

Brantlinger, Patrick (1986), 'Victorians and Africans: The Genealogy of the Myth of the Dark Continent' in Gates, Henry Louis ed., *Race, Writing and Difference*, Chicago, London: The University of Chicago Press

Broderick, Dorothy M (1973), *Image of the Black in Children's Fiction*, New York, London: Bowker

Brown, Lloyd W ed. (1973), *The Black Writer in Africa and the Americas*, Los Angeles: Hennesy and Ingalls, Inc.

Calvert, Peter (1982), *The Concept of Class: An Historical Introduction*, London: Hutchinson

Carothers, J.C (1954), *The Psychology of Mau Mau*, Nairobi: Government Printers

Carothers, J.C (1953), *The African Mind in Health and Diseases*, Geneva: World Health Organisation

Clark, J. P (1977), *The Ozidi Saga*, Ibadan and Oxford: Ibadan University Press & Oxford University Press

Colson, Theodore (1973), 'Derek Walcott's Plays: Outrage and Compassion' in *World Literature Written in English*, Vol. 12, No 1

Conrad, Joseph (1962), *Heart of Darkness*, Englewood Cliffs: Prentice Hall

Cook, David & Okenimkpe (1983), *Ngugi wa Thiong'o: An Exploration of His Writings*, London: Heinemann

Coultard, G. R. (1962), *Race and Colour in Caribbean Literature*, London: Oxford University Press

Cudjoe, Selwin R. (1980), *Resistance and Caribbean Literature*, Athens, Ohio: Ohio University Press

Dathorne, O. R (1974), *The Black Mind*, Minneapolis: University of Minnesota Press

Dathorne, O. R (1981), *Dark Ancestor*, Benton Rouge and London: Louisiana State University Press

du Bois, William (1965), *The Souls of Black Folk*, London: Longmans

Depestre, Réné (1973), 'Problems of Identity for the Black in Caribbean Literatures' in *Caribbean Quarterly*, Vol. 19, No. 13

Duerden, Dennis & Pieterse, Cosmo (1972), *African Writers Talking*, London: Heinemann

Eagleton, Terry (1976), *Marxism and Literary Criticism*, London: Methuen

Edwards, Viv (1986), *Language in a Black Community*, Clevedon: Multilingual Matters

Eliade, Mircea (1959), *The Sacred and the Profane*, San Diego: Harcourt Brace Jovanovich

Eliade, Mircea (1965), *The Myth of the Eternal Return*, New Jersey: Princeton University

Enekwe, Ossie (1987), *Igbo Masks: The Oneness of Ritual and Theatre*, Lagos: Nigeria Magazine Publication

Fanon, Frantz (1967a), *Black Skin, White Masks*, trans. Charles L.Markmann, New York: Grove Press, Inc.

Fanon, Frantz (1967b), *The Wretched of the Earth*, Middlesex: Penguin Books

Finn, Julio (1988), *Voices of Negritude*, London: Quartet Books

Fonagy, Peter & Higgit, Anna (1984), *Personality Theory and Clinical Practice*, London: Methuen

Fordham, Frieda (1961), 'The Shadow in Jungian Psychology and Race Prejudice' in *Race and Class* Vol. II, No.2

Freire, Paulo (1972), *Cultural Action for Freedom*, Harmondsworth: Penguin Books

Freire, Paulo (1972), *Pedagogy of the Oppressed*, Harmondsworth: Penguin Books

Freire, Paulo (1978), *Pedagogy in Process: The Letters to Guinea-Bissau*, London: Writers and Readers Publishing Co-operative

Gates (Jnr), Henry Louis ed. (1984), *Black Literature and Literary Theory*, New York, London: Methuen

Gibbs, James (1986), *Wole Soyinka*, London: Macmillan

Goody, Jack (1977), *The Domestication of the Savage Mind*, Cambridge: Cambridge University Press

Gordon, Chad & Gergen, Kenneth J. ed. (1968), *The Self in Social Interaction*, New York: John Wiley

Gorlach, Manfred and Holm, John A (1986), *Varieties of English around the World*, Amsterdam/Philadelphia: John Benjamins Publishing Company

Gottrik, Kacke (1984), *Apidan Theatre and Modern Drama*, Goteborg: Almquist and Wiskell International

Goveia, Elsa (1970), 'The social Framework' in *Savacoa* No 2

Grotowski, Jerzy (1968), *Towards a Poor Theatre*, New York: Simon and Shuster

Gugelberger, Georg ed. (1985), *Marxism and African Literature*, London: James Currey Ltd

Gutkind, P. C. and Waterman, eds. (1977), *African Social Studies*, London: Heinemann

Hall, C. S. and Lindzey, G (1978), *Theories of Personality*, New York, Chichester

Hamner, Robert (1981), *Derek Walcott*, Boston: Twayne Publishers

Harrison, Deborah Sears and Trobasso, Tom (1976), *Black English: A Seminar*, Hillsdale, New Jersey: Lawrence Erlbaum Associates Publishers

Hatch, James (1980), 'Some African Influences on the Afro-American Theater' in *The Theatre of Black Americans*, Vol. I, Errol Hill (ed.), New Jersey: Spectrum Books

Henderson, Ian (1958), *The Hunt for Kimathi*, with Philip Goodhart, London: Hamish Hamilton

Hill, Errol ed. (1980), *The Theatre of Black Americans*, Vol. II, New Jersey: Spectrum Books

Hill, Errol (1985), *The Trinidad Carnival: Mandate for a National Theatre*, Austin, Texas: University of Texas Press

Hopkinson, Slade (1977), "'Dream on Monkey Mountain' and the Popular Response" in *Caribbean Quarterly* Vol. 23, No. 2

Jahn, Janheinz (1968), *A History of Neo-African Literature*, New York: Faber & Faber and Grove Press

Kachru, Braj B. ed. (1982), *The Other Tongue*, Urbana, Chicago, London: University of Illinois Press

Kardiner, Abraham and Oversay, Lionel (1968), 'On the Psycho-dynamics of Negro Personality' in *The Self in Social Interaction*, eds. Chad Gordon and Kenneth J. Gergen, New York: John Wiley and Sons Inc.

Katrak, Ketu (1986), *Wole Soyinka and Modern Tragedy: A Study of Dramatic Theory and Practice*, New York: Greenwood Press

Katz, Stephen (1980), *Marxism, Africa and Social Class: A Critique of Relevant Theories*, Montreal: McGill University Occasional Monograph Series 14

Killam, G. D. (1973), *African Writers on African Writing*, London: Heinemann

King, Bruce ed. (1979), *West Indian Literature*, London: Macmillan

Knox, Robert (1850), *The Races of Man: A Fragment*, Philadelphia: Lea & Blanchard

Kwofie, Emmanuel (1976), *The Grammar of Spoken French in the Ivory Coast: A Study in Second Language Acquisition*, Grossen-Linden: Hoffmann-Verlag

Leaky, Louis (1952), *Mau Mau and the Kikuyu*, London: Methuen

Leaky, Louis (1954), *Defeating the Mau Mau*, London: Methuen

Lindfors, Bernth & Schild Ulla ed. (1976), *Neo-African Literature and Culture: Essays in Memory of Jaheinz Jahn*, Wiesbaden: Heyman

Lindfors, Bernth ed. (1977), *Forms of Folklore in Africa*, Austin: University of Texas

Lloyd, Peter (1982), *Third World Proletariat*, London Allen & Unwin

Lowenthal, David (1972), *West Indian Societies*, London: Oxford University Press

Lukacs, Georg (1971), *History and Class Consciousness: Studies in Marxist Dialectics*, London: Merlin Press

Lyn, Diana (1980), "The Concept of the Mulatto in some Works of Derek Walcott' in *Caribbean Quarterly* Vol.26, Nos 1 & 2

Mannix, Daniel P. (1963), *Black Cargoes: A History of the Atlantic Slave Trade*, London: Longman

Mannoni, Octavio (1968), *Prospero and Caliban: The Psychology of Colonization*, London: Methuen

Maughan-Brown, David (1985), *Land, Freedom and Fiction*, London: Zed Books

Memmi, Albert (1968), *Dominated Man: Notes Towards a Portrait*, New York: Orion Press

Memmi, Albert (1974), *The Colonizer and the Colonized*, London: Souvenir Press

Mischel, Walter (1976), *Introduction to Personality: A New Look*, New York, London: Holt, Rinehart and Winston.

Moore, Gerald (1981), 'Soyinka's New Play in Gibbs, James ed. *Critical Perspectives on Soyinka*, London: Heinemann

Ngũgĩ wa Thiong'o (1972), *Homecoming*, London: Heinemann

Ngũgĩ wa Thiong'o (1977), *Petals of Blood*, London: Heinemann

Ngũgĩ wa Thiong'o (1981), *Writers in Politics*, London: Heinemann

Ngũgĩ wa Thiong'o (1983), *Barrel of a Pen*, London: New Beacon Books

Ngũgĩ wa Thiong'o (1986), *Decolonising the Mind*, London: Heinemann

Ngũgĩ wa Thiong'o, (1993), *Moving the Centre: The Struggle for Cultural Freedoms*, London: James Currey

Nichols, Charles (1963), *Many Thousand Gone*, Leiden: E, J. Brill

Nkosi, Lewis (1981), *Tasks and Masks*, Essex: Longman

Nwoga, Donatus ed. (1967), *West African Verse*, London: Longman

Nwoga, Donatus ed. (1976), *Literature and Modern West African Culture*, Benin: Ethiope Publishing Corporation

Obiechina, Emmanuel (1973), *Culture, Tradition and the West African Novel*, Cambridge: Cambridge University Press

Obiechina, Emmanuel (1986), "Africa in the Soul of Dispersed Children: West African Literature from the Era of the Slave Trade" in *Nsukka Studies in African Literature* No 4, pp. 101-160.

Ogunba, Oyin (1975), *The Movement of Transition*, Ibadan; Ibadan University Press

Ogunba, Oyin & Irele, Abiola eds. (1978), *Theatre in Africa*, Ibadan: Ibadan University Press

Ogunbiyi, Yemi ed. (1981), *Drama and Theatre in Nigeria: A Critical Source Book*, Lagos: Nigeria Magazine Publication

Okagbue, Osita (1987), 'Theatre on the Streets: Two Nigerian Samples' in *Maske und Kothurne* 33

Okagbue, Osita (1990), 'The Dialectics of Content and Form in West Indian Theatre' in *New Literatures Review* (Summer South)

Okagbue, Osita (1996), 'Language and Identity in West African and West Indian Theatre' in *Culture and Identity: Selected Aspects and Approaches*, eds. Suzanne Sterne-Gillette, Tadeusz Slawek, Tadeusz Rachwal and Roger Whitehouse, Katowice: Uniwersytet Slaski

Okagbue, Osita (1997), 'The Strange and the Familiar: Interculturalism between African and Caribbean Theatre in *Theatre Research International,* Vol. 22, No. 2

Okagbue, Osita (2004), Exile and Home: African in Caribbean Theatre' in *A History of Theatre in Africa*, Martin Banham ed. Cambridge: Cambridge University Press

Okagbue, Osita (2007), *African Theatres and Performances*, London: Routledge

Okagbue, Osita (2008), 'Deviants and Outcasts: Power and Politics in Hausa *Bori* Performances' in *New Theatre Quarterly*, Volume 24, Issue 03 (August) pp 270-280

Okpewho, Isidore, Boyce-Davis, Carole and Mazrui, Ali (2001), *African Diaspora: African Origins and New World Identities*, Bloomington and Indianapolis: Indiana University Press.

Omotoso, Kole (1982), *The Theatrical into Theatre*, London: New Beacon Books

Osofisan, Femi (1978), 'Tiger on Stage: Wole Soyinka and the Nigerian Theatre' in Oyin Ogunba and Abiola Irele, *Theatre in Africa*, Ibadan: Ibadan University Press

Ottenberg, Simon (1975), *The Masked Rituals of Afikpo: The Context of an African Art*, Washington: Henry Art Gallery and University of Washington Press

Parekh, Bhikhu (1982), *Marx's Theory of Ideology*, London: Croom Helm

Platt, John, Weber, Heidi & Liam, Ho Mian (1984), *The New Englishes*, London: Routledge and Kegan Paul

Parsons, Talcott (1968), 'The Position of Identity in the General Theory of Action' in *The Self in Social Interaction*.

Rawick, George (1972), *The American Slave: From Sundown tom Sunup*, Connecticut: Greenwood Publishing Company

Ray, Benjamin C. (1976), *African Religions: Symbol, Ritual and Community*, New Jersey: Prentice-Hall Inc.

Reynolds, Edward (1985), *Stand the Storm: A History of the Atlantic Slave Trade*, London: Allison and Busby

Ricard, Alain (1983), *Theatre and Nationlaism: Wole Soyinka and LeRoi Jones*, Ile-Ife: University of Ife Press

Roberts, Peter (1988), *West Indian and their Language*, Cambridge: Cambridge University Press

Rodney, Walter (1973), *How Europe Underdeveloped Africa*, London: Boyle-L'Overture Publications

Ruark, Robert (1955), *Something of Value*, New York City: Doubleday

Ruark, Robert (1962), *Uhuru*, New York: McGraw Hill

Said, Edward (1978), *Orientalism,* London: Routledge

Shelton, Austin J. ed. (1968), *The African Assertion: A Critical Anthology of African Literature*, New York: Odyssey Press

Soyinka, Wole (1988), *Art, Dialogue and Outrage*, Ibadan: New Horn Press

Soyinka, Wole (1976), *Myth, Literature and the African World*, Cambridge: Cambridge University Press

Taylor, Patrick (1986), 'Myth and Reality in Caribbean Narrative: Derek Walcott's *Pantomime*' in *World Literature Written in English*, Vol. 26, No.1

Tiryakian, Edward A (1968), 'The Existential Self and the Person' in *The Self in Social Interaction* by Chad Gordon and Kenneth J. Gergen eds. New York: John Wiley and Sons Inc.

Traore, Bakary (1972), *The Black African Theatre and Its Social Functions*, (trans.) Adelugba, Dapo, Ibadan: Ibadan University Press

Turner, Victor (1967), *The Forest of Symbols: Aspects of Ndembu Ritual*, Ithaca: Cornell University Press

Turner, Victor (1969), *The Ritual Process: Structure and Anti-Structure*, Middlesex: Penguin Books

Upton, Carole-Anne (1998), 'The French-speaking Caribbean: Journeying from the Native Land' in Richard Boon and Jane Plastow eds. *Theatre Matters: Performance and Culture on the World Stage*, Cambridge: Cambridge University Press

Van der Leeuw, G (1963), *Sacred and Profane Beauty*, London: Weidenfeld and Nicholson

Walcott, Derek (1978), 'The Muse of History' in Edward Baugh ed. *Critics on Caribbean Literature*, London: George Allen & Unwin

Walcott, Derek (1989), 'Profile of a West Indian Writer', *The South Bank Show* (ITV, January 15)

Walcott, Derek (1998), *What the Twilight Says: Essays*, London: Faber and Faber

White, Hayden (1973), *Metahistory: The Historical Imagination in Nineteenth Century Europe,* Baltimore: The John Hopkins University Press

Wilde, Oscar (1966), *Complete Works*, London: Collins

Williams, Eric (1945), *Capitalism and Slavery*, Chapel Hill: University of North Carolina Press

Williams, Eric (1970), *From Columbus to Castro: The History of the Caribbean 1492-1969*, London: Deutsch

Williams, Eric (1962), *History of the People of Trinidad and Tobago*, Port-of-Spain: PNM Publishing Co

Zuesse, Evans (1979), *Ritual Cosmos*, Ohio: Ohio University Press

INDEX

.

www.ingramcontent.com/pod-product-compliance
Lightning Source LLC
Chambersburg PA
CBHW070448100426
42812CB00004B/1232